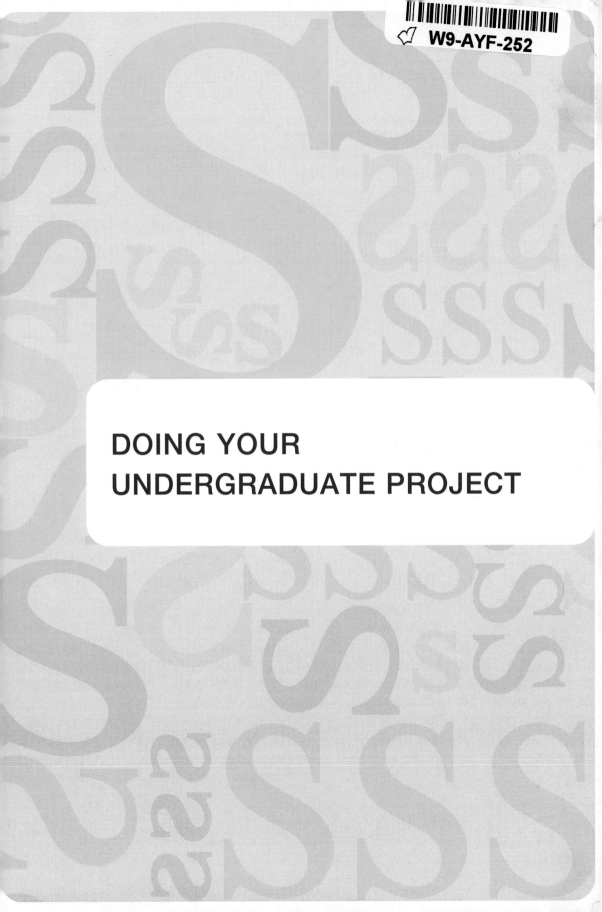

DOING YOUR
UNDERGRADUATE PROJECT

SAGE
Study Skills

DOING YOUR UNDERGRADUATE PROJECT

Denis F. Reardon

SAGE Publications
London • Thousand Oaks • New Delhi

SAGE Publications Ltd
1 Oliver's Yard
55 City Road
London EC1Y 1SP

SAGE Publications Inc.
2455 Teller Road
Thousand Oaks, California 91320

SAGE Publications India Pvt Ltd
B-42, Panchsheel Enclave
Post Box 4109
New Delhi 110 017

British Library Cataloguing in Publication data

A catalogue record for this book is available
from the British Library

ISBN 0 7619 4206 8   978 0 7619 4206 1
ISBN 0 7619 4207 6   978 0 7619 4207 8

Library of Congress Control Number available

Typeset by C&M Digitals (P) Ltd., Chennai, India
Printed in Great Britain by The Cromwell Press Ltd, Trowbridge, Wiltshire
Printed on paper from sustainable resources

Contents

List of figures and tables

Figures

Tables

Preface

An important requirement of many undergraduate courses in UK universities is that students do a major piece of research work, referred to as a project or dissertation. Whichever of these is required, the work is usually done during the final year of a three-year full-time degree, the equivalent period during a part-time degree, or is at least started and may be completed during the placement period of a sandwich degree, which may be of four years' duration. The time allowed for completion of the work is normally at least the two semesters of the final year and may be as much as 12 to 15 months if started during the sandwich placement. Precisely what a particular academic department requires will be determined, at least in part, by the nature and discipline of the degree being read, and will be specified in the course regulations. However, whatever an academic department specifies, most projects have much in common in terms of shape, form and style and in terms of the parameters within which the work has to be done. In essence, this book is concerned with both managing and doing the undergraduate project to reflect the fact that the undergraduate may be regarded as unique in the sense that he or she will be both the project manager and the researcher – and will manage herself or himself because, under university rules, the project normally has to be done as an individual piece of work.

This book is written primarily for undergraduate students and draws on experience gained from more than 30 years of teaching undergraduates about project work and supervising projects undertaken in the workplace by full-time and part-time students and by sandwich students on placement. These students have ranged in age from direct entrants from secondary education to mature students returning to learning in their 30s and 40s. Much has been learned from these students about factors that can affect project work, including lack of confidence in their ability to manage what many of them regard as a very substantial and daunting piece of work, through inadequate professional skills such as time management and work scheduling, lack of knowledge of basic writing skills, underdeveloped intellectual potential, and no recognition or understanding of ethics. Thus, advice is given on all that is involved in undertaking a project, from the choice of the topic through writing the proposal, reviewing the literature, selecting and using methods of investigation, recording, interpreting and discussing results to drawing conclusions and writing the final report.

Though the book is intended primarily for undergraduate students, experience gained from teaching and assessing professional diploma students studying project management has provided some insights into difficulties that many of them experience due to having to manage full-time employment, part-time study and life. It became clear that diploma and degree students have much in common in respect of managing what amounts to a full work schedule during the period of their courses. They need much guidance, but the demands of work coupled with part-time study do not give much time for tutorial support. Therefore, this book is provided to supplement such support and to substitute for it becoming, in effect, a set of tutorials on project management, suitable for undergraduates and, to a large extent, non-graduate diploma students.

Acknowledgements

This book would not have been written without the encouragement that I received from former colleagues in the School of Information Studies at the University of Central England in Birmingham. In particular, I would like to thank Chris Hart, with whom I shared much of my teaching in the later years of my career at UCE. Over the years from 1970, I had developed a range of materials to support classes that I was teaching in undergraduate project management and Chris suggested that I should develop these materials into a guide for undergraduates. He also put me in contact with Sage. I owe much to Anna Luker, from the editorial department at Sage. She has been very supportive and encouraging, providing suggestions and insights, and much helpful advice. Other former colleagues whom I must thank are Barbara Chivers and Clare Nankivell, both of whom provided constructive criticism of some of the material that evolved into this book. Indirect contributions came from the many students who attended my classes over the years. Students are usually very forthcoming with comment and opinion on class materials provided by tutors. I was fortunate in that my students were very helpful and positive in the opinions that they offered. Also, their performance in project work was the source of much useful but 'unconscious feedback' on the value of my Project Manual and my paper on Literature Reviewing that were provided to each student at 'project time' and which have been incorporated, with modifications, into this book.

Denis F. Reardon
Tamworth 2005

1 The Value of a Project

How to use this book

The main purpose of this book is to serve as a guide for the preparation, management and presentation of an undergraduate project to be undertaken during a degree course in the humanities, arts, or social sciences. It is intended to answer the sort of questions asked by undergraduates and to enable them to 'break down' the seemingly rather daunting process of managing what is usually the most important piece of course work that they will undertake during their degree course. Because of the similarities and over-lapping definitions of project and dissertation at different universities, much of this book may be applied judiciously to the preparation and writing of a dissertation.

The chapters represent the main elements of the undergraduate project research process. The experience referred to earlier has shown that students have found that breaking down the project process into these elements has provided them with a systematic and structured way of tackling their work. The chapters are arranged in an order that has proved helpful over many years, though each may be used independently to understand specific aspects of managing and doing your project. Thus, there may be repetition of certain points in some chapters rather than provision of references between chapters. As well as introducing this book, this chapter is intended to explain the practical value of doing a project and its importance in your future career. Also, it provides a guide to assist you in deciding what type of potential researcher you are by showing you how to identify your strengths and weaknesses and your likes and dislikes in respect of your general knowledge and understanding, and of the subjects that you have studied on your course. From this, you should be able to develop sound ideas of what you could and could not do as a project topic.

Chapter 2 is designed to assist you in preparing your mind to do your research work and so provides a detailed description of what a project is and what research is, because experience has shown that many students do not realise what is involved in either of these. It is useful to understand the context within which the research is to be done since this will enable the literature search and review to be better informed and will help to 'prove the value' of the work to be done. Attention is drawn to the importance of ethical conduct in research and, finally, the administrative matters that are such important contributors to a successful project are set out.

Many students have difficulty in choosing a topic for their project. Sometimes the difficulty is of their own making, as they do not seek advice or guidance from tutors or supervisors. They appear to hold the view that only they, the individual students, should be involved, but 'do not know where to start'. **Chapter 3** takes you from 'an idea for a topic' to the hypothesis and shows how to develop one through analysing the topic, formulating the research question and creating a knowledge map – all of which will help you to choose and know your topic intimately.

Most university departments will require a project proposal from you and this will have to be considered satisfactory by your tutors before you are permitted to proceed with your project. Many students neglect the proposal. Do not fall into the trap – a trap of your own making – by thinking that it is an easy task to prepare a proposal or that you can do it whilst 'getting your research underway'. A well-prepared, well-structured proposal will act as an excellent desk reference tool throughout your research, and in **Chapter 4** you will find out how to write one.

In **Chapter 5**, the way to plan your project is explained. This is another element that is often neglected by undergraduate students on the basis that 'I don't need to plan because I know exactly what I want to do'. Can you always recall exactly what you want to do? A well-made plan will act as a detailed reminder and route map for your research, making sure that you know what must be done, when it must be done and what is needed to do it. The planning method provided is based upon the life cycle approach to project management, which is systematic, structured and quite straightforward and has been used with success by many students.

There are risks associated with every aspect of life, not least with undergraduate project work. Generally, the risks are small, even insignificant, but there are occasions when a major risk event has severely adverse effects on a project. Learn how to assess and manage risks; such learning will be useful in professional employment after graduation. In **Chapter 6**, the risks that may be associated with your project and possible ways to assess and plan for them are discussed.

There are many books available on research methodology and so **Chapter 7** alerts you to methods that have been frequently used in undergraduate projects. Choice of method is critical to the success of any project, so how do you choose methods appropriate to your topic? This chapter contains guidance on what methods are available, how to choose methods suitable for your investigation and how to use them. You must review the literature of your chosen subject to ensure that you know what has been done before and this makes reviewing the literature the most important research method that you will use. As it is regarded as so important, a separate chapter, **Chapter 8**, provides a detailed examination of the literature review, how to do it, and how not to do it.

Chapter 9 focuses on how to use the results that you will obtain in your investigation. Experience has shown that many students either substantially under-use their results because they do not realise their significance or try to make too much of them, possibly due to their enthusiasm for the work. An undergraduate project is not likely to produce world-changing outcomes since it is intended more as a proof of ability to research than as a results-oriented piece of work, though the results are important.

Chapter 10 is devoted to writing the project report. This is a seemingly arduous task, difficult to start, to plan and to finish, yet if you approach it systematically and give yourself enough time, you will find that it is very satisfying. After all, it is the story of your research and is the only proof that you have done your project. This chapter contains guidance based upon more than 40 years of writing, reading and assessing reports at undergraduate, postgraduate and professional levels.

What will be learned from this book?

The project is intended to be a major learning vehicle, so it is important for you to know exactly what a project is, why you have to do it, and how to do it. Therefore, in using this book, you will begin the process of learning to be a project designer, manager and a researcher. You will acquire a range of skills and understanding that may be transferable to other situations. The main skills and understanding that you will need to complete the project successfully are listed in Box 1.1.

You will learn what research is and how to do it, what is required of a researcher in terms of qualities and attributes, and what is demanded in respect of standards in research, recognising that, at this stage, you are doing undergraduate work.

In the time available to do an undergraduate project, normally no more than 20 hours a week for 30 to 50 weeks, it will not be possible for you to get very detailed knowledge of each of the skills listed, but you will gain sufficient knowledge and experience to understand what is required for successful project completion.

Box 1.1:   Skills and understanding needed to complete the project

- Project planning and management
- Time management
- Work scheduling
- Risk assessment and management
- Resource planning and management
- Ethical behaviour and standards
- How to self-audit your skills
- Reflection – an essential intellectual process for the researcher
- Report writing
- Subject knowledge
- Research – a body of intellectual and practical skills, many of which are dependent upon the topic in which the research is being done.

Why do a project?

Your university requires a project for several reasons. One of these may well stem from opinions that have been offered by senior figures in commerce, government, and industry, namely that graduates are lacking in project management skills. These opinions reflect the fact that much nominally routine work done in commerce, government and industry has a lot in common with project work since it is done in discrete time, work and resource frames. Therefore, your degree includes project work to give you the opportunity to begin to develop project planning and management skills and research skills that will be valuable in employment after graduation. However, as the project is done at undergraduate level, it is not intended that you should seek to do what is often called leading edge, ground-breaking or wave front research that might produce a major contribution to the body of knowledge in your chosen topic area. Indeed, such work requires substantial knowledge of the subject field and considerable research experience. Nor is it intended that your investigation should result in a definitive solution to a specified problem, proof of a theory or the development of an innovative idea or product.

The project is intended to enable you to grasp the fundamentals of research, whether theoretical or practical, and of project management. To achieve this, your project must normally be simple and straightforward. It will enable your tutors and examiners to determine your ability to define, design, do and deliver a piece of research. Thus, it will be the way that you plan, organise and do your research that will be under test, more than the subject content and topic-specific results or outcomes of the research, though these will be of significance. In other words, your project is a learning vehicle that will enable you to gain essential academic, professional and practical skills and, when completed, will enable you to demonstrate your capabilities. Keep in mind that a project that is well done will be an impressive addition to your curriculum vitae.

The general aims and objectives behind the project and its assessment

The aims are statements by which you declare your intentions in carrying out your project. They are the purposes that you expect to fulfil by doing your project. In the case of your undergraduate project, certain general aims will be established for the project by your academic department to enable your tutors and examiners to undertake the required assessment of your skills. These aims relate directly to what you have to prove about yourself as an investigator or researcher. They are concerned with the extent to which you have to learn research and project management skills and use them appropriately in the definition, design, planning, completion and reporting of your project. Can you cope with what is involved in doing a major piece of investigative work? Can you do the work and report it in a way that conforms to academic standards? You will establish other aims in consultation with your tutor and these will relate to the specific investigation that you will do. All the general aims will normally be set out in the project briefing issued by your tutor and should be repeated in your project proposal. The briefing will usually also contain the objectives and assessment criteria, and administrative and regulatory details relevant to the project. The precise form in which the general aims are given to you will depend upon the subject that you are studying for your degree, the nature of the project that you choose to do, and the regulations of your university.

The aims are summarised in column 1 of Table 1.1: *General aims, objectives and assessment criteria*, in which they are presented together with the objectives and the criteria for assessment. This table enables the links that must exist between the aims, objectives and assessment criteria to be identified. There must be direct and logical links between your objectives and your aims; the linkage is one of dependency. Similarly, there must be links between the assessment criteria and the objectives. In the final analysis, the best way to assess your potential as a project worker or investigator is to determine how well you have conformed to accepted practice and to measure the quality, extent and manner in which you achieve your objectives, using agreed criteria.

At first reading, the general aims may appear rather daunting. Yet they are not if you recognise that the earlier parts of your course have contained elements that will have introduced many of the underlying skills and knowledge necessary to help you to fulfil these aims. These skills will be honed as the project progresses and you will develop others as a direct result of doing the work. Similarly, your knowledge of the subject area will be expanded and deepened. In order to fulfil these aims, you will have to achieve the general objectives specified for the project in the project briefing. Typical objectives are listed in column 2 of Table 1.1.

The objectives are the achievements that you must attain in order to demonstrate whether the aims have been fulfilled. The aims and objectives may be differentiated in general terms by regarding the aims as qualitative intentions and the objectives as quantitative intentions. Thus, objectives are measurable or quantifiable. For example, one aim of the project is: 'To test the student's ability to interpret and evaluate data and information gathered during research'. This is primarily concerned with the intellectual skills that enable you to 'tease out' meanings, trends, patterns, relationships, causes, solutions and explanations of results using, for example, analysis, synthesis, integration and appropriate presentation of the results. This aim is, therefore, linked to the second objective: 'To demonstrate the ability to use the research skills acquired whilst on the course, by satisfactory completion of a major piece of research work'. The extent to which this objective is attained will be demonstrated by the methods that you have chosen, the effectiveness and efficiency with which you have used them, the quality of the results obtained by using these methods, and the soundness of the analysis, interpretation, evaluation and presentation of the results.

Recognise that, although particular objectives are linked to particular aims and particular assessment criteria, such linkages are not exclusive. The achievement of a particular objective may ensure that parts, or all, of more than one aim are fulfilled. Similarly, one specific assessment criterion may link to more than one objective. When assessing your project, tutors and examiners will have created in their minds an image of your work based upon your stated intentions. They will also have created in their minds a 'quality framework' within which they will place your project and by which they will assess it. This framework will be an integration and synthesis of the assessment criteria, not a set of 'tick boxes' linked to specific criteria.

Table 1.1 General aims, objectives and assessment criteria

Aims

To enable the student to design and carry out research in an academic, professional, commercial or technological environment.

To provide the opportunity to use research skills acquired whilst on the degree course.

To encourage the development of an ethical, systematic, rigorous approach to the selection and use of research methods.

To encourage the development of an ethical, systematic, objective approach to the collection and use of data and information.

To test the student's ability to interpret and evaluate data and information gathered during research.

To test the student's ability to provide a cogent, reasoned and objective argument based upon data and information obtained by research.

To test the student's ability to manage a substantial and demanding piece of research using project management skills.

To test the student's ability to write a formal document reporting research.

Objectives

Demonstrate the ability to formulate an hypothesis, establish a research question and prepare a proposal for its investigation.

Demonstrate the ability to use research skills acquired whilst on the course, by satisfactory completion of a major piece of research work.

Demonstrate the ability to manage research using project management skills, by completing a project to agreed parameters.

Produce a report that demonstrates the ability to apply the written communication skills developed during the course.

Demonstrate oral skills, utilising learning gained by doing the work, in a viva and during seminars and tutorials.

Demonstrate recognition of the academic standards, including ethical standards, essential in the undertaking and reporting of research work, by applying these in the work done and reported.

Assessment criteria

The quality of the project proposal in terms of its clarity, definition, precision, realism and objectivity and its relationship to the outcomes of the project.

The appropriateness and quality of use of the research methods.

The scope and quality of the literature search and review.

The quality of analysis, synthesis, integration and evaluation of the data and information gathered.

The quality of the argument based upon the data and information gathered, both in the research and from the literature reviewed.

The quality of use of project management skills.

Adherence to academic and professional standards, including ethical standards.

The quality of the report in terms of the structure and the clarity, brevity, precision and accuracy in the use of language.

The assessment criteria are used primarily to determine whether the project objectives have been achieved and, if so, the extent to which they have been achieved. Thus, they are more than just parameters to measure your research results. They will also be used to assess the quality of the learning gains that you have made as a consequence of doing the project. In other words, the criteria are intended to assess your potential as a project 'manager' and research investigator. They are not just measures of how good the research itself was.

When tutors assess the project report, it is certain that they will use a range of criteria that may include some or all of those listed in column 3 of Table 1.1. Therefore, it is important that you have a clear understanding of the general aims and objectives and of the assessment criteria before the research work is started. They may be listed and explained in a project brief given to you when the 'project period' of your course starts. You should discuss these with your supervising tutor or course director in order to be completely clear as to what is required of you in terms of breadth, depth and quality. In other words, undertake careful preparation before you start on your project. You know almost from the start of your course what will be required of you, at least in general terms, and so you can form some of your ideas gradually over 12 to 18 months before the project period is upon you.

Qualities and attributes of a researcher

The project is designed to test your potential as a project planner and manager and to test your ability to carry out the project that you have planned. Thus, you will have to prove yourself as a researcher or investigator, though at a fairly elementary level. As your abilities as a researcher will be assessed, it is useful to explore the features of a researcher. This will help you to determine the extent to which you enter the project phase of your course with an understanding of what you must be in order to fulfil the project requirements. What qualities/attributes do you have or can you develop that will possibly mark you out as a potential researcher?

All researchers will demonstrate some of the qualities or attributes that are essential to the proper and satisfactory conduct of research. Most of these are developed by experience rather than being inherent in a researcher. Your project is a major tool for encouraging this development explicitly, though development will have begun much earlier, perhaps even before you enrolled on your degree course. The course work that you have already done, such as essays and seminars, will have demanded of you that you show certain qualities and attributes in order to meet the assessment criteria and so successfully complete the work. Your hobbies may have contributed to development of certain qualities. For example, many hobbies require persistence and the ability to concentrate for lengthy periods of time, and demand great attention to detail and accuracy – qualities that are valuable in a researcher.

What else is desirable in you as a researcher? A critical attribute is objectivity. All researchers must be able to carry out their research in an objective manner and with an open mind. In essence, the researcher must be able to 'stand back' from the matter being investigated and consider all aspects of the research work in a completely dispassionate manner. There must not be any predisposition to particular points of view, no seeking to prove a point or an hypothesis. However, enthusiasm and a strong interest can and should accompany objectivity. Opinions, conclusions and any proofs related to the research topic must be formed as a consequence of the research, not in order to shape and form it. Therefore, do not allow yourself to become a slave to an idea, a method or a theory. Nevertheless, it is the case that all research, to greater or lesser extent, is value-laden. Thus, there is nothing wrong with you having a point of view as long as you recognise this and rigorously examine your attitude to your proposed topic. What assumptions have you made? Are they valid assumptions, do they have a sound basis? Is there any possibility that you may have a personal bias, an enthusiasm or some preconceived notion or notions to which you are particularly strongly attached and which you cannot 'leave behind' when starting your research? Do not despair if you recognise such 'errors'. It is natural for people to have preconceptions. Preconceptions suggest that we may have quite strong opinions on, or enthusiasm for, particular matters. We are entitled to these and they may prompt ideas for research. However, it is important for you to recognise your preconceptions and enthusiasms and to ensure that you compensate for them during the course of your project. You must ensure that they do not have a prejudicial effect on the objectivity of your work.

Other attributes include the ability to think analytically, and to synthesise ideas – of others engaged in research on or writing about the topic, those you had that prompted your research and those that you form as a result of doing the research. The researcher has to be able to think inductively, that is, to build up individual ideas into mental constructs, for example, representing clear images of problems, processes or the hypothesis and research question being investigated. It is also important for you to be able to think deductively, that is, have the ability to reason from the general to the particular, for example, being able to infer from examination of a known construct what the constituent parts are, how they are related and what the relative significance is that these parts have in the overall construct.

Absolute honesty is a fundamental requirement in all researchers. It is essential that all researchers act with integrity at all times. Indeed, whatever their field of research and whatever their seniority in that field, all researchers must conform to a code of practice appropriate to the field in which they are researching. It is common for universities, research institutes and professional associations to have a code of ethics that will include specific elements devoted to research. This code will include an unequivocal require-ment to abide by high ethical standards when designing, conducting and reporting research. Responsible conduct in research is dealt with in Chapter 2.

Summary

When you enrolled on your degree course, you committed yourself to doing a project at some time during the course. At enrolment, the project was 18 months to 2 years off and, from such a distance in time, did not appear to be threatening. Also, it is possible that you had only a hazy idea of what would be involved and that you would have a year or more to do it. However, when the project period is a semester away, the 'threat' seems substantial. How can you deal with this threat? By preparing for it, by learning just what a project is and how to go about formulating your ideas, by learning about yourself and what is involved in being a project researcher. The discipline required of a researcher begins before the project is formulated, training your mind to do research, and discipline in the acquisition of the 'rules' of research, from the initial idea through to the submission of the final report, reflection on the work and the viva based upon the research. The learning gains achieved by doing a project will prove to be valuable in professional life. Therefore, it is worth the effort to ensure that this work is carefully prepared and well presented. Pay close attention to the aims, objectives and assessment criteria; together they provide quite detailed and systematic guidelines on how to do the project.

Further Reading

Allan, Barbara (2004) *Project Management: Tools and Techniques for Today's ILS Professional.* London: Facet.

Martin, Paula K. (2001) *Getting Started in Project Management.* Chichester; New York, N.Y.: Wiley.

Moore, Nick (1999) *How to Do Research* (3rd edn). London: Library Association Publishing.

Young, Trevor L. (2003) *The Handbook of Project Management: A Practical Guide to Effective Policies and Procedures* (2nd edn). London: Kogan Page.

2 Preparing to Do Your Project

This chapter is intended to help you to clarify your mind when preparing to do the project and to help you to realise that you can do it. When about to start any project, however small, the route to successful completion will be made clearer, straighter and smoother by proper preparation. Your undergraduate project is small in comparison to industrial and commercial projects but is big to you as the individual who has to do it alone. So, what are you letting yourself in for in your chosen project? How can you prepare yourself for this substantial piece of work? What commitment are you making?

To answer these questions, we will firstly define and discuss what a project is, and then we will consider in some detail what research is and why it is done. We will examine why it is important to adopt and maintain a responsible attitude to the conduct of research and show some consequences of not doing so.

Preparation must also include the establishment of the administrative procedures that will be essential in keeping control of your project. Therefore, having considered what is involved in what may be described as the intellectual aspects of research, we must now consider what is involved in administration of your project. When doing research, you will create or cause to be created a range of types of documentation – the project records. Some of this documentation will be forms that you will have designed for recording information and data gathered as the project research progresses. Other documentation will include material from reading the literature and from sources such as organisations with which you may co-operate or communicate and from people from whom you may obtain advice and guidance. Thus, there are several more questions that will be addressed in this chapter under a discussion of the administration of the project.

What is a project?

The work involved in professional, scientific and technical employment in government, commerce and industry may be regarded as consisting mainly of two types – routine work and project work. As first-degree courses are now usually regarded as preparation for employment of particular kinds, it is important that these courses should include the development of project management capabilities in undergraduates. It is also important that the project experience provided by the course should be as realistic as possible, though recognising that there is no perfect substitute for real-life work-based projects. Thus, although the undergraduate project is small, if it is properly designed and undertaken, it can provide a valuable experience in which much is learned that is pertinent to the larger-scale projects of government, commerce and industry.

Box 2.1:   The difference between a project and a dissertation

The regulations and guidance governing undergraduate dissertations and projects at different universities provide substantial similarities in the definitions of each, leading to a blurring and potential confusion between the two. It is useful to draw a distinction between the two.

   For the purpose of this book, a project is regarded as primarily a practical investigation, seeking new information and/or data and is often work-based. It is defined more precisely below.

   A dissertation is regarded as a substantial academic piece that has clear, specific academic aims and that incorporates the evidence of the student's ability to treat critically, analytically and objectively a particular focus of study. All the information and data that are studied are taken from existing published and unpublished but accessible sources. It is a means for a student to demonstrate understanding of the prevailing situation in respect of that focus, such as the body of theory being used to explain a particular phenomenon and possibly to produce new analyses and syntheses of existing ideas.

The term *project work* is used quite loosely at times, resulting in nearly everything that is done in some working environments being labelled as projects. To have a clear understanding of what routine work is and what a project is and for the purposes of this book, it is useful to define the two types of work so that the differences between them can be understood.

Box 2.2: Definition – Routine work

The day-to-day administration, meetings, problem solving, interviewing, dealing with customers, in other words – running things so that the daily business of product or service provision of the organisation continues to happen.

Box 2.3: Definition – Project work

Projects are stand-alone, discrete 'packages' of work that are usually outside the routine work of the organisation but normally linked to it through a domain of common interest that may be a product or service of the organisation or a related problem.

Projects invariably have precise terms of reference that include a defined topic or matter of interest, a specified time frame, a prescribed resource package that includes people and finance – and clearly defined scope, aims and objectives, and methods of investigation. It is also common for them to have some specified outputs, known as outcomes or deliverables. Your project will have terms of reference and a time frame that are prescribed by the degree course regulations. Normally, you will select the topic and define the project in consultation with your tutors. The aims, objectives and methods of investigation will stem from the agreed project definition and from the project brief issued by your tutor.

For you, the undergraduate, the project is a significant piece of investigative work requiring the use of many basic research skills. Some of these skills, such as logical, analytical and critical thinking, writing, interpreting and evaluating relevant subject literature, information and computing technology skills, communication skills, time management and work scheduling, will have been acquired, at least in embryo, during earlier stages of the course being followed or even prior to joining the course. Many of these skills will be reinforced and others will be developed whilst undertaking the work for the project. There are many books containing advice and guidance on how to hone many of the skills that you will need for studying, including those valuable in doing your project. The book by Rudd (1989), *Time Manage your Reading*, and that by Lashley and Best (2003), *12 Steps to Success*, are useful desktop tools and will provide help in developing important transferable skills.

The project must be the work of the individual student, though tutors within the department or school to which the student belongs invariably provide guidance. It is important that you, the student, retain control of your project. It may be the case that, when on sandwich placement or if you are a part-time student, you are researching a topic that is of value to your workplace; so much so that your section leader or line manager effectively takes control. This may lead to a research design being produced that is more suited to the requirements of the workplace than your university. This may, in turn, lead to the data analysis and interpretation being undertaken by the section leader so that the results are produced to the schedule, form and style that the organisation requires. You lose control of your project and, because the section leader has designed the research and done the analysis and interpretation of results, the work is not yours. In such a case, little if any of the intellectual input to the work is yours, even if you have discussed the results with the section leader. Similarly, if you are doing an academic project, as a full-time student, it may be that your academic supervisor very heavily influences what you choose, how you do the project, what you put in the project report and how you write it. In effect, you are too closely supervised and the project becomes your tutor's with you acting as a project assistant. In either case, your project will not fulfil the terms of the degree and so will not satisfy the examiners, normally resulting in failure. Your project is only yours if you make the significant intellectual and management contributions, and this should be evident throughout your report.

How big should the project be?

Projects may be broadly described as small, medium or large. The description is based mainly on the time frame allowed and the resource requirements to complete it. Thus, a project may require anything from one hour to many tens of thousands of hours and involve resources ranging from a few pounds to many millions of pounds and from one person to thousands of people.

An undergraduate project is a small project since it involves one person – you, the student – and little finance (the costs of stationery and working materials, some processing and binding and, perhaps, some travel costs connected with library visits or interviewing subjects of study). The time taken to complete your project should usually not exceed 800 hours. Thus, it is a small project in comparative terms but appears large for you as it is the first such piece of work that you will do and you are entirely responsible for its completion. The time frame suggested is a guide not a specification and individual universities may have specific requirements that require a time commitment substantially different from this figure.

It is usual for the total time allocated to a project to be determined in relation to the number of standard modules to which it is equated by your academic department or university. If the project has the value of three standard modules and the project proposal is valued at one standard module, as may be the case, then the total credit value will be 48 if your university values individual standard modules at 12 credits. Total dedicated study time for such a module is normally 120 hours, to which it is reasonable to expect you to add at least 30 hours. This gives a minimum of 600 hours to be allocated to the project, usually over two semesters, even a whole year for a project undertaken by a sandwich placement or part-time student.

Your commitment to the project and your enthusiasm for it would suggest that you would devote more time to it, which is why the figure of 800 hours is suggested. This will include formulation of the project proposal, preparation of which will often begin before the nominal start date of the project. The 800 hours will average out at 20 hours per week allowing for the inter-semester periods. Recognise that these time frames are guides, not prescriptions. It is clear, therefore, that even though classified as small, an undergraduate project still requires careful preparation, including planning and management in order to meet the specified aims and objectives both within the degree course regulations, which will include the time allowed, and within the project itself.

Another factor that may be used to determine the size of the project is the number of words that the academic department permits you to use when reporting your research. Careful consideration of your topic, its definition, including any limitations you impose upon it, and the methods you use investigating it, when taking into account the number of words permitted, will suggest a natural size to the project. Most undergraduate projects are limited to between 10,000 and 12,000 words, working possibly on the basis that a standard module normally requires course work equivalent to approximately 2,500 to 3,000 words. Some universities impose penalties for exceeding the prescribed figure and for falling substantially short of it. If you prepare, plan and design your project well, and if you accept that you must write it with good structure, grammar and appropriate vocabulary, and with clarity and brevity of style, the number of hours required for planning, doing and writing up the project may be estimated with reasonable accuracy.

You must realise that the word length that you have to submit is not the total number of words that you will write when making your final report. You will have prepared and revised several drafts before being satisfied that you have something worth submitting.

You may write as many as three or four times the number of words that are in the submitted version of your final report. This is usual. It is one of the reasons for the careful project planning and management recommended.

What is research?

In general terms, research is a process concerned with finding out something, seeking data and information to enable an unknown to be explained, a problem to be solved or a cause to be discovered. The *Shorter Oxford English Dictionary* offers a more succinct definition.

Box 2.4:   Definition – Research

An investigation directed to the discovery of some information, fact, or facts by careful study of a subject; a course of critical or scientific inquiry.

Note that the emphasis is upon *careful study* and *critical inquiry*. Major implications of these terms include the need for careful preparation of the research, its topic, definition, scope, aims and objectives, and the systematic and objective conduct of the work.

Our individual perceptions of what research is are probably governed as much by the ways of researching within our own particular subject area or discipline as by a dictionary definition. For example, the scientist or technologist relies largely upon observation and experiment for the acquisition of data and information when researching, using accepted, even standardised methods of investigation, and behaving and reporting according to certain standards. Much scientific and technological research is carried out in purpose-built laboratories. A feature of scientific and technological research is control – of the environment, of methods and their use, of subjects of study and of the writing and presentation of the outcomes.

The laboratory of the historian, archivist, information scientist and many humanities researchers is largely the documentation available – textual and non-textual – that has been produced perhaps over a period of many years, even centuries. Some of the documents may be original documents such as treaties, graphical material, art objects, speeches and minutes of meetings; others may be contemporary reports of events that may be in textual, audio or visual forms. An information scientist may utilise secondary sources such as bibliographies, indexes and bibliographic citations as research data sources. For example, it may be that the information scientist seeks to establish whether research in a subject is growing in importance and may use literature activity, that is, frequency and growth rate of publication – in journals, patents, conference papers and similar – as a measure of research activity.

The social scientist, on the other hand, may regard the whole of society as a potential laboratory within which to research. Such research may be concerned with expenditure patterns of social groups, attitudes of different age groups to the quality of broadcast media in a community, or a comparison of attitudes of different ethnic groups to crime and punishment. In broad terms, the social scientist studies people in a wide range of contexts to seek to understand the attitudes and behaviour of individuals in groups. As with researchers in science, technology, the humanities and the arts, the social scientist uses recognised and accepted methods of investigation and conforms to specified standards of behaviour in conducting research.

So, whatever the subject area involved, research is a process of investigation and questioning. There are three questions we can pose when contemplating research. These are:

1. **Why do people research?**

2. **What is being researched?**

3. **How is it being researched?**

The answers to these questions will trigger many subsidiary questions, the number and nature of which will be dependent upon the particular topic being investigated. One way of exploring the three initial questions is shown in Figure 2.1 – *Answering the three questions*. Some of the answers to the questions are explored in the text below

Why do people research?

The general answer is that there is something that they wish to know and the only way to find out is to do the necessary research. The precise answer to the question 'Why?' will depend on factors such as the particular subject of interest; pressures to meet demands for innovation; critical concerns about problems affecting products or services of an organisation; or for no other reason than that there is a gap in the knowledge map of a subject area and the researcher considers that it would be interesting or useful to fill it.

One of the strongest motivators to research is the desire to achieve a specified goal. A widely publicised example of this is the determination of the USA to put a man on the moon before the end of the 1960s decade. This prompted intensive research

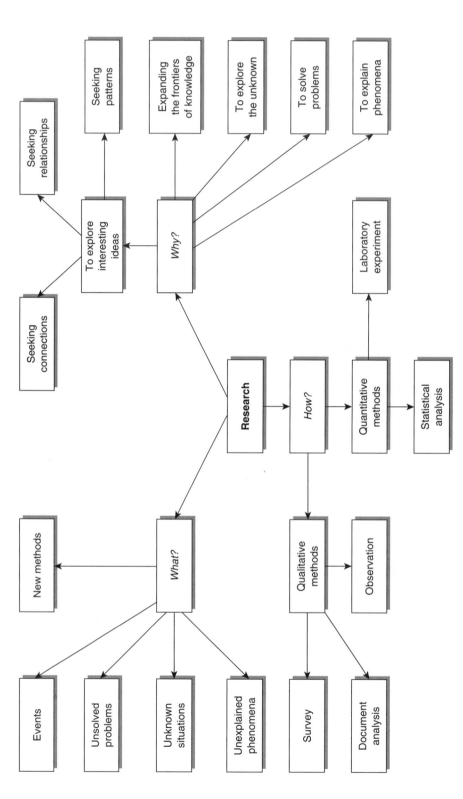

Figure 2.1 Answering the three questions

to develop or design new materials, processes, vehicles and equipment, and to gain understanding of the way that humans would react both psychologically and physio-logically in an environment into which they had never before ventured. Many tens of thousands of researchers in a very wide range of disciplines became involved to achieve the overall objective, which took nearly nine years to achieve.

What is being researched?

The answers to 'What?' will be closely linked to the answers to 'Why?'. For example, researching because there is a problem with the integrity of a particular product such as an all-weather garment, immediately suggests that what must be investigated is con-nected with one or more of the following: the design of the product; the materials; the manufacturing processes; or the environment or circumstances in which it is being used by those who are experiencing the problem. Other reasons for researching may be prompted by innovation in materials or processes that could be applicable to a particu-lar organisation. For example, there may be a new material that has been developed for one specific purpose. The material may have interesting properties that suggest that it may have potential for use in other applications. It has often been suggested that the non-stick surfaces in cooking utensils resulted from research in the US space programme to find high temperature materials for use on re-entry vehicles. Some med-ical treatments have been found to have useful, even potentially life-saving, alternative uses, for example, aspirin was developed as an analgesic but is now recommended for use by people who suffer certain heart conditions. Rapeseed oil was originally produced for human consumption in cooking, but it is now also used in some parts of the world as a relatively low-pollutant producing fuel for motorcars. Research is undertaken to discover or to test these variant applications.

Some researchers are interested in ways of doing things rather than particular products, processes, or behaviour patterns of consumers. A social or political scientist may want to find a new way of measuring the impact of a particular government policy on a specific section of the national community. Is there a more accurate or more certain method of finding out what people truly think? Other researchers may seek new meth-ods of producing existing products either to improve productivity or product quality, or to reduce production costs. Caterers may need new ways of preparing, cooking and preserving certain foods to minimise the risk of food poisoning and satisfy health and safety regulations. Investment managers and business analysts may seek new ways of measuring risks associated with share buying in order to improve the degree to which they can safeguard their clients' money.

When you have to choose your research topic, you may consider investigating some method or methods used within your subject area. Suppose that you are studying to be a teacher and will be placed for teaching practice in a primary school that has a high proportion of pupils from ethnic minority homes and most of these pupils are first generation immigrants. Is there one agreed method of teaching English successfully to such a diverse group? You may settle on an investigation into methods of teaching English to multi-ethnic classes in which many different mother tongues are spoken. Thus, your research is method focused.

How is it being researched?

There are many different methods used in research, some of which will be specific to a particular subject, others will be more generally applicable. All methods may be generally categorised as either quantitative or qualitative. Some of these may be used in what is called desk research. Others may have to be used in fieldwork or laboratory work. The researcher uses quantitative methods to gather measurable data. Examples of such data are: the number of students enrolled on fine arts degree courses in UK universities in a particular year; the proportion of a specific age group that smokes cigarettes; or the expenditure on leisure activities in different regions of a country. Qualitative methods are used to gather information about matters that are not measurable, for example, why undergraduates choose their courses of study, or why people buy the records of particular singers or orchestras.

Neither group of methods is exclusive to any particular subject or discipline. Media and marketing analysts would use qualitative methods to gather awareness and opinions about radio or newspaper advertising, or to assess viewers' opinions of a new television drama series. They may also use quantitative methods to measure the size of the audience or the change in sales volume that followed a new advertising campaign.

Social scientists may use both quantitative and qualitative methods in a project concerned with, for example, a comparative evaluation of the social inclusion policies of selected local authorities. Qualitative methods would be used to elicit the opinions of the people at whom the policies were directed and of the providers of the services designed to fulfil the policies. Quantitative methods would be used to measure the number and sizes of groups – ethnic, social and cultural – at whom the policies would be targeted, the finance and other resources used to implement them and the proportions of the original target groups considered to have benefited from them. A classic example of research that relies on quantitative methods is the UK national census that takes place every ten years. This census is designed to gather quantitative data about the entire population. The data are subjected to statistical analyses to produce information that will be used by central government in the formulation of many of its policies, such as those concerned with taxation, and with spending on health, social services and education.

Why a code of ethics is necessary

Why should a guide to research mention ethics? Because it is essential to ensure that the integrity of the research process and ethical behaviour become second nature to all researchers. That is why it is considered in this discussion of research preparation. High ethical standards must be instilled into all researchers from the start of their careers. You must realise from the start of your career as a researcher, and it starts with your undergraduate project, that you must at all times behave ethically. There are important reasons why this must be so. Successful research brings various benefits to the researcher, to the sponsors of the research and to the institutions in which the research is undertaken. Among these benefits are prestige, recognition by peers, and the potential for substantial material gains for the individuals and organisations involved.

Therefore, it is possible to envisage circumstances in which a researcher is tempted to breach a code of ethics, to behave unethically, for example, by manipulating survey samples or falsifying data to achieve a particular outcome. It is often difficult to fathom the motives of people who behave in this way. The reasoning may be that this is not in breach of the code, but is merely the making of adjustments to achieve what is 'obviously the correct result'. Such reasoning is faulty and constitutes misconduct. There are other motivators to unethical behaviour and it is worth examining what research misconduct is, in order to understand it and realise some of the consequences.

Research misconduct

Misconduct in research does not commonly feature in the professional and academic press, but this does not mean that it is rare. It does make newspaper headlines when it involves notable individuals or results in harm to people. However, there have been sufficient significant cases over the past 10 to 20 years for the interest in research integrity to have taken on a higher profile in responsible organisations. The importance now attached to responsible conduct in research by national governments, universities and professional associations is clear from the publication of policies and codes of research ethics. However, these bodies do not usually insist on the wide publication of breaches of their codes and of the consequences for offenders.

To illustrate how seriously misconduct is now taken, it is worth considering the work of one of the more prominent bodies in the area of research integrity. This body is the

US government's Office of Research Integrity (ORI) and it does, as a matter of policy, publish its findings in cases of misconduct in research. It promotes integrity in biomedical and behavioural research supported by the (US) Public Health Service at about 4,000 institutions worldwide (ORI). Although it focuses on scientific disciplines, there is much that can be learned by all researchers. In its promotion of integrity, the ORI supports research on research integrity, and is currently intending to commit $1,500,000 to support such research in 2006. The ORI has a website – http://ori.dhhs.gov/ – that includes a newsletter, notifications of conferences and reports on research integrity and findings in cases of misconduct. A Research Conference on Research Integrity in November 2004 is an indicator of how seriously research integrity is taken in official circles in the US. The conference included coverage of prevention of research misconduct, fostering a responsible conduct of research culture, and appropriate handling of allegations of research misconduct. It becomes clear from the reports published by ORI, and from the conferences with which it is associated, that misconduct in research is not a rare occurrence and does, occasionally, involve people who hold senior research posts. Detection of such misconduct is much more likely due to the considerable resources and effort now devoted to discovering those responsible for it, whatever their seniority as researchers.

Integrity is an attribute that must govern all aspects of the research process and so the requirement for ethical behaviour is not confined to the generation and use of research data. It is a requirement throughout the research process from the initial thinking and research design, through formulation of the hypothesis and research question, selection and use of methods and design of data capture instruments, selection and use of subjects for study, reviewing the published work of others, and writing your own report on your research. For example, human subjects of study in a survey must not be identified, embarrassed, or their social, physical or mental well-being jeopardised by your research. Your results must not be used in any ways other than those originally set out in your accepted research proposal. You must report all that your work discovers whether it supports your original hypothesis or not.

Remember that your research is designed to *test* your hypothesis not to *prove* it. From the moment that a potential researcher begins to think about a topic, there is the possibility that unethical behaviour may become involved. The researcher may seek to prove a particular hypothesis and design the research to try to ensure this. This immediately jeopardises the research because the intention should be to test the hypothesis. 'Seeking to prove' suggests strongly that the researcher has a subjective view that the hypothesis is valid and wants to show this. Subjectivity of this kind is not a sound attribute for a researcher.

Box 2.5: Some forms of research misconduct

- Fabrication of evidence, data or results
- Falsification of evidence, data or results
- Selective use of evidence to support an hypothesis
- Choosing and using only experimental samples that will produce evidence supporting the hypothesis
- Suppression of evidence
- Claiming another's work as your own.

Discussion of ethics in research often seems to concentrate on research involving humans or animals. Yet there are many other forms of research misconduct that constitute unethical behaviour and their implications should be clearly understood. Particular forms of misconduct may result in a chain of consequences that may have far-reaching effects, not only for the perpetrators but also for their colleagues or co-workers, for those for whom the research was done or who were intended to benefit from the outcomes, and for those who will subsequently read the 'misconducted' published work. Bear this in mind when the circumstances at a particular point in your project work cause you to consider 'cutting corners' or 'taking a chance' in order to overcome a seemingly intractable problem. Or, indeed, unwittingly, you may do something that amounts to research misconduct. It is worth examining briefly some of the forms of research misconduct (see Box 2.5) that have been identified over the years in order to alert you to the dangers inherent in such behaviour.

Fabrication of evidence, data or results

The fabrication of data is a deliberate attempt to mislead your peers. It may involve the creation of records of interviews that never took place; adding extra numbers to categories of subjects observed; or adding to answers to specific questions in a survey. Never forget that your work may become the starting point for other workers who will rely upon it. They may accept material that you claim to have discovered. Think of the implications.

Falsification of evidence, data or results

Falsification usually involves the manipulation of evidence acquired so that an idea or expectation has stronger support than would otherwise be the case. For example, interviews with hastily selected, 'carefully prepared' subjects may be included in a survey at a late stage in the research to try to overcome failure to do sufficient interviews of properly chosen sample subjects within the allotted time. Again consider the implications for those involved in the research when the misconduct is discovered. This may result in co-workers who were not aware of the misconduct, being tainted by association and having their scholarly reputations tarnished. If results of the research have been published, there is the problem of making sure that the possible invalidity of the false evidence is made available to all those who read the publications. If several years have elapsed between publication and discovery, work in the intervening period, in which others have relied on the evidence, may no longer be reliable. These were implications in the case of Fujimura outlined in the Box 2.6, *Faking the past – Archaeological fraud*. A case that may become a classic similar to that of Fujimura involved Professor Reiner Protsch, a German anthropologist. Protsch was found to have systematically falsified dates on many 'Stone Age' relics (Harding, 2005) adding thousands of years to their ages.

Box 2.6:   Faking the past – archaeological fraud

As an illustration of the fabrication of evidence, a case that could become a classic is that of Shinichi Fujimura, a Japanese archaeologist. Media reports (see www.nationmaster.com/encyclopedia/Shinichi-Fujimura) disclosed that he had lied about finding stone artefacts at an archaeological site. These finds seemed to suggest that Japanese civilisation was 700,000 or more years old. A journalist showed that Fujimura had buried the tools himself and then discovered them later. Thus, he fabricated evidence. What are the implications of this misconduct? The initial one is that the work on the site in question is rendered valueless. Japanese history reverts to being no more than 70,000 to 80,000 years old. Fujimura is obviously shamed and will have destroyed his scholarly reputation. His co-workers, who will have relied upon him for learning and guidance, may have their reputations at least tarnished by association with him.

   Other implications stem from the fact that Fujimura's career as an archaeologist spanned at least 20 years. His fabrication of evidence in this one case calls into question the validity of all his other work. During his career, he worked at many other sites. Investigation by the Japan Archaeological Association found that 159 sites had been tampered with. Publications may have appeared carrying reports of the work. Fellow archaeologists will have been associated with him in those digs and may have been co-authors of some of the reports. Publications by other archaeologists may have cited these reports, and these chains of citations could extend over several years. How will these now intellectually and academically tarnished publications be traced? How will the fact that they may contain fabricated evidence be declared to the readers who may access them in libraries or databases around the world, and who may not have read of Fujimura's admission of research misconduct? The fabrications will remain in the public domain indefinitely; the careers of others who were dependent at least in part on the work done with or by Fujimura may be adversely affected, even founder. Indeed, school textbooks may have to be rewritten.

Selective use of evidence to support an hypothesis

A researcher may have a great enthusiasm for and be committed to a particular hypothesis. During the research, much evidence is gathered. Analysis of this evidence challenges the validity of the hypothesis. This challenge may not be very strong but is significant. The researcher decides that leaving out some of the evidence that counters the hypothesis modifies the situation and leads to the hypothesis apparently being strongly supported by the research. It is wrong to do this; all evidence should be reported and analysed. Discovery may occur when others try to replicate the research and do not get the same strength of support from their evidence.

Choosing and using experimental samples that will produce evidence supporting the hypothesis

This suggests quite strongly that the researcher has always been intending to prove a point, to ensure that a particular hypothesis is seen to be as stated in the research plan or that particular objectives had to be achieved. The research will have been designed around the central intention of achieving this proof. When others read the report and possibly try to replicate the research, there is a strong likelihood that the misconduct will be discovered.

Suppression of evidence

There are several reasons why researchers have suppressed evidence. One is that the evidence gathered may clearly and completely invalidate an hypothesis, or even destroy long-held beliefs of the researcher who has built a substantial reputation or career on them. Suppression of the evidence that invalidates the hypothesis may be the only way that the researcher sees to preserve both reputation and career.

Research today is often sponsored, as very few individuals can afford to be independent researchers. The sponsor of the research may have a legal entitlement to ownership of the data and information gathered in the research. Unless there is an agreement to the contrary, it is the sponsor's intellectual property, paid for by the financial support provided. In such cases, there may be occasions when suppression results from pressure from vested interests. It may be that the results of the research show that a retail product, a service or a television advertising campaign does not reach the performance guaranteed for it. Another possibility is that publication of the research would coincidentally publicise something that a sponsor would prefer to keep confidential. For example, I supervised an undergraduate project on the potential market for certain future products then under development by a major industrial corporation. Publication of the project report, even if only in the university library and in the student's academic department might have resulted in disclosure of significant features of the corporation's acquisition plans in a very competitive international market place. In fact, the student was initially given permission to use the information but a change in departmental management resulted in a different management policy being imposed, leading to the permission being rescinded at a very late stage in her project. Such conflicts of interest, between commercial confidentiality and academic freedom to publish, may be very difficult to resolve. Students have found difficulty in accepting what they have regarded as censorship of their work but the corporation was entitled to limit access to the work. Suppression of evidence in such a case may be considered perfectly reasonable by all parties, though it is more properly regarded as preservation of confidentiality.

Claiming another's work as your own

This may take the form of plagiarism, which is knowingly representing the work of others as your own. It may be that you take and use the results of another without that person knowing, that you claim a particular method or a research instrument as your own when it was suggested to you in private discussion with another researcher, or that you copy significant parts of a text written by another author. These instances must be viewed as theft of intellectual property. There is no excuse for this.

The consequences of research misconduct

People who act unethically are seeking an advantage that they consider they may not be able to achieve by fair means, or they are not inclined to invest the necessary effort in their work. In the commercial, industrial or academic research world, those acting unethically would probably have estimated the risks and consequences of their actions. Undergraduates who seek advantage by unfair means usually do not measure the risk nor do they identify the possible consequences. Even when consequences are considered, they are not regarded as likely to be severe. This may be the case with the cheating that goes on with essays and similar routine course work. Such actions usually lead only to the loss of some credits. The records of discovery and consequences usually remain confidential and are destroyed after a relatively short time. The situation is very different in the case of cheating in research. There are significant consequences that may stem from research misconduct (see Box 2.7).

> **Box 2.7: Possible consequences stemming from research misconduct**
>
> - Loss of respect and recognition by peers
> - Effective ending of academic and research career prospects
> - Possible criminal proceedings
> - Notification to the relevant professional organisations
> - Notification of the offence to journal editors or book publishers.

Loss of respect and recognition by peers

At its simplest, it may have an influence on the quality of references provided by those who know of the misconduct, such as personal tutors and heads of academic departments. What is more damaging is that you may be regarded as a person with whom it is not worth working. Indeed, you may become something of a pariah in the research community in your subject and possibly beyond. It will become very clear that a cheat is considered to be without scholarly integrity. The effect of this is unquantifiable but will be traumatic to most people. The opportunity to form networks of people who would be potentially useful contacts or future research collaborators would be lost. Ask yourself, 'would you want to work with a cheat?'

Effective ending of academic and research career prospects

Academic and other research institutions cannot afford to have on staff any researcher whose reputation is intellectually tarnished – there is too much at stake in terms of prestige and the financial support from research funding bodies. Also, the academic department that detects misconduct in an undergraduate's research will almost certainly ensure that the student is not considered for postgraduate research – if allowed to graduate. What organisation would want to take a chance on a cheat? The possibility that you would cheat again would be considered as high. Would the risk be worth taking? Would clients accept your presence close to their research?

Possible criminal proceedings

This is an extreme outcome and will depend upon the nature of the offence. Some misconduct does include misuse or fraudulent use of research resources. The case of Protsch is relevant – see p. 24.

Notification to the relevant professional organisations

The offending researcher's professional association or society will be notified of the misconduct. Think of the implications – possible expulsion from these organisations; loss of professional status and recognition; and loss of career and professional advancement. The financial consequences and the loss of self-esteem could last a lifetime.

Notification of the offence to journal editors or book publishers

This is necessary if the research has been published, which is very likely as the 'publish or perish' attitude prevails in many research institutions. Also, there is often a requirement to publish sponsored research, particularly when the sponsor is a public body. Think of the implications for the researcher and for those who have been associated with the researcher or have relied upon the research. How widely known will the misconduct of the researcher become? How easily would the researcher be able to get articles and books published after having gained a reputation as a cheat? How easy will it be to get further research support?

Detecting research misconduct

Experienced researchers in all fields will have considerable knowledge of what is possible, who is doing research in what areas, what the credible methods available are, and what is possible within specified time frames and with specified resources. They will often be able to recognise research of doubtful validity. Fortunately, the great majority of researchers adhere to high ethical standards. Careers and reputations depend on this but, more importantly, it is essential that those who use the outcomes of research have confidence in them. In an extreme, lives may depend on research results. Also, researchers build on or use the work of others in a range of ways when doing their own work. They must have confidence that they can trust the earlier work. Otherwise, dependent work, undertaken over a period of possibly several years and involving many researchers in that time, may collapse if it has been founded on falsehoods. This may have grave consequences for all the innocent researchers in the research stream that may flow from or involve the use of tainted work. It may also have very significant financial implications.

Your tutors and examiners will have the experience and knowledge to spot possible misconduct in your research. How will they do this? Sometimes co-workers will notify the relevant authority if they have detected what they perceive to be misconduct. However, much detective work can be based upon the research report. As your report will nominally be the definitive document about your research, your tutors and assessors will pay very careful attention to a range of features that may give clues as to the integrity with which you did the research reported. Some features are more obvious than others. There are several ways in which misconduct is detected. Box 2.8 and the text below highlight some of them.

Box 2.8:   Some ways in which research misconduct is detected

- Whistle blowing
- Debatable magnitude of data sets for the programme size reported
- Data are 'too perfect'
- Failure or inability to produce data reported in the project report
- Inability to replicate the work reported
- Text is plagiarised.

Whistle blowing

Some organisations, such as national governments and industrial corporations, are establishing procedures to facilitate this (Kaplan, 2001). There have been instances in which a third party has advised a tutor that an unfair advantage has been sought. The worst cases in my experience featured the copying of almost all of a project. In one of the cases, the project had been done two years previously in the same department; in the other case, the project done by a student on a similar degree course in another university had been copied. In both cases, supervising tutors were alerted by third parties.

Debatable magnitude of data sets for the programme size reported

In other words, how did the researcher manage to do so many interviews, survey so many companies, study so many television programmes or analyse so many portraits within the time frame? How was so much done within such a limited resource envelope?

Data are 'too perfect'

Everything fits the required outcomes absolutely without any problem and without even marginal departures from perfection. There are no rogue data, no gaps or inconsistencies, and no inexplicable results. The research proceeded exactly according to plan. This is not the norm and is unlikely in an undergraduate project.

Failure or inability to produce data reported in the project report

This may be due to carelessness in record keeping but is often likely to be the result of data invention at the time the true results are being analysed and found to be insufficient. With no time to do more data gathering, the researcher 'creates' some.

Inability to replicate the work reported

This may be due to a badly written methodology section. However, if your tutor has ensured that this section is properly done and adhered to, then the possibility is that at least some of the results have been taken from elsewhere, falsified or have been fabricated.

Text is plagiarised

Your tutors and examiners will be relatively widely read and knowledgeable about your topic, so they will be familiar with the mainstream research, the significant authors, the important developments and theories, and the general trend of thinking. They will also have their particular specialisms. Thus, they will almost certainly have encountered anything of pertinence to your topic. Also, some universities exchange information on undergraduate project topics. There is software available to test written work for similarity to published work and there are many websites that provide tutors with help in detecting plagiarism. Tutors recognise that the web has provided students with great opportunities to obtain material that some have used to gain unfair advantages in their course work, including project work. Now tutors use the web when they doubt the origin of a student's work. I have, within the last ten years, been involved in the assessment of two undergraduate projects, each of which contained very substantial amounts of plagiarised material. In one case, at least 90 per cent of the submitted project had been downloaded from the web, slightly rearranged and had some section headings changed. In the other case, significant parts of a book, amounting to several thousand words, had been submitted as the project. Chapter headings had been changed and the first paragraph of each of several chapters had been relocated within the text. Both students were failed and the students lost the opportunity to gain a good degree.

Since plagiarism is one of the most frequently encountered forms of cheating at undergraduate level, and as it is known to extend to use of copied material in major projects, it is worth discussing in more detail. As a researcher, you must demonstrate integrity in the attribution of ideas of others that have in some way encouraged, enlightened, or inspired you, or provided or explained something of use to you in your research. You must always inform your reader of the source of your ideas. This is more than a tradition, it is a scholarly imperative. If there are any ideas in your report that are not attributed to other people, then the reader normally has the right to assume that the unattributed ideas are yours. However, it is understood that some ideas are part of the generally accepted substance of the subject and so attribution is implicit since those knowledgeable in the subject will readily recognise their origins. For example, it is unlikely that there will be citations to the major contributions of Boyle, Darwin, Einstein or Newton in current publications in the particular sciences. 'Everybody knows' their contributions, they are part of the foundations of their subjects. Citation in these cases is often described as implicit. Every subject has its famous and fundamental contributors to whom no attribution is considered necessary, by convention rather than rule.

At this early stage in your development as a researcher, it is better to attribute than not to attribute. Students who use, without attribution, the work of others, even when they, the students, try to modify it to make it fit their style, will not recreate the work in their own style. Your tutors will be familiar with your style and so will quite readily detect any imported or recycled text. They will 'see the joins' between your words and the plagiarised words, and between words from different sources if you have imported text from several documents.

Since all research builds on the work of others in some way, it is unlikely that a research topic that has never before been thought about and discussed in some forum, and to which nothing relevant has been published, will feature in an undergraduate project. Attribution to others of the ideas that you have gained from reading about their work, or from discussions with them, is the recognised way of paying the intellectual debt that you owe to them. It will also demonstrate to your reader that you have made yourself aware of what has gone before in the topic being researched and that you have familiarised yourself with the methods, arguments, explanations, theories and processes pertinent to it. In summary, you will have shown that you have authority and support for your research and that you have learned from what others have done – you are 'well read' in your research subject. Thus, you will avoid the possibility of plagiarism and begin to establish your potential as a researcher.

Administration of the project

When we hear the word 'administration' we often form a mental image of filing cabinets, clerks and files of documentation. Whole departments in organisations are dedicated to administration. Why is there so much administration? Because effective management and control of an organisation depend on knowing in great detail precisely what has been done, when it was done, who did it and why it was done.

Surely you want to be able to control your project as effectively as an organisation controls its business? You want to be able to 'put your finger on' precisely what you did, created or thought or needed, with the minimum of effort. You want to know exactly where you have reached in your research plan without having to wade through masses of unorganised notes, discs, emails, papers or articles.

Recognise that at any given time during the life of your project, you must know exactly what you have accomplished, what your thoughts are, what you have to do and when you have to do it. Therefore, it is important that you create a system for keeping records and all other documentation that you or others create as a result of your project being done. It may seem bureaucratic, even pedantic, to do this. However, there comes a time in all research when it is helpful to be able to review progress or to refer back to some previous thoughts. Good notes on what you have done, with explanations of why you have done things and their outcomes, plus other relevant documents will ensure that the review is of good quality and is productive. You will save yourself time and trouble. You will have control of your project.

What documentation will be needed?

There are certain basic documents that all researchers should create and keep. These include the notes made during the development and definition of the topic for research, including notes of discussions with tutors and workplace supervisors. These notes are essential and form the foundation of the project proposal, which is another critical document. Writing of the project proposal is considered in Chapter 4, *Writing the Project Proposal*. The project plan will be developed from the proposal, which will contain an outline of the way in which you intend to do your research – the project plan in embryo. What may be termed a companion to the project plan is the project diary or log. In this you will record everything that happens, as it occurs, that is pertinent to the project, together with explanations and opinions.

Other documentation will include all correspondence relating to your project, notes of telephone conversations and interviews pertinent to the project, records of all items included in your literature review, questionnaires and other data capture instruments created for your research, and transfer or summary sheets on which, for example, you may record interim totals of responses to individual questions from questionnaires or from interviews. You should include notes explaining all the methods that you use in your research, together with any modifications to them with reasons for the modifications, and also include any principles or formulae that you use to analyse, interpret or synthesise your research data.

What form will the documentation take?

Project records may take many forms (see Appendix 1 and Chapter 4 of Orna with Stevens (1995)). It is quite common nowadays for many research records to be in electronic form, even the project diary. However, even in electronic form, there are substantial differences between the designs of records. For example, the format of a record for an item for your literature review will be very different from that for the record in which you summarise the interim totals of responses to questions from a customer survey. Some correspondence may take the form of emails, some may be conventional letters, and others may be internal memoranda. Do not forget the notes made in meetings, telephone conversations, and attendance at exhibitions, courses, seminars and tutorials relevant to the topic of your project, and even notes from casual meetings that may be relevant.

The project plan

The proposal will include the general time and work schedule for the project. This must be developed in detail to give a clear and precise indication of all that is involved in doing the project. It will provide a breakdown of the work into suitable units and show exactly when each of these units will begin and end and how they are related. This schedule provides a detailed plan of what you intend to do, when you will do it, and how you will do it in order to complete the project. It represents your sensible intentions and is usually worked out in consultation with your tutors. The plan can usefully be displayed as a series of horizontal charts (see Appendix 2), the first of which provides a monthly breakdown of the significant events, activities and processes with interim aims and objectives. Each month can then be displayed as a chart in which the events, activities and processes are presented on a day-by-day basis. Each chart should show the dependencies between activities and should also identify those activities that are independent. Do not forget to include holidays and an allowance for slippage. Slippage is important since it is rare that a project keeps exactly to plan. Allow some days, strategically throughout the project period, to accommodate the possibility of sickness – yours or a critical contact's – and failure to keep to timetable with activities such as interviewing, questionnaire surveying and utilisation of information technology facilities.

The project diary

This is also called the research diary or research log. However it is known, it has a particular function and that is to provide a record of the project as it progresses. In the diary you will record what has been done, when it was done, what problems were encountered, how they were resolved if at all, variations in the project plan and why they were done, contacts made and used, and why they were used, times of meetings with your tutor and workplace supervisor, and the subjects of discussions with them, and personal opinions on the progress. It is recommended that every individual item entered in the diary should be dated and timed and includes a record of all people who were concerned with a particular item, giving brief notes of their contribution. It may be that there are several items recorded on one day and that a week or more might pass before it is necessary to make another record. Events worth recording may occur in clusters between which some time may elapse before the occurrence of other noteworthy events. A simple page-a-day diary would suffice since each day is unlikely to be so full of critical or significant activities as to justify anything larger.

Interim research summaries

As you will not be devoting all your time to the project work, it is worth making a summary of progress periodically, a reasonable period being from four to six weeks. In some courses, the summary may be called a situation paper since it is a statement of the situation in respect of your project at a particular time. This can act as a quick reminder of where you have reached when you return to the project after some time away, perhaps doing course work for a final year module. It will also act as a memory aid in discussions with your tutor or workplace supervisor. These summaries can be straightforward typed reports of usually no more than 300 to 500 words. Remember to date and number them so that together they form a 'history' of your project. Properly done, they will be very helpful when the time comes to write the final report.

Personal reference documents

There are certain routine documents that all students should keep, particularly if they are in a workplace or on a sandwich placement. These include the contract of employment, information about health and safety, security, and the use of certain controlled facilities such as design and print, and bulk mailing. These documents may contain useful information about confidentiality, ownership of intellectual property, responsibilities and liabilities, and the provision of support and training in the use of equipment and facilities that may be useful in the project. They will normally be in company house style and should be filed for reference. Your university may provide documentation in which sources of help in skills enhancement, project report production and special information and library facilities are listed.

During your research, you will need to design forms on which to record data and information gathered. It is almost certain that you will have to design these forms yourself unless your university department or your employer has standard forms that you could use. Some of the forms will be highly specific, to be used to collect only one sort of data or information. Others may have more general use.

General records

These are the nearest that you should get to a general-purpose form. They may be used for recording details of, for example, visits to interviewees, telephone conversations, casual meetings, and attendance at seminars, tutorials, and courses relevant to your research. When designing these forms, make clear provision for naming the type of event being recorded and for the names of people directly involved, the venue of the event, and the date and time. Include sufficient space for notes of the subject discussed and for your comments, clearly distinguishing between the two. Some records may require the use of continuation sheets, for example, when reporting an extended interview with a tutor. It could prove useful to note significant general records in the project diary.

Literature review records

Each item that you read and review for your project must be noted. You will extract data or information from the literature that is pertinent to your research. It may be that you obtain useful data that may be added to or compared with your research results, you may gain some insights into a particular method that you plan to use, or you may gather explanations and opinions about your topic. When you design the literature item review record form (see Appendix 3), you must take into consideration all the different gains that you may make from the literature. Allow for all these so that you do not have to redesign the form some time into your research. Essential elements in the form are the name or names of the author or authors of the item that you are reviewing and a clear identification of the literature source, using a referencing standard. You may usefully add further sections in the form, in the first of which you should put the notes of the ideas that you have extracted from the item. The next section could contain what you have learned from it and your opinion of the contribution that the item makes to your research. Then you could indicate the extent to which, if at all, the item links to any other items that you have included in your review, showing the nature of the links, for example, the item may support what you have read elsewhere, challenge it or refute it. Remember to cross-refer from the other items to the current item. In your form design, you could even make provision for links in a separate section. A further section could be designed for you to include key words that indicate what the main thrust of the item is, for example, methodology, results, theories, or data capture instruments. Finally, it is important to make a note of the exact location of each item reviewed. You will prepare and write your literature review over a relatively long period during the project and your learning gains in reviewing will be substantial, causing you to rethink what you have gained from items reviewed earlier. Many of the items will have been used in or borrowed from a library or document file. Having the exact location, even to the extent of a library book number or shelf mark, or filing code, will make your job of retrieval much simpler. Examples of literature review record forms that I designed for my own and my students' use are given in Appendices 3 and 4.

Data capture instruments (forms to record results)

A critical process in all projects is recording the results of the investigation as it progresses. The data and information being gathered by the research will be the working material from which you will develop your arguments, conclusions and recommendations. You may well have substantial amounts of data and information to collect. Therefore, it will be very helpful for you to produce suitably designed forms on which to make your records. These instruments may be questionnaires, interview report forms, grids for recording the positions of objects by geographic location, or catalogue entries for fashion items, photographs or archaeological finds. For example, it is quite common for undergraduates to choose a project topic that requires the use of questionnaires to capture data or information. Be very careful. Questionnaire design requires great care – see Chapter 7, *Methodology*. A questionnaire is not something that can be 'dashed off' in a couple of hours. It requires specialist help if the data or information captured are to be good and useful. The social sciences section of a good academic library will carry many books that have sections devoted to questionnaire design. You should make sure that you consult a suitable authority before finalising any questionnaires. Certainly consult your academic tutor. If you are doing a work-based project, you may be fortunate enough to have appropriate expertise available in your employing organisation. Record your thinking in respect of the structure, form and content of each question and the order of questions.

You must exercise tight control over the administration, distribution and completion of questionnaires. This control could range from a well-written, concise guide to recipients on how to complete it, to a detailed set of guidance notes for the person or persons, including you, who perhaps will be interviewing to gain the required information. Other parts of the control will be the recording of distribution and return, using a controlled distribution list to keep clear, precise notes. Transfer sheets on which to accumulate data from individual questionnaires and summary sheets on which the data from transfer sheets are to be summarised, should also be designed. It may also prove useful to create a comments summary sheet to record comments made by respondents that do not lend themselves to counting since they are qualitative rather than quantitative. An additional useful record will contain your justification and explanation of the design and nature of the questionnaire, the reasons for its use, commentary on any problems in its administration and use, results from the pilot testing of it, and feedback about it from respondents.

Correspondence

Correspondence comes in many forms, including emails, type-written letters, facsimiles, hand-written letters and notes, and voice mail. Although it may seem extravagant to do so, it is worth printing copies of all electronic correspondence. This is because you may not always have access to the system on which you receive and store your electronic correspondence. Also, it makes it possible and it is more useful to group your documents by subject content, rather than related documents having to be grouped by the form in which you have received them.

How will the documentation be organised?

Time, date and number all project records. These records will include all completed questionnaires and interview forms, your notes of the activities and interactions in the project work, and notes from internal and external documentation that you reviewed to prepare and undertake the project. Solicited and unsolicited comment and opinion, where relevant, should also be recorded. Note on the documents the subject, time and date of receipt of each item of correspondence; do not rely on the date of despatch or the postmark.

If your main data capture instrument is a questionnaire, then the distribution of the questionnaires could be recorded, indexed or arranged in one or more of a number of ways, for example, by class of subject or by organisation, depending upon the nature and purpose of the records.

Box 2.9:   Some ways of arranging the records created when doing your project

- Alphabetically by recipient
- Chronologically by date of distribution
- Categorically, e.g. by type of employment of recipient
- Alphabetically by interviewer
- Quantitatively by size of organisation
- Alphabetically by nature of business or product type
- By standard ethnic or cultural grouping of recipient
- By age of recipient
- Alphabetically by subject
- Classified by subject.

Notes from internal and external literature discovered as a result of the literature searching that is an integral part of the project, could be organised by subject categories as broad or as specific as you consider appropriate. These categories may reflect methods, materials, styles, events, processes, results, theories, comments and opinions, depending upon the topic of your research. Correspondence should be indexed under originator or sender (who?) and arranged under content category (what?).

Why go to so much effort? Because this sort of effort expended at the initiation of the project will enable your time to be used more effectively. Also, by providing the means to monitor the progress of the project, it will help you to ensure that sufficient data and information are collected for the outcomes of the project to be meaningful. Finally, keep back-up copies of all electronic documents, and keep all documentation in a secure place. I have known several occasions on which disaster has struck, such as fire, and theft of project files. In some of those cases, the students concerned had not kept all their records secure nor had they made back-up copies of at least the critical files and located them away from the main files.

Summary

Successful projects are founded on thorough and effective preparation. In this chapter, the elements of good preparation have been introduced and explained. The project is the first significant piece of research for most undergraduates and so attention has been given to precisely what a project is and how to determine the amount of time to devote to it. Also, the need for an understanding of what research is, why and how it is done, and the importance of integrity in research have been considered in some detail. Record-keeping is critical to good management of your project and so the design, production and organisation of documents on which to record all the data and information that your research generates have been discussed.

Further Reading

Halding, Luke (2005) History of Modern Man Unravels as German Scholar is Exposed as Fraud. *The Guardian*, 19 February, 2005.

Kaplan, Elaire (2001) The International Emergence of Legal Protections for Whistleblowers. *The Journal of Public Inquiry*, Fall/Winter 2001, pp. 37–42.

Lashley, Conrad and Best, Warwick (2003) *12 Steps to Success* (new edn). London: Continuum.

Orna, Elizabeth with Stevens, Graham (1995) *Managing Information for Research*. Buckingham: Open University Press. (See particularly Chapter 4, pp. 59–73.)

Rudd, Shirley (1989) *Time Manage Your Reading*. Aldershot, Hampshire: Gower.

3 Choosing a Topic

A project may be 'work-based' or 'academic'. The work-based project is strongly practically oriented and usually has a developmental element in it that will have potential utility for the workplace. It is an investigation that focuses on some aspect of the working environment in which the student is undertaking a sandwich placement or is employed. The aspect may be a service or an element of a service offered by the employing organisation. It may be concerned with a problem that has been identified and that needs investigating with a view to finding a solution. It may involve the feasibility of changing existing or introducing new structures, procedures, equipment, services or techniques. It may be devoted to an examination of external factors that may affect the services or products offered by the employing or sandwich organisation in some way or ways currently not clearly understood.

The academic project will normally be a theoretical exploration or a piece of desk-based research. For example, this may be an investigation of the current position of particular developments in, or affecting some aspect of, a subject or area of professional endeavour relevant to the student's degree course. It may be a comparative analysis or synthesis of existing and available information and data on some aspect of importance and topicality in the chosen subject or profession.

Whether your project is to be work-based or academic, selection of the topic for it requires clear and disciplined preparation. In this chapter, factors that will assist you in making an informed choice of topic are considered. Ways in which the selected topic may be refined and used to develop the research question that will be addressed in your project are discussed.

Give yourself no more than six weeks to settle ideas for the topic of your project, though experience has shown that most students agree project topics well within that period. You may wish to begin consideration of possible topics before the nominal start date of the period during which the project has to be undertaken. This amount of time is not suggested lightly. It enables discussions to be held with tutors, workplace supervisors if appropriate, and with colleagues, of topics that might be suitable for investigation as your project. Some roundtable discussions with fellow students can often prove fruitful. Fellow students bring current experience obtained in a variety of environments and this can give pointers to, for example, possible limitations on ideas, additional perspectives, or novelty in approach. It is not unusual for the person who is not familiar with a particular subject area to be able to spot flaws or interesting and possible unique features worth exploring, that someone very close to the subject may miss or take for granted. You will eventually settle upon a possible topic for your research project, but to do the research, you need an hypothesis.

The hypothesis

Very early in the research process, it is necessary to formulate the hypothesis that the research will be designed to test. What is it, what is its significance, and how does it relate to your research? Few students understand what an hypothesis is and often begin their research without clarifying their thoughts. This will usually lead to problems as the research develops. So let us take two definitions from authoritative reference sources and use them to develop our understanding.

Box 3.1:   Definition 1 – Hypothesis

A provisional supposition which accounts for known facts, and serves as a starting-point for further investigation by which it may be proved or disproved.

Shorter Oxford English Dictionary

Box 3.2:   Definition 2 – Hypothesis

Supposition put forward as a basis for reasoning or investigation.

Oxford Guide to the English Language

These definitions demonstrate the essential role that the hypothesis plays in research. Note that the word 'supposition' features in each definition, and this forms the starting point of investigation. In effect, in order to proceed with an investigation, the researcher is stating, 'suppose for me that the following is so …'. The supposition must be much more than a whim or fancy in the mind of the researcher. It must have a reasonably sound and objective basis for being offered, and is often based upon facts and experience gained over a reasonable period of time of, for example, a problem or a phenomenon. The formulation of the hypothesis and its possible development into a thesis are shown in Figure 3.1, *The hypothesis explored*. From the start, you must be clear in your mind that you are not doing the research to *prove* your hypothesis; this is explicit in the first of the definitions given and implicit in the second. You are doing the research to *test* your hypothesis.

Let us consider Figure 3.1 in more detail. The 'research question' is developed to test the hypothesis that you have formulated as a result of considering your strengths, weaknesses and areas of interest. The word 'IDEAS' is used in Figure 3.1 to illustrate what is involved in exploring the hypothesis. It is presented as a group of specific, related processes that together sum up what is involved in the general research process that you will use to do your project.

'**I** – investigation' may be regarded as a process of careful study;

'**D** – discovery' relates to the capture of data, information, possible explanations, problems, and 'interesting things' that might be relevant;

'**E** – evaluation' relates to evaluation of the results, data and information gained in the research and from reported work of other researchers to determine their relevance to the research question;

'**A** – analysis' is applied to your results using accepted principles, and to the work of others, to determine the features of the results;

'**S** – synthesis' relates to the process of bringing together data and information from your research and, possibly, of data and information from other sources.

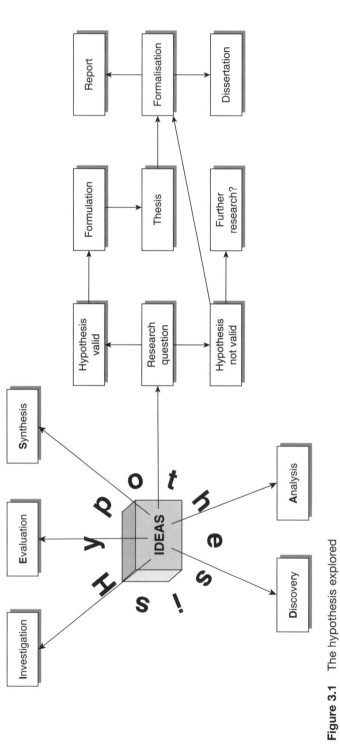

Figure 3.1 The hypothesis explored

The purpose of analysis and synthesis is to look for relationships or links, for example, to explain phenomena, support the hypothesis or otherwise, or solve a problem. If you use these processes effectively and efficiently, you will normally be in a position to formulate your thesis. This will be based upon interpretation of the evidence from your research and may include the work of other researchers.

Your research may show that your hypothesis is either valid or invalid. If it is shown to be valid, then you will have progressed to the point at which you can formulate a thesis. That is, you will have confirmation, for the time being, of a coherent, logically and objectively developed and integrated set of ideas as the best current explanation of, for example, a phenomenon that caused you to form your hypothesis. It will relate directly to the aims and objectives of the research and to the research question. You will present your thesis as a formal report or a dissertation, the form being determined by the regulations of your course.

Supposing that your research clearly establishes that your hypothesis is invalid. Is your work wasted? Have you failed your project? The answer to both these questions is – not necessarily so. You will need to review in detail, and with great care, everything that you did during your research, from the initial thinking to the final discussion. You will need to check the hypothesis. Is it logical, is it objectively developed and clearly expressed? Is the research question logically, objectively and clearly developed from the hypothesis? Is the research design appropriate and well defined? Are the methods well chosen and properly used? Are the project records clear, systematic, complete, precise and accurate? Are your arguments logically and systematically developed? Have you used your data and information logically and rationally? If you can honestly answer these questions positively, then your work is not wasted.

Objective reflection will enable you to determine all that you have learned from your work. Failing to prove the validity of something can be as valuable as proving its validity. In essence, you have proved that something is not so, according to the knowledge currently available. This can be useful to others researching in the same field. It may be that your failure to prove the validity of the hypothesis is the starting point for further research because, in your review of your work, you find interesting and thought-provoking leads that you or others can follow.

Is your project a failure? Can you still pass if your hypothesis is invalid? The answer to the second of these particular questions is 'yes'. However, this will depend upon the quality of every element of your project. Remember that the project is not primarily intended to get a research result by finding a solution to a problem or an explanation of a phenomenon. As you are an undergraduate, your project is intended primarily to test your project management and research skills. The fact that you have conducted work

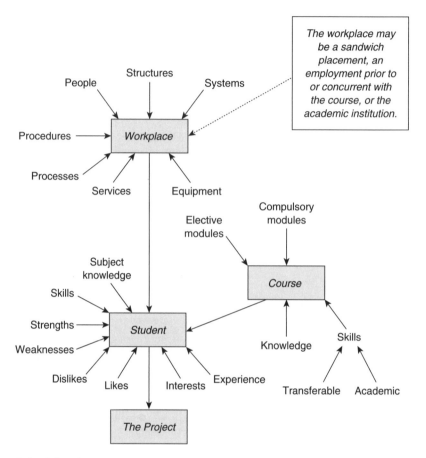

Figure 3.2   Informing your topic choice

that invalidates your hypothesis and that you have reported it objectively, will be an element in your favour, if this invalidation results from good research. You may have proved that you have the makings of a sound researcher. Your tutors will be able to advise as to the extent that invalidation of your hypothesis affects the grading of your project, if it affects the grading at all.

The relationship between you, your course and the workplace

There are three interacting elements that can provide considerable assistance in the process of choosing the topic for your project. The first of these is you, the student. In Figure 3.2, *Informing your topic choice*, the contributions that you, your course and, for sandwich and employed students, the workplace can make, are presented. If your project is based in your university department or school, there are contributions that this 'workplace' can make to choice of topic. For certain questions, the answers will help you to produce quite detailed profiles – of you, your course and the workplace. The answers will also help you to firm up your ideas about possible topics. Some are suggested here but do not regard this list as exhaustive.

Your personal profile

You are a combination of experience, interests, likes and dislikes, strengths and weaknesses, skills, and knowledge. One way in which you can represent this combination is to create a series of lists of those elements of which you are composed. For example, list in two parallel columns your weaknesses and strengths, and categorise them into academic, professional and personal. You may find that particular strengths may go some way to counter-balancing particular weaknesses. Similarly list your likes and dislikes. Complete the exercise by setting out your experience, interests, skills and knowledge. Be cautious when creating these lists. Over-assessment of your abilities, strengths and experience, for example, may lead you to choose an unrealistic topic. It will help to clarify your thinking about yourself if you create a personal profile.

It is important to undertake an honest and objective assessment of yourself. This will enable you to avoid taking on too great or too demanding a topic. Proper self-assessment will help you to set realistic parameters and to capitalise on your interests, strengths, competences and abilities. Consult your personal or course tutor or a close friend.

What are your academic and professional strengths and weaknesses?

Box 3.3:   Academic and professional strengths?

- Are you good at solving problems such as 'people problems'?
- Do you enjoy handling data, or figures such as statistics?
- Do you enjoy or find easy the use of information technology?
- Are you more practically or more theoretically oriented?
- Are you inductive or deductive in your approach to situations?
- Are you creative or logical in your approach to problems?
- Do you brief yourself thoroughly before undertaking a task?

The answers to these questions will not often be an outright *yes* or a *no*. They may be represented on a scale ranging from an absolute *no* to an absolute *yes*. For example, you may think that you are 'fairly good' at solving people problems, relatively weak at statistics, and 'attack a task head on' without much preparation. These answers would put you somewhere between *yes* and *no*, as most of your fellow students would probably be. The position on such a scale indicates your degree of strength or weakness. Do not worry about this; learning about yourself helps you to change yourself to advantage.

What are your personal strengths and weaknesses?

Box 3.4:   Personal strengths?

- Are you a 'loner' or do you prefer to work as a member of a group?
- Are you good or bad self-manager?
- Are you good or bad at time management and work scheduling?
- Are you an initiator, a leader, a follower, a manipulator?
- Are you a self-motivator, a good communicator, a contemplator?
- Are you persistent, dedicated, easily put off or sidetracked?
- Are you an innovator, or a developer of the ideas of others?

You will probably not have considered yourself from several of the points of view evident in these questions. This is not something to worry about. They are rather formal descriptions of 'people types' and most undergraduates will not have had need to think about themselves in these ways. Now is a good time to start since you may need to deploy skills implicit in these questions when doing your project, particularly if it is a work-based project. Again, the answers will be on a scale somewhere between *yes* and *no*.

The course profile

Now that you have your personal profile, turn to the course as a source of inspiration for ideas. You will have chosen certain electives from what was possibly quite a wide range of subjects. What did you choose and why? If you examine your electives very carefully, you may detect certain common features in them. For example, the course work in each may have demanded that you work in groups, or that you work on your own to produce well-argued theoretical papers. Conversely, there may have been a substantial practical component in each of them. The fact that you chose them to add to the compulsory core modules, suggests that there was some underlying feature that appealed to you, perhaps because it linked to a career choice that you intended to make. How do the demands of the electives link to your personal profile? Do they make use of your academic strengths and skills? Do they enable you to avoid subject areas that relate to your academic weaknesses? Do they enable you to exploit some of your interests? Do not ignore the core modules. In these there may be theoretical ideas or fundamental principles that you could usefully consider, for example, in relation to a workplace if you are taking a sandwich degree or are an employed student.

What elements or modules of the course have you enjoyed, been most interested in, inspired or stimulated by, or put off by? For example, if you have enjoyed research-oriented modules and gained good grades for them, this would suggest that you have some of the qualities necessary to be a researcher, such as objectivity and analytical and systematic skills. You may have found laboratory-based work devoted to problem-solving of particular interest.

You may have preferred those modules in which you were able to work alone without the need to co-operate with fellow students or interview human subjects of study. Conversely, you may have enjoyed modules in which the course work required you to work in small groups.

You may have determined that you are not comfortable with the sort of work that requires relatively extensive and intensive research of subject literature. However, recognise that the literature search, analysis and review processes are essential components of any project work. Therefore, you must not avoid this work but judicious choice of subject can reduce, though not eliminate, the amount and intensity of literature reviewing needed in a particular project.

Or is there a tutor whose subject knowledge, academic attitude and qualities as a teacher and leader of a research team, have triggered your interest in some specific topic for which he or she would be an ideal supervisor?

Recognise and be honest about your limitations. For example, you may have an opinion about some of your abilities that may not coincide with reality. Seek an opinion, from your tutor or workplace supervisor, about any project topic before you become so keen upon it that you insist upon doing it. Your opinion is subjective, perhaps strongly so, and you may seek to justify it or prove it in a suitably constructed and conducted piece of work. Such an attitude contains dangers but, if you realise this feature of yourself, you can turn it into a good learning experience.

The workplace profile

Finally, consider the contribution that the workplace, pre-course or concurrent with the course, can make. The term 'workplace' is used here to describe the place of employment of sandwich students, of part-time students and of full-time students who are working during their time on course. It is also used, when appropriate, to describe the academic institution in which full-time students are studying and may be doing their project. A workplace may be generally defined as an organisation in which activities and resources interact to provide products or services or both. The activities may range from scientific, technological and industrial, to commercial, managerial, governmental, educational or social. The resources will include finance, people, physical structures, equipment, materials, and energy supplies. How do any of these relate to what you have studied on your course and, particularly to the strengths and knowledge identified in your personal profile? By carefully comparing your personal profile with the workplace profile and your course profile (the total of what you have studied, not the course as a whole), you will be able to produce a reasonably clear picture of a subject area plus available skills and abilities from which it should be possible for you to choose a project topic. So, what can the workplace offer you?

Your employer, sandwich placement organisation or academic institution, may have several areas of its services or products, which managers consider should be investigated. Some or all of these may be suitable as they stand or could prove suitable with modifications. Some may never be suitable, however modified. A topic recommended by the employer does have certain advantages, such as a specified amount of time within the working week to do the project. You should ensure that this time is used to the full since the employer or tutor may have determined the precise time frame necessary to complete the work satisfactorily. The work may even be integrated into your job. In comparison, an academic project will normally have time scheduled into the course timetable. If you take advantage of advice from the employer or tutor, you will use the time effectively and efficiently.

It may be that you will be given appropriate resources to do the work. If you are working on a topic that is not of interest to the employer, you may find that there is little or no time allowance made for your work. Also, you will have to find any finance, software, stationery, and equipment necessary to do the project. However, if you are working on an employer's topic, you will usually find that the necessary resources will be provided within sensible limits and, possibly, support for attending short training courses related to the project work. The resources may even extend to the printing and binding of a certain number of copies of your project report.

Your employer or tutor may already have substantial amounts of useful data and information suitable for a project. Also, assistance may be provided in the design of appropriate data capture instruments, and in the analysis and interpretation of data and information captured as part of the project. However, it must not be done for you.

It is important to realise that there are potential dangers in involving the employer too closely in the project. For example, a change in your line manager may result in certain permissions received from the previous manager being revoked with a consequent loss of access to resources, data or important assistance being provided. The employer may decide to manage the project to ensure that it satisfies some internal agenda and it therefore ceases to be your project. Indeed, the consequent change may result in you not being able to meet some or all of the aims and objectives of your work, or may require removal of data or information from your project. A similar situation may arise with an academic project if your tutor is very knowledgeable in your topic and has great enthusiasm for it. In such a circumstance, it may be that your tutor uses you as little more than a research assistant, having 'taken over' your project. It can sometimes require diplomacy and tact to resolve such a difficult problem. In order to deal with an employer or a tutor who has effectively assumed control of your project, you will need to refer to your course regulations. These will make clear the extent of the assistance that you are permitted to receive.

Finalising the topic

So now you have a fairly clear idea of what topic you want to investigate. It is easy to suggest that the sooner a decision is made on a topic, whether doing a work-based or an academic project, the sooner work should start. Be cautious; do not rush into the work. Having settled on a topic area, not the specific topic, think about it, for example, in the context of the workplace. Box 3.5 contains questions that are worth asking and answering before finalising your topic. Most of the questions are also relevant to an academic project. Think carefully about each question before answering it. It will take you some time to gather the necessary information to answer these questions. You will be able to answer some of the questions only after consulting with a line manager in the workplace or with your tutor. You may also need to consult library catalogues, bibliographic specialists in your university library, maps, transport timetables and, possibly, fund holders from whom you may be able to obtain finance to support at least travel and subsistence, and even printing and binding of the project report.

Box 3.5: Finalising the topic

Questions that you should ask yourself before finalising your topic include:

- Do you sufficiently understand the specialist vocabulary of the subject within which your topic lies?
- Will you have to travel between sites either to examine some service features or to interview staff?

(Continued)

Box 3.5:   (Continued)

- Will you need to have ready access to:

  - files of records
  - databases of published information
  - information technology
  - data processing facilities
  - spreadsheets
  - word processing
  - document design facilities?

- How much of the available literature on the topic is in English?
- If there is a substantial proportion of the literature in foreign languages, do you have access to translations or translation facilities? Recognise that specialist topics usually require specialist translators.
- Will you have to provide a money budget for any part of the work?
- When and how will the money be provided?
- Can you perceive, after careful consideration, any obstacles of an organisational, individual or personal nature that may have an adverse effect on the progress or success of the project?
- Problems encountered with work-based projects include commercial and industrial confidentiality, with associated limitations on usability of certain information. Also, there may be particular microcultures in an organisation that do not work well together, or there may be a hidden agenda in a particular department.

If your responses to this sort of thinking are all reasonably positive and you have clearly and accurately identified possible stumbling blocks to progress and are sure that you can surmount them, then you are in a position to go ahead with the chosen project topic.

Topic analysis

The main purpose of topic analysis is to formulate the research question or questions that will be addressed in your project work. The topic that you have chosen will not yet be specific enough for you to investigate it exactly as chosen. It will be necessary to analyse it to determine precisely what it is in the topic that calls for investigation. The process of topic analysis is critical and should be approached in a systematic manner. A systematic approach to topic analysis and research question formulation is presented in Figure 3.3, *The research question.*

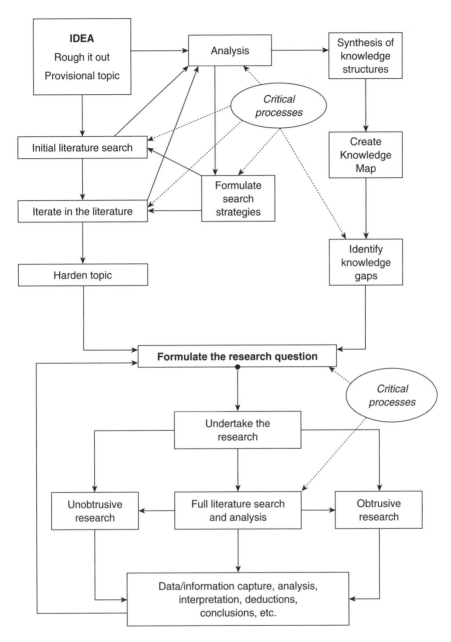

Figure 3.3 The research question

What is involved in topic analysis? This question has a two-part answer. The first part is concerned with analysing the topic from the point of view of its subject content. The second part is concerned with its nature and context.

Content analysis

In order to understand the content, it is useful to identify what the various component parts of the subject are. What are the main categories of components in the subject? Is it a subject in which materials and processes appear to dominate? Or is it a subject in which period, place and people are of most significance? For example, the main components of medicine are the human body, its organs and parts, diseases, treatment, and specific therapies. In religion, the religious system, doctrines, sacred books or tracts, icons, events and people are significant. Architecture is concerned with types of building, parts of buildings, building form and function, building processes and materials, styles, period and place. Transport is concerned with the medium in which the transport occurs – land, sea, air and space – and with transport vehicle, vehicle function such as military or civil, passenger or freight, and motive power. Commerce may be analysed into type of service offered, such as banking, insurance or broking, methods, forms of finance, and time. Management is a very wide-ranging subject and includes finance, personnel or human resource, strategic, functional, tactical and operational management, knowledge, marketing and customer relationship management. It involves processes, activities, structures, situations, products, services, and locations.

The social sciences are generally concerned with people, mainly in formal and informal groups. The groups may be social classes, religious, ethnic or racial groups, communities at local, regional, national and international levels or leisure groupings such as sports crowds and theatre audiences. The social scientist studies such matters as the processes of group formation and coherence, the beliefs of groups and the behavioural characteristics of members and their groups. With all subjects, there are the theoretical and practical aspects from which some valuable project topics may be identified.

The analysis can be taken to greater detail. For example, the treatments in medicine may be analysed down to type of treatment, such as chemotherapy or radiotherapy, and chemotherapy can be analysed down to individual drug treatments. Another example is literary fiction; we can analyse the literary form that is fiction down to genre such as science fiction, detective fiction, romance and adventure. Fine arts may be analysed to medium, form, mood, materials, processes and tools, style, period and artist. These examples are not exhaustive but do illustrate the sort of detail in which a topic can be analysed. You will have to determine the extent and intensity of your topic analysis by deciding precisely what you will need to specify in the aims and objectives of the project.

Nature and context of the topic

When you have analysed the content of your topic, you will have a much greater understanding of it and its place in the overall structure of the subject or discipline of which it is a part. Now it is time to think about the nature of the topic and then the context in which it is to be considered. The nature of the topic relates to whether it is theoretical, practical or developmental, or involves problem-solving and decision-making. There are certain questions that you can ask that will help to you to understand why it is important to determine the nature of the topic. The first of these is – *What is explicit about it?* In other words, what is clearly evident as a result of the existence of the topic? For example, you may be considering a problem of a major backlog of products ready for distribution in a wholesale warehouse. There may be clear evidence of insufficient work force, of fluctuating delivery of despatch notes and infrequent arrival of vehicles to take despatched products. This may lead to a second question – *What is inferable from it?* In other words, because the problem exists and you have identified the explicit aspects of it, what can you infer from this evidence? You may consider it reasonable to infer that the warehouse management is not functioning effectively or efficiently, or that the transport management is not up to scratch. Do not settle for these inferences; look for other possibilities. A third question prompted by your initial findings could be – *What is predictable from it?* Backlogs of the type identified are very likely to result in failure to keep to agreed delivery schedules. In turn, this will lead to customer dissatisfaction, even to loss of orders. Developing questions of this kind will help to clarify and add precision to the definition of your topic.

It is important to realise that the context of your project is more than the workplace or academic environment in which you are doing it. Both are made up of the work force, the buildings, equipment, systems, facilities, materials and other resources necessary to produce the products or services. Also, both are almost certainly operating in a competitive market place, with the attendant pressures and problems stemming, for instance, from local, national or international economic conditions. There may be a substantial regulatory framework within which your organisation has to operate. Your topic is embedded in this sort of quite complex context. Therefore, it is important for you to recognise and understand precisely what the context is within which you will have to undertake your project. For example, competitive and economic pressures may have severe effects on many of the work force, resulting in substantial adverse attitudes to their work. They may prove unco-operative when you try to gather their opinions on the potential benefits of a change in certain work practices, although this is less likely in an academic environment. Such investigations will almost certainly be regarded as a threat to employment in a non-academic environment since, if implemented, they will bring change. In difficult times, change is often seen as impending job losses. Further contextual features to identify include the methods, processes, materials and equipment related directly to the topic of your investigation, and the people who are working on the matters that are an integral part of your topic. All these features should be established precisely so that you can prepare a clear and exact definition of the topic in its specific context, including all actual and potential influencing factors.

The research question

It may seem to you that establishing the topic content, nature and context is unnecessarily complicated. Certainly, it appears complicated but in reality it is quite straightforward and relatively quickly done. If your preparatory work – including consultation with tutors and workplace supervisor and your personal, course and workplace profiling have been carefully done, you should establish content and context in a week. You will then be in a position to begin formulating your research question.

What do we mean by research question? In undertaking research, you are seeking to find out something. You are not taking a random mental walk around the universe of knowledge. You will be in a subject area that you know generally and may well have quite detailed knowledge of parts of it. The areas about which your knowledge is indistinct or non-existent should provoke in you at least a questioning frame of mind in which you are asking: *What is there? Why is it so? How do I find out about it?* It is a general feature of research that it is done to answer questions. These questions will be specific; such specificity enables you to define precisely what you seek and may suggest methods to be used in your research. Also, well-structured and precise research questions will provide a very good starting point for formulating the initial search strategy that you will need in order to start your literature search and review. Research questions usually begin with an interrogative pronoun such as: *Who? Which?; What?,* or an interrogative adverb such as: *Where?; When?; Why?*

Formulating the research question requires time and care and is an essential part of the overall research process. It does have several valuable outcomes, one of which is the confidence that you will have in your project since the research that you do will be built on a firm and clear foundation.

Let us assume that you have had what you regard as a promising idea for your research. Now list some questions about the topic that you would like answered. Five or six questions should be enough. Regard these as provisional questions. Think carefully about them. They should be realistic, clear and to the point. Choose one of these questions and use it as a search strategy to do a quick literature search, producing no more than three or four items, to find out what you can about the subject of the question. Repeat this process with the other questions in your list. Analyse the content of the literature obtained from the searches. This will help you to get to know the particular aspects of your topic reflected in the questions. Eventually, you will reduce the number of questions to one or two. You may even 'harden' the topic sufficiently to formulate the research question at this point.

You may discover many things from the literature, for example, theories, problems, events and methods of investigation relevant to the question and, therefore, to your chosen topic. Use what you have discovered in beginning to develop a picture of the structure of the subject. The content analysis already conducted will have produced the subject components of your topic. In all subjects, these have a logical order into which they can be arranged to create a picture of the structure of the subject. If we take the subject of architecture, the order that we settle on for our project purposes could be: Building type, components, details, materials and processes. Components of religion could be organised according to the order: religious system; doctrines; sacred writings; sacred buildings; religious artefacts; events; people.

Creating a knowledge map

Now that you have an idea of the structure of your topic, you can formulate sharper, more precise strategies to undertake more extensive searching of the literature. Outputs from this searching will enable you to do two things, which can be run in parallel. The first of these is that you will be able to produce a much more clearly defined topic. The second is that you will be able to build a more detailed and thorough picture of the structure of the subject of which your topic is a part. This 'knowledge map' will contain areas of uncertainty and gaps. This is to be expected because you are relatively new to the subject and because you have not undertaken a detailed and exhaustive search and review of the literature of the subject. Indeed, if the map were complete with no areas of uncertainty, it would suggest that you would have considerable difficulty in finding something to investigate. So what is a knowledge map?

Box 3.6:   Definition – Knowledge map

A knowledge map is a graphical presentation of the structure of the knowledge that exists in a given universe of interest, or focus of study or specific interest, in which the knowledge is categorised, and the relationships between knowledge components are identified and indicated.

The knowledge map will enable you to determine your degree of understanding of the chosen topic area and to clearly establish the domain of interest that is your project topic. The boundaries of this domain will be precisely defined and within the domain the subject components will be displayed. A well-drawn knowledge map can lead to the generation and understanding of the relationships between concepts within the specific domain of interest to you. These relationships will be identified as dependent and independent, subordinate, co-ordinate and super-ordinate. Within the picture of the subject structure that you now have, there will undoubtedly be some areas of uncertainty and gaps in the structure. The uncertainties and gaps suggest possibilities for research. Discussion with your tutor and taking account of your preliminary literature searching and sharpening of your project topic will assist you in selecting a gap or an uncertainty as the possible source of your research question. However, it will be possible to clarify some of the uncertainties and fill some of the gaps by the detailed and intensive literature search and review that you undertake as one of the essential parts of your main project research. (The literature review is discussed in detail in Chapter 8.)

Some criteria to be satisfied

The undergraduate project has already been defined as small, and there will normally be only one research question to be addressed. However, this question must satisfy the same criteria as the questions in a large research project. We can represent these criteria as a series of questions.

Is the research question interesting to the researcher?

It is important that the question should be interesting to the researcher because, among other things, research is time-consuming and may at times be tedious whilst the routine tasks are undertaken. These tasks may be very extensive if much data and information are to be gathered, particularly if some are difficult to track down. The research mind accepts this and, with good project planning and management, tedium may be reduced or eliminated.

Is the question too broad, too narrow or just right?

A question that is too broad may cause lack of clear understanding and vagueness in determining what is required, leading to opportunities for misinterpretation resulting in inadequate research. Another possible problem is that broad questions may require substantial effort, resources and time to answer, and none of these may be available to you. If the question is too narrow, there will not be sufficient substance in your research to justify having done it. Also, it is very unlikely that a project built on a question that is too narrow will gain a pass grade.

Is the research question simple and straightforward?

Complex, difficult to understand questions mean that there may be room for various interpretations with the potential for inadequate or fruitless research. So, the simpler and more clearly and precisely expressed the research question, the better able you will be to produce a satisfactory research design.

Does the question have relevance?

When answered, will it reveal new knowledge, new explanations of, or insights into existing data, information or knowledge appropriate to the subject domain of the research? If you are able to give positive answers to these points, then it is relevant; if not, the work has no value and, therefore, no relevance.

Can it be researched?

Is it answerable? Is it feasible in the time and with the knowledge, methods and equipment available to you, the researcher? You must be able to give a positive response to each of these.

What data or information do I need to answer it?

Is the scope of these data or information measurable? Will the data or information be accessible, in the time and with the facilities and resources that are available to you? Discussions with your tutor or supervisor are valuable in answering this.

Is the question of such quality that it will enable you to produce useful outcomes? Is there any value in the research prompted by the question?

Do not choose a bland, unremarkable question because it deals with something that will be easy to research and write up. Such a question may ensure that you obtain a pass grade for your project report but the uninspiring work will not impress the examiners nor will it be satisfactory proof that you have research potential.

Is the question ethical?

Will there be risks to subjects of or participants in the research? Will there be a need for written informed consent from the subjects and participants and will you be able to obtain it? Will there be any potential for conflict of interest, for example, between you and the organisation in which you are researching? Will the research result in you gaining access to information of a confidential, sensitive or personal nature and will you be able to ensure its security? Is there a code of research ethics to which you must conform, either within your university or within the organisation in which you are researching? This criterion must be met.

Some examples

We now have an idea of the general shape and form of a research question. Let us examine two examples of potential research questions.

1. A business education question – too broad?

Assume that you are a business studies undergraduate student on sandwich placement in an insurance company. You want to do a project on business education. Consider the research question:

> *How do in-house training courses in business management provided by employers in the business sector compare with university degree courses in business studies?*

Is the question interesting to you, the researcher?

By the time that you have to choose a project, you will have been on your business studies course for nearly two years. In that time, you will have formed an opinion about the quality and value of what and how you are being taught. Your opinion of the course and the lectures, seminars, learning facilities and teaching staff may be good or bad, or somewhere in between. The organisation to which you are going for your sandwich placement may provide training courses itself or may have contracted out to a professional institution the provision of tailor-made short courses. You would like to find out if these in-house courses are better preparation for work than your degree course. So the first criterion is satisfied.

Is the question too broad, too narrow or just right?

It is too broad. As worded, the potential field of research is the whole of business and the whole of education for business. Normally, no single organisation will be able to find the resources or devote the time necessary to investigate the topic as expressed in the question.

Is the question simple and straightforward?

It is not expressed simply or in a straightforward way but it could be refined to provide a question suitable for fulfilling the terms of an undergraduate project. Clearly limiting and defining the particular university courses and in-house courses that you intend to study could achieve this. Additionally, it would prove sensible to limit the universities to specified regions and limit the businesses by size and to particular parts of the business sector. Sample sizes and survey methods you intended to use would be critical.

Does the question have relevance?

There certainly is relevance in the question from at least three points of view. First, an answer to the question would help you to determine whether you are making the best preparation for your career in business. Second, if the research to obtain data and information is well designed and undertaken, the results would be of value to business organisations planning staff training and development programmes. Third, it would prove useful to your university and to other educational institutions providing business studies courses by giving some insights into what businesses require of their employees.

Can it be researched?

If the topic is clearly and precisely defined, if the aims and objectives are realistic and the research parameters carefully and realistically established, then it should be possible to do useful research on the topic.

What data and information do I need?

The number of university degree courses and universities is finite and reasonable, and so the business studies students will be reasonably accessible. Also, the number of employers offering in-house training courses should be discoverable. Therefore, there will be measurable data and appropriate information obtainable. Provided the size of population to be surveyed and the sample sizes for your study are soundly determined, the research as more narrowly defined could be carried out in the time frame available.

Is the question of such quality that the outcomes will be useful?

There will be value to the research if properly done. There will be employers and universities interested in the outcomes. For example, it may prove useful to the tutors who manage your degree course, for example, in the development of case study material for use in your course, or in the establishment of sponsored studentships. If well done and well reported, your research may be used to inform recruitment programmes of some business enterprises, even leading to the development of formal links with particular universities.

Is the question ethical?

When doing your risk assessment for the project, you will identify whether there will be any ethical matters requiring your consideration. The question may seem simple from the ethical point of view, however, there may be situations when you will have clear need to consider the ethics. For example, in surveying staff of a business organisation, you may be offered access to personnel files. Appropriate permissions must be obtained, from the individual staff and from the organisation. In interviewing individual staff or university students, you may elicit information or opinions that are of a very personal and possibly controversial nature. You should make clear to the interviewees that their informed consent is required before they take part in your research and before you use their contributions. You may need to consider treating the interview records as confidential and representing interviewees and others who offer opinions as anonymous respondents.

In conclusion

The question, as originally posed, met most of the criteria in general terms but failed on the important one of broadness. It is very unlikely that the question as framed would be researchable. However, it does have much merit and this is shown by the relative ease with which it could be refined to make it possible for you to develop a research topic that you could do in the time frame allowed for your project.

2. A question of option choices – just right?

There will come a point in your topic analysis when you arrive at the question that appears to be precisely what you want to research. You may be fortunate enough to settle upon the question at the start or be given your research question by your tutor. Let us examine a question that seems to be just what you want. This time, assume that you are a student on a fine arts degree course in which it is possible to choose a specialism from a range that includes sculpture, painting, and textile design. There are about 200 students on your degree course among whom there are many students from overseas and from a range of ethnic minorities. You decide to explore the possibility that there might be a relationship between the national and ethnic origins of your fellow students and the specialisms that they choose. After discussion with your tutor, you develop the following question:

What is the distribution of specialist option choices made by students on the fine arts degree at my university in relation to their national and ethnic origins?

Is the question interesting to you?

It is often difficult to be clear about why something interests you. In this case, during your time on your course, you will have registered perhaps subconsciously, then consciously the variety of ethnic and overseas students working around you. The fact that you now want to find out more about them suggests a greater than average interest in the subject.

Is the question too broad, too narrow or just right?

Embedded in your question is a clear definition of the population that you wish to study. This population is of a reasonable size, and features that you will need to consider as possible parameters are readily identifiable and realistic. As you begin the design of your project, you may decide to extend the research to cover the religious and cultural backgrounds of the students. The necessary research could be completed in the project time frame.

Is the question simple and straightforward?

Yes, it is clear and the research necessary to answer it is readily designed and accomplished.

Does the question have relevance?

It does, from at least two points of view. First, successful completion of the work will satisfy your interest. Second, if your research is thorough and sound, the results may prove relevant to recruitment to your course.

Can it be researched?

It is certainly researchable at undergraduate level. All the elements necessary for the research – mainly course documentation and the subjects of the research – are relatively easily accessible, being available within your academic department or your faculty. The methods that you would need are straightforward and simple to use.

What data or information do you need?

Many of these are implied by the question. National and ethnic origins, and religious and cultural backgrounds and the specialism choices will be essential data. Information that would prove valuable would be reasons why students had chosen their particular specialisms. All these will be readily obtainable.

Is the question of such quality that the outcomes will be useful?

Yes. Your work may prompt further work by your tutors with a view to deciding how they could develop or redesign the course or how they could determine what specialisms to offer to particular cohorts. Recognise that your research gives a picture only of the situation at a particular time in your degree course. Other universities may use your work as a starting point for work of their own. When results of work from all universities offering similar fine arts degree courses are aggregated, it may be possible to generalise conclusions, perhaps regionally or nationally. Marketing of relevant courses to ethnic and religious groups in the UK, and internationally, may be more informed as a result of your work, either directly or indirectly.

Is the question ethical?

Nominally it is. Ethical concerns will arise when you design the research and select the methods by which you will obtain your data and information. Think about the features that you wish to identify in order to answer the question. Think also about the uses that you and others may make of the data and information that you gather. You must realise that you will be requiring disclosure of what some individual students, and students from particular backgrounds, may regard as very sensitive. Very careful consideration must be given to the way in which you will elicit the data and information. You may have to guarantee anonymity and will need to obtain informed consent to access and to use the data and information.

In conclusion

The question, as orginally posed, met all of the criteria, some explicitly, the others implicitly. The research population is clearly defined and limited and the subjects are accessible. Data would be available from organised systems. It would be important to recognise the potentially sensitive nature of some interview questions. Properly done, the research should produce useful outcomes.

Summary

Choosing the topic for your project is an important process and it is not easy. However, every year thousands of students do it and produce successful projects. How do they do it? They give time and thought to choosing a topic and take advice available from tutors, line managers, library staff and others with relevant knowledge and experience. The importance of the project should bring home to you the value of careful preparation. Such preparation is not difficult if you are systematic and follow the guidelines given in this chapter. The factors that should ensure an objective and sensible choice of topic have been examined. Much can be learned from analysing yourself, your course and the environment in which you will do the project. Formulation of the hypothesis and your research question was explained and criteria to help you to refine and 'sharpen' it were offered and discussed with examples.

Further Reading

Bell, Judith (2005) *Doing Your Research Project* (4th edn). Buckingham: Open University Press.

Blaxter, Loraine, Hughes, Christina and Tight, Malcolm (2001) *How to Research* (2nd edn). Buckingham: Open University Press.

Hart, Chris (1998) *Doing a Literature Review: Releasing the Social Science Research Imagination*. London: Sage Publications. (See particularly Example A. Justifying your topic, pp. 198–204.)

4 Writing the Project Proposal

The importance of the proposal

You now have a topic for your project. So you now have to write the proposal that will explain how you intend to do your work and what your research capability is. The proposal is an important document because it embodies the project's reason for being and so it is examined in detail in this chapter, paying particular attention to the main concerns expressed by students. Let us begin by discussing briefly some aspects of the project that students often do not give enough attention to when preparing the proposal.

First, you must realise that the proposal is a formal document intended to persuade in order to gain support for the work that you propose. Its persuasiveness lies more in its content than in its style. However, style is important in so far as the proposal should be informative, explanatory, clear and succinct and should not leave any possibility of misinterpretation of what you intend to do and how you intend to do it.

Second, it should be structured in such a way that the readers are led to answers to questions they will have. These will relate, for example, to the extent of your abilities to do the work, whether or not you have the required objectivity and precision of thinking for research, and the appropriateness of the proposed work to the subjects that you have studied and the depth of knowledge and understanding that you bring to the research.

Third, the proposal seems to be a major endeavour and it is. It is also very important but realise that there is always help available so make sure that you use it. Your university may provide you with a standard format or a convention or template to use when writing your proposal. The format will normally consist of a set of standard headings that you are recommended to use when writing the proposal. These will provide systematic guidance on how you should proceed and help you to order your thoughts appropriately. Additionally, there will be tutors available when 'project time' comes around. Use them. There may be a series of project preparation classes such as seminars and tutorials offered in your academic department. The fact that they are available should suggest to you that your tutors consider them important, so prepare for them and take part.

Fourth, there should be copies of proposals written by students from previous cohorts that you will be able to consult. Again, use them, with tutor approval. If you take advantage of this help, you will be able to prepare a sound proposal. It is unlikely that your degree regulations will permit you to proceed with the project until your topic has been approved. Experience over more than 30 years has shown that students who take advantage of the help available invariably gain approval for their proposals. Yes, composing and writing the proposal are demanding but thousands of students prepare successful proposals every year.

Finally, writing the project proposal requires careful preparation and clear, logical thinking. Remember that the overall objective in researching, however simple or complex the research, is the advancement of knowledge in a particular subject area. What is the knowledge that you seek about your chosen topic? You will have thought about your topic, done a preliminary review of the pertinent literature, discussed this and your topic with your tutor and your workplace supervisor if you have one, and created your knowledge map. You will have formulated your hypothesis and established your research question. When beginning the first draft of the proposal, you must keep this question clearly in your mind. This will clarify why you are doing the project and so there will be less chance that you will allow yourself to be sidetracked during the investigation. Also, you will be more likely to develop clear and unequivocal aims and objectives.

Feasibility of the proposed research

A critical step in preparing the proposal is establishment of the feasibility of your proposed research. There are several perspectives from which feasibility may be viewed. First, from the time viewpoint – will there be enough time to do all the work required, including an allowance for the unexpected, known as 'slippage time'? Second, from the skills availability viewpoint – do you have or can you readily acquire the skills necessary to complete the work required? You may be able to get someone to help you with some aspect of your work, provided that this aspect is not a significant matter within the project; for example, you would be allowed help setting up software. Third, from the scope viewpoint – is there enough 'breadth and depth' in the proposed topic to warrant investigation? Fourth, from the relevance viewpoint – is the topic relevant to the specific environment within which the work is to be done or to the general professional needs, directions and environment? Does it have relevance to some part of your course? It should. Finally, from a political viewpoint – is the proposed work likely to impinge upon matters of a sensitive nature, to 'offend' decision-makers or policy-makers, or clash with current policy trends, attitudes and decisions within the intended working environment?

Your university department convention for proposals may specify a particular structure. This will have, as one purpose, the clear indication of what you must put into your proposal, which makes your job relatively straightforward. Most proposal structures have at least seven components in common and these are examined below.

What is involved in preparing the proposal?

A research proposal is a highly structured document and the process of preparing a proposal is very systematic, see Appendix 5. Therefore, use the headings of the sections of the proposal as a guide to preparing it. These sections are clearly indicative of what should be written into them and they are usually organised into a logical order. Whether the proposal is for a piece of 'pure' theoretical research undertaken within your university department or for a work-based product or service development or problem-solving project (if you are on a sandwich placement or are an employed student), the basic structure of the proposal will be the same.

1. Working title

This should be no more than a general but succinct representation of your topic and the intent of the project. The title of the final report submitted may well be substantially different from the working title. The working title should imply the breadth and depth of the topic. It can then function as a brief and useful summary and a general reminder whenever your thoughts need bringing back into focus or back into line with the original intent. This may be the case if you have been away from your project for some time due, for example, to pressures of other work or a holiday.

2. Scope

This statement describes the extent of the project and should be brief, clear and to the point. It should clarify the working title and give a clear indication of the breadth, depth and overall coverage of what is to be investigated in the project. If there are any limitations to be imposed on the work that are not clear from the general statement of scope, these should be stated.

3. Aims

These are general statements of the intent behind the project work and the product of the work. They are statements that encompass the ultimate purpose of your proposed research.

4. Objectives

These are clear, succinct statements of the intended outcomes of your research. They will state specific achievements that you must make in order to demonstrate that your research is successful and that the aims have been fulfilled.

5. Justification

This is an explanation of why the project is being done and should be done. The intention is to demonstrate clearly why the resources in terms of your time, time of other staff (do not forget that tutorial and workplace supervision is a contributing factor here), costs of travel, stationery, equipment utilisation, and use of facilities such as design and print, should be expended on your project. The resource demands made by your research may be minimal because of its very nature as an undergraduate project. Nevertheless, it is worth the learning experience of justifying a piece of research.

6. Methodology

In this section, you describe and explain the methods that you will use in doing your research. Therefore, you must clearly explain how you will gather the data and information that you will need, how it will be recorded, and how it will be processed. The techniques and methods, equipment, systems and procedures that you use should be clear to a reader who does not have the opportunity to question you about them. Therefore, the description of proposed methodology should be clear and unequivocal so that you can develop it in detail when writing your final project report. Recognise that the methods chosen must be suitable for the fulfilment of the aims and the achievement of the objectives. In fact, they must be logically linked to the aims and objectives. When preparing this section, keep in mind that your methodology should be so well described in your final report that another researcher should be able to replicate your work without having to consult you on any aspect of your methods.

7. Provisional work schedule

This is a general indication of the timetable of the work during the project period. Therefore, it will be sufficient to break the period into major segments, perhaps month by month initially, giving an indication of the start and finish dates of what you intend to do in each, provided that there are no problems. Analyse what is involved in pursuing the work; break down the work into components; determine what dependencies there are between individual components; determine the order in which the various components, both dependent and independent, need to be investigated. It is useful to build in slippage time to enable the unexpected to be accommodated. The project period normally lasts for at least 6 months and may be as long as 12 months. You may get sick, people critical to the research may get sick or be unavailable when needed. Equipment malfunction, service failure and other matters beyond your control may occur that interrupt the scheduled work, even causing severe delays to completion of parts of your work or to the project itself. Fit the work to a sensible and rational time plan. Take into account all aspects of the work and try to identify factors that may influence adherence to the plan. Recognise that some influences cannot be forecast and so some form of contingency must be built in to the plan. Distribute slippage sensibly throughout the project period; do not put in a single week or fortnight somewhere in the second half of the period, as some students have done. Tutors will have the necessary experience to guide you on slippage allowances but note that your project submission date will not usually be extended since it is built into your course schedule. Understand that matters such as slippage allowances are a normal part of project planning and management.

There are other headings under which individual university departments may require some information. These may be concerned with resource demands, risk analysis, and possible benefits and outcomes of the proposed research:

Resource demand

Realise that the resources necessary to undertake the work proposed amount to more, often much more, than the person doing the work. At undergraduate project level, provision of required resources is usually the responsibility of you – the researcher. Remember such matters as access to databases, libraries, and people (as advisers or as subjects of investigation). You may be fortunate in that a workplace employer may make resources available, for example, design and print for preparing a questionnaire and postage for mailing it, and in the production of the final report.

Risk analysis

Identify what may be likely to have adverse effects on the proposed work. Determine the extent to which it may be possible to foresee potential problems and the measure of control that it may be possible to exercise over their resolution. Be objective in determining possible risks. Remember that not every problem is a risk and that it may be possible to anticipate some risks. Remember, also, that a reasonable definition of risk is 'potential departure from the norm' and that a problem is a 'situation requiring a solution' – not a difficulty that cannot be resolved. Risk is usually ignored by or does not occur to the undergraduate planning and doing a project. Yet there are risks attached to all work and so a detailed consideration of risk assessment and management is given in Chapter 6. Tutors in your academic department will have experience of risk analysis and management, and contingency planning; consult them.

Potential benefits and outcomes

These may be specific to a particular workplace or general to a section of the profession or to the profession as a whole. They should include personal gains such as subject and research understanding, skill acquisition, insights and self-confidence. There may also be benefits to your university department or to your course. However, be cautious in identifying possible benefits and outcomes.

Preliminary literature review

Some universities require that students include a brief review of the literature pertinent to the research topic; usually no more that six items need be captured. This is usually an indicative review done to ensure that the chosen topic is of value and is currently being discussed in the published literature, and that you are able to capture pertinent literature and use it properly to prepare for your research. Remember to cite and list the references that you have consulted for the review. Some tutors may require that you present a bibliography of the main items that you will consult during your research. These may include standard works on methodology and theories, and reports of similar research.

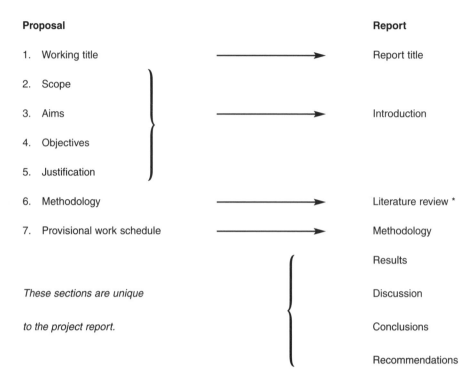

*This section has been located before the methodology section in the report because the literature will provide most, if not all of the methods that will be used in the project. Also, the format suggested by some course documentation puts the literature review section before the methodology section even though the literature search and review processes are research methods.

Note: A more detailed version of this figure is provided in Appendix 6, Relationship of the project proposal to the project report.

Figure 4.1   The links between the proposal and the report

How is the proposal linked to the final project report?

The relationship between the proposal and the report is very strong. The structure of the proposal is similar to that of the report and so it can act as a series of pointers to what the report should contain in each of its sections. The links between the sections of the proposal and those of the report given in Figure 4.1, are developed in detail in Appendix 6, *Relationship of the project proposal to the project report* to make clear how strong they are. The working title provides a reminder or reference point when returning to the research after a short period away. The title of the final report need not be determined until the report is complete. The function of the report title is different from that of the working title since it is more an identifier of the report than a memory jogger – regard it as the name of your report.

These links are emphasised because experience has shown that some students never refer to their research proposals once they have been submitted and approved, and many rarely do so. Yet failure to refer to your proposal may prove to be a fatal mistake so far as the success of your project is concerned. The approved proposal is a critical document. It defines what you are permitted to do and is the foundation of your research and the route planner for the work.

Ultimately, the project report exists only because the proposal exists. As it is assessed before the project report is completed, it will have a tutor's comments and opinions attached. Thus, there are good reasons why it should always be to hand as a working copy on which you can write comments as your research progresses. These comments will be opinions – yours and your supervisor's – or will amplify, clarify or extend various parts of the proposal and will have value when you begin to write the final project report.

The scope, aims and objectives act as controls on the research since their effect is to define the research in terms of its boundaries and intended outcomes. They should not be varied significantly once you have started your research, as together they constitute a statement of what you will be doing and why you are doing it. Any significant changes will change what it is that you intend to do and in such a case, it will normally be necessary to prepare a new proposal or, at least, a statement of project variation that will require approval. Normally, you will not have the time to do this. However, as your research progresses, you may receive feedback that suggests quite clearly that one or more of the objectives cannot be achieved. It is possible to abandon an objective provided that it is not a critical one. For example, in the case study reported later in this chapter, one of your objectives may be to interview every one of the 72 councillors mentioned. The demands on the time of some of the councillors, particularly those who chair important committees or represent the Borough Council on national organisations, may be such that you are not able to meet them within the time frame that you have allowed for the interviews. You can legitimately abandon the comprehensive survey that you intended and accept perhaps 50 interviews. You should note whether those not interviewed include all who chair the committees of the council, since it could be suggested that they would be more likely to read all available sources of information. The information gained from these interviews will still be useful. This will not invalidate your research since the primary purpose of your project is to enable you to demonstrate that you can do research and plan and manage a project.

The justification section of your proposal will be very useful when you are writing the discussion, conclusions and recommendations sections of your report. For example, when discussing your results, you may find that they reinforce the reasons why you proposed to do the research. Conversely, it may be that your results contradict or challenge what you understood from the literature when preparing your proposal. In this case, you may have found a gap or weakness in the knowledge existing in your chosen topic area. Therefore, it is important that you are clear, logical and objective when preparing the justification for your research. When you begin to write your project report, the scope, aims, objectives and justification sections of your proposal will make a significant contribution to the introduction in the report.

The methodology section of the proposal contains key controllers of your work. You must use the methods that you have proposed since these are what your tutor has approved. There is a clear and essential link between the methods and the objectives of the research. The methods will have been chosen as together they are the means by which the objectives might be achieved. Again, this section will give very good guidance on the content of the corresponding section in the final report.

Literature reviewing is an important, even critical, method that is common to almost all research. The indicative review in the proposal provides a significant element of the authority for doing the research and for the methods you propose to use. It also provides a starting point for the full review that is an essential part of the final report. The items in the preliminary review in the proposal must feature in the full review since they helped in the formation of the argument for your research. The full review is normally so significant that it is usually presented in a separate section in the final report and is often located before the methodology section since it provides detailed information on the methods that you will use in your research.

The work schedule, which may be varied as the research progresses due to force of circumstances, is a statement of what has to be done and when. Having ready access to this will mean that potential problems may be anticipated sufficiently early to reduce or eliminate their possible effects. It will also enable you to check off what has been done and to make any reasonable amendments that have been agreed with your tutor. The schedule should not be very tight but should contain provision for slippage to allow for the things that can go wrong even in the best-planned research. Notes made on the schedule during the research, for example, relating to difficulties encountered in interviewing subjects or explaining problems in accessing databases for pertinent literature, will be useful when writing the report and when reflecting upon what you have done once the project is finished.

A well-annotated proposal can be helpful particularly when analysing and trying to understand your results and when writing your discussion. Individual students have added blank pages to the proposal and used it to produce a very detailed contemporaneous commentary on their research. As these notes will reflect the structure of the proposal, they will feed directly into corresponding sections of the report. You are recommended to do this, as it will have the advantage that the notes will be made when the ideas are fresh in your mind.

The two sections of the report that have to wait until almost the end of the project are the conclusions and the recommendations. There is no direct link between the proposal and the report so far as these sections are concerned since both sections can come into existence only after the results have been analysed and discussed. These two sections are entirely dependent upon the research being completed before they can be written. You may be tempted to begin drawing conclusions, even to think of possible recommendations when results begin to be gathered. This is unwise, so do not do it even if over half the results are complete, since late results may alter an emerging picture quite significantly.

The proposal seems to be rather a complicated document to prepare when you probably have no previous experience to rely on and particularly when it is the foundation of perhaps the most important piece of work that you will do for your degree. Therefore, it is useful to consider an example in which every one of the suggested sections of a proposal is illustrated. This is a realistic proposal, having been developed from a project that was completed by an undergraduate whom I supervised. There are some tips on writing a proposal that you should bear in mind when writing your own and when examining this example.

Box 4.1: Some tips on writing a proposal

A proposal is more than a proposal – it tells the readers much about the proposer. Therefore, the drafting of it is an important matter.

A well-structured proposal is easy to read and understand, and helps the proposer to clarify her/his thinking. It also leads to the answers to a reader's questions.

Avoid breaking up the text with extensive and detailed diagrams. These can be intrusive and may antagonise the reader, resulting in the reader being unfavourably disposed towards your proposal.

Read aloud your proposal at a reasonable pace. If any parts of it sound tedious to you or to a listener, then these parts will almost certainly be tedious to the tutor who has to approve it.

(Continued)

Box 4.1 (Continued)

Start writing for your target readers with your aims and objectives clearly in mind.

Write for the people who are going to read it. How much specialist knowledge do they have of your subject area? For example, you have to convince your academic tutor or tutors, so you should write in the tone 'this is what I would like to do ...'. A copy for a workplace supervisor may have the tone 'this is what I intend to do'. This is because the project is a demand of your course not your workplace.

A well-structured proposal with good layout makes a good impact. Remember that the proposal may be the *only* evidence to the readers that you exist – the proposal *is* you in such a case.

You will usually need to work through several drafts before it is in the necessary condition to submit. Each rework will enable you to refine and sharpen your case. Allow a reasonable time lapse between each draft.

Consult your tutor before finalising the proposal.

The importance of supervision of the project, from proposal to final report

On approval of your proposal, a tutor will be allocated to act as your academic supervisor during the project period. If you are on a sandwich placement as part of your degree or are an employed student, you may also have a workplace supervisor appointed by your employer if undertaking a work-based project. These supervisors bring to your project work extra value in the form of knowledge and opinions about your topic based upon possibly extensive workplace experience. However, always keep in mind that the project is designed to fulfil academic criteria set by the requirements of your degree course, and these must take precedence over those set by the workplace. Much more often than not, it is possible to 'merge' the requirements of both, resulting in a final outcome of the project that is beneficial to the student and valuable to the workplace and the course.

Supervision is a critical process in the initial development of your project and in its progress and final, successful completion. Your proposal should include provision for what you may regard as the minimum amount of supervision that you consider necessary. Determine this in consultation with your tutor, who may be guided by the course regulations in which a supervision schedule may be recommended. It is useful for you to work with your supervisors as a 'steering group' for your project. The group should meet periodically, say, every month to six weeks depending upon how long the project period is, to discuss progress, review your research plan and decide on the next stage of your work. If your project is work-based, these meetings will enable you to ensure that a balance is maintained between the requirements of your degree course and the possibly strong advice and guidance offered by your workplace supervisor. One of your responsibilities will be to keep records of all meetings involving you and either or both of your supervisors. These will prove useful when writing the final project report. They will help you to identify when the supervisors have provided possibly conflicting advice. They will also demonstrate your recognition of the importance of regular communication during your research.

A sample project proposal – Riversbridge Borough Council

Let us suppose that you are a student on a public administration degree course. You have been allocated a sandwich placement with a local authority called Riversbridge Borough Council. The borough has a total of 24 electoral wards, each of which returns three councillors. Your placement is for 12 months, beginning on 1 September and ending on 31 August the following year. You are particularly interested in local politics and have followed the proceedings of the Borough Council for some time. During that time, you have noticed that some of the councillors appeared to be much better informed than others and as a consequence, the Council debates often seem to be unbalanced. You intend to use your placement to establish the reasons for the apparent differences between the councillors in debate, and to find an explanation as to why some councillors are better informed than others.

When you take up your placement, you discover that there is an information service provided to the councillors by the information services section of the local public library. These take the form of a monthly abstracts bulletin of journal articles, a weekly news bulletin, and a quarterly review of current official and legal documents relevant to the operations of the Borough Council. These services are delivered to all 72 councillors. The public library has to meet the entire cost of the services. The costs are substantial and there is no evidence available to suggest whether the services are either useful or cost effective. After discussion with your tutor and your workplace line manager, you decide that a study of these services will make an ideal topic for your project. You prepare the following proposal to submit to your tutor.

The proposal in Figure 4.2 is clear, succinct and complete. It is a proposal that can be completed within the nominal time schedule – an academic year. The work proposed is realistic for an undergraduate, calling into play many of the skills that have been gained during earlier parts of the course plus personal transferable skills. It would make demands upon objectivity, determination, tact and diplomacy of the student and will require consideration of ethical matters. In other words, satisfactorily pursued, it will provide a significant learning experience. It would be approved. Having studied the example carefully, now apply what you have learned from it to the following scenario. If you spend five or six hours analysing the scenario, spread over two days to give yourself time for reflection, you should be able to form a reasonable outline of a proposal.

Value and use of current awareness services to councillors – a study

Working title

A consideration of the value and use of the current awareness services provided by the public library information services section for the elected representatives on Riversbridge Borough Council, using analysis of relevant management information and data, and interviews with the councillors.

Scope

The current awareness services currently offered to elected representatives to Riversbridge Borough Council will be carefully reviewed. The resources used in the provision of these services such as finance, people, and consumables will be identified and quantified. The ways in which the services are delivered will be examined and the opinions of the recipients will be gathered by means of structured interviews. The literature will be searched for information on similar services and on methods appropriate to such an investigation. The pertinent literature will be reviewed. Contact will be made with other local authorities that provide information services to their elected representatives to obtain data and information for comparison. Some determination of the cost effectiveness of the services will be made.

(Continued)

Aims

To quantify the cost of the current awareness services provided to the elected
representatives to Riversbridge Borough Council.
To determine the value of these services to the elected representatives.
To produce a report on the current awareness services and their potential for
development.

Objectives

On completion of the project, the main outcomes will be:

- A review of the current awareness services provided to elected
  representatives.

- An assessment of the cost and effectiveness of the services.

- An assessment of the value of the services to the representatives.

- Some proposals on possible developments in the services.

(Continued)

Justification

Current awareness services, in the form of a monthly abstracts bulletin of journal articles, a weekly news bulletin and quarterly reviews of current official and legal documents, have been provided for 20 years, initially to committee chairmen and their deputies. Their provision to other members of Council has grown by request as elections have brought changes in the Council membership and as appreciation of the importance of information has grown.

Anecdotal evidence and performance in debates in the Council Chamber suggest that some members do not use what is sent to them. Also, there are no clear figures on the costs of producing and distributing the outputs of the services. Estimates vary by orders of magnitude since some of the costs are absorbed in the general printing and mailing and other operating costs of the public library. This lack of clarity is not acceptable in a time of severely restricted budgets in local government.

It is considered timely to examine the services to identify the use made of them and their value to the users. This will provide information that will enable the costs and effectiveness of the services and the users' perceptions of their value to be established. The results of the investigation will be reported to the Council to assist it in making decisions about the future of the services.

The justification should be kept succinct and should contain the essential elements of the existing situation that you intend to investigate. It should 'set the scene' in which your work will focus and include the background and general information upon which your opinion and that of your tutor or workplace supervisor have been based. It should also include what you intend to gather in doing the work and what the destination of the results will be.

(Continued)

The literature reviewing process must be recognised as a critical element of the methodology section and must include all documentation. An indicative review must feature in the project proposal and a full review must feature as an important, possibly critical element in the final report.

Methodology

Available internal documentation on the setting up and running of the services, including the justification for them, will be reviewed and analysed. This documentation is expected to contain information on production and distribution costs, circulation, content, and special purchases such as official documents and reports relevant to the interests of the Council, for inclusion in the services.

The published literature will be searched, surveyed and reviewed in order to discover available material on similar information services to identify common features, comments and opinions, and possible learning from them.

The use of the services by the 72 councillors and their perceptions of the value of the different outputs will be established by structured interviews followed by analysis of the interview transcripts.

A questionnaire will be mailed to local authorities that have been identified as providing information services to elected representatives. The main purposes of this questionnaire will be to obtain details on precisely what is offered, what the costs of the services are and comments and opinions on the perceived value of these services. It is expected that this questionnaire will provide some data and information for comparison purposes.

The interview is a reasonable method to use in this research, as all councillors normally will be readily accessible within the time frame of the project. It is also important to note that each interview may be as long as an hour, giving a total of at least 72 hours of notes to transcribe. If the interviews are to be tape recorded, transcription of such a number will take a substantial amount of time. Written notes may be transcribed more quickly particularly if you prepare a script to use in the interviews. Therefore, transcription time must be built into the project work schedule.

As the questionnaire is to be mailed to recipients, you must include an explanation of it and notes for guidance on how it should be completed.

(Continued)

Provisional work schedule

1–31 July	Discussion with tutor, preliminary literature review, may include some internal documentation.
1–31 August	Vacation.
1–15 September	Start placement.
	Discussion with workplace supervisor; identification of elected representatives; first draft of proposal and discussion with tutor.
	Create project documentation and records system.
15–30 September	Finalise project proposal and submit to tutor.
1 October –	Begin scheduling interviews with elected representatives, formulate scripts for interviews.

Do not arrange more than one a day, and no more than three in a week. Thus, you will require 72 days spread over 24 weeks.

Begin full literature search, survey and review, including internal documentation.

The review continues until the beginning of June.

Prepare first progress report and discuss with tutor and workplace supervisor.

(Continued)

| 1 November–30 April | Do interviews with elected representatives. |
| | |

Allows six weeks for slippage due to cancellation and rescheduling of interviews.

Transcribe interview notes or tapes.

As soon as possible after each interview.

Design and test the questionnaire intended for other local authorities; amend as necessary and distribute.

| 1–15 December | Discussions with staff who prepare the information services to elicit detailed information and data on costs, processes, special purchases, materials and distribution. |

Return of questionnaires from local authorities – begin analysis of information and data.

Send reminders if necessary.

Prepare second progress report and discuss with tutor and workplace supervisor.

| 1 December–28 February | Literature search and review continues. |

Begin draft of parts of report – the introduction, literature review and methodology sections.

Begin analysis of interview transcripts.

(Continued)

1 March–31 May	Prepare second draft of report, including results and analysis of local authority survey and provisionally complete literature review.

Sometimes new material is published that you and your tutor consider must be included in the review after its nominal completion date.

1–15 April	Prepare third progress report and discuss with tutor and workplace supervisor.
1–30 June	Complete analysis of interview transcripts and write the review of the results. Quick recheck of current literature.
1–15 July	Prepare third draft of report, submit to tutor and workplace supervisor for consideration.
15 July–15 August	Final recheck of current literature. Complete final draft of report, taking account of comments from tutor and workplace supervisor. Oversee production and binding. Reflection followed by exit discussions with tutor and supervisor. Submit project report to tutor – two copies; copy to workplace supervisor.

This gives your tutor and workplace supervisor time to comment and detect errors of fact, breaches of ethics or similar matters that may be corrected relatively easily.

Figure 4.2 The proposal

An exercise in writing a proposal

You are a student on an information technology degree course and you have been allocated a sandwich placement at a sixth form college. Prior to you starting at the college, the Governors determined that it would be advantageous to install an intranet linking all classrooms, teaching staff rooms, the college library and IT technicians in order to enable access to the Internet for all students and teaching staff, and to permit them to use the electronic information services, access to which is currently available only in the library. You have to prepare a proposal embodying this for formal approval by the Board of Governors of the college.

Some information about the college that will help in preparing the proposal is given here. This should be enough to draft an outline of the proposal. However, you may assume extra information provided that it is reasonable and proportionate to the scenario. The college has 650 students working for A-levels, GNVQs, BTECs, and various GCSEs. There are 35 teachers, two professionally qualified library staff and two IT technicians. Thirty-eight classrooms with student capacities ranging from 15 to 40, are distributed approximately equally between two three-level buildings either side of a quadrangle. Four of the classrooms are dedicated information technology suites, one for each course. Each of the four course leaders (A-level, GNVQ, BTEC and GCSE) has an office, the rest of the teaching staff share ten offices, the two IT technicians share an office, and the library staff share an office. There will be other information and data relevant to the college but that is not necessary for you to know or take into account in writing the proposal.

Some tips on working

- **Analyse the scenario for facts, data and information.**

- **Determine what is implied within the scenario.**

- **Determine what may be inferred from it.**

- **Make reasonable assumptions about the knowledge of the individual Governors.**

- **Think about the purpose and mission of the college.**

- **Installation must be complete within an academic year – the time line is important.**

- **You must complete the project within the year to meet your course requirements.**

- **Do your initial literature search very early on in the project period.**

- **Request access to internal documentation.**

- **Remember ethical considerations.**

- **Remember that costs are a critical factor in educational projects.**

- **Examine the experience of other colleges that have installed intranets.**

Summary

In this chapter, you have been given a way of working that should enable you to prepare a proposal that will meet the requirements of your course. You must recognise the importance of your proposal. In realising the link that exists between the proposal and the final project report, the critical and valuable role of the proposal becomes clear. Each section of your proposal links directly to a section or sections of the final report and, if logically and objectively prepared, will 'feed into' the report. You will find your research proceeds more smoothly and the writing up of the final report will be made simpler. Also, those who will assess the proposal will more quickly find answers to their questions. They will want to know what you want to do, how you are going to do it, what you intend to use to do it, and when and how long the research will take. The way of working described has been used successfully for many years by undergraduates tutored by the author. An example of its use is provided and explained in order to demonstrate the value of the systematic, structured approach.

Further Reading

Moore, Nick (1999) *How to Do Research* (3rd edn). London: Library Association Publishing. (See particularly Chapter 3, pp. 29–43.)

5 Planning the Project

You have prepared yourself mentally to do a project, you have chosen your topic and have written your research proposal. Your proposal provides a general statement of what you intend to do that is sufficient for your tutors to decide to approve it. However, it is not a detailed plan of exactly how you will do the research in terms of time, methods, activities and resources. The proposal is the starting point for your project plan. You should use it to build the detailed plan of just how you will do your research. Formulating this plan will take some time but it will be time well spent since a good, clear and detailed project plan will give you an exact definition of what is to be done and within the prescribed time frame. Properly done, it will provide a route map that will enable you to keep precisely on track throughout your research. It will necessarily have to be agreed with your tutors and will act as a guide to them and to your workplace supervisor if you have one, since they will not be so closely engaged in the research as you.

The research plan is the foundation upon which the success of your project depends. At undergraduate level, planning the project is not a complex task but it does require objective and logical thought. In this chapter you will be provided with basic guides that you can use to produce your plan.

The project life cycle

How do you start to draw up your plan? One useful method is to consider the idea that a research project has a life cycle, since this will give clues as to how the plan may be structured. The life cycle is shown in Figure 5.1. The idea of the project life cycle is valid whatever the size and nature of the project, the larger and more complex the project, the more detailed and extensive the life cycle will be. The cycle shown is for an undergraduate project and so is relatively straightforward. This cycle traces your project from the initial idea through the preparation of the research plan, doing the research, including the analysis of the results, the determination of whether the aims and objectives have been realised, to submission of the final report and reflection on the research once it is complete. The cycle is presented in four stages: Define – Design – Do – Deliver.

The '**define**' stage is concerned with establishing precisely what you will be investigating: the scope, aims, objectives and limits of the work, and justification for it. It also defines the project in terms of the resources that will be needed, such as finance and people, consumables, facilities and equipment. The resources and other requirements should be carefully estimated since, in the normal course of events, it is not possible to change requirements significantly once a project is underway. Such a detailed definition is necessary because the design of the project is heavily dependent upon what will be available to do the research. For example, you may be distributing relatively complicated questionnaires in such numbers that they require machine analysis on return from respondents. The initial design of these questionnaires and their subsequent setting up for machine analysis can be complicated, time-consuming and costly. If you intend to interview subjects, remember that transcription of tape-recorded interviews may require substantial time and the assistance of appropriately skilled clerical staff. Also, you may have to take into account ethical matters.

The '**design**' stage covers the preparation of the research plan, focusing on scheduling the activities involved into a carefully worked out timetable. It is important to take into account any dependencies that exist between particular activities, and to schedule activities so that there is not any chance of work overload during any period of the research. Also, in this stage, you will build in the scheduling of resources and facilities required for particular activities. A critical feature of this stage is the choice of methods to be used in your research. You may choose methods that are accepted as standard for your subject, you may modify existing methods, you may design your own or you may use a combination of these. Whatever you decide, you must explain your methods clearly so that any researcher could do the research just from reading your plan. The times when you will start to use the various methods chosen and when you will finish using them must be shown on the plan. In essence, this stage is concerned with breaking down the work into small, discrete components and fitting them into appropriate places in the time allowed for the project.

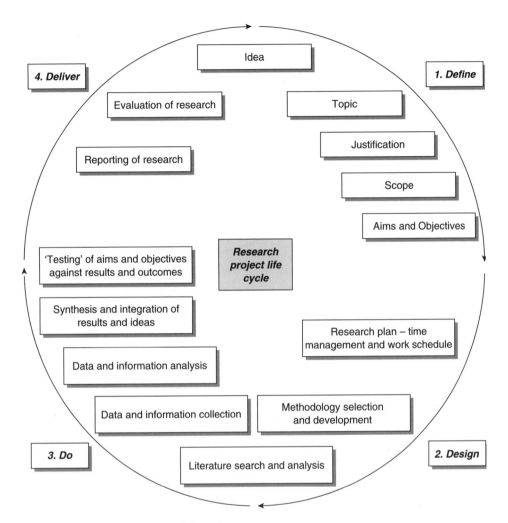

Figure 5.1 Research project life cycle

Four questions should be answered by the way that you present this stage: *What do I have to do? When do I have to do it? Where do I have to do it?* and *What do I need in order to do it?* Mentally prefix each of these questions with the word 'precisely'. Remember that your project has built in constraints – the main ones being the fixed time frame within which you have to do the project and the requirements established by your degree programme and university.

The third stage is concerned with **doing the research**. This is the stage that many students consider to be 'the project'. It is what they want to get started on almost immediately and often neglect the preparation that constitutes the first two stages and which provides the foundation that is essential for a good project. Going straight to this stage is likely to result in a project that, at best, may be reasonable and, at worst, a failure. A critical element in this stage is the literature search and the analytical review of the pertinent items found. This part of your research requires a substantial amount of time and will extend from the very beginning of the project period to approximately six weeks before the end of it. Thus, this stage overlaps the preceding stages, of necessity, and for good reasons. There is much to be gained from the literature, ranging from project management and research methodology to research results, theories, explanations and opinions. The literature review is dealt with in detail in Chapter 8.

The final stage of the life cycle is the **delivery** of the results and outcomes of your research. It is at this stage that you test the results and outcomes against the aims and objectives that you established for the research. Have you met them, completely, partially, or not at all? The extent to which you have met them or failed to meet them, and the reasons why, will inform much of your discussion and may influence your conclusions. A major activity at this stage is the writing of the final project report. However, it is unwise to leave the drafting of the report until the previous stages are all complete. In fact, this is another stage that overlaps the earlier stages to advantage. You are advised to start the first draft of the report during the definition stage of the project. This first stage provides some essential content of the report, which must contain the aims, objectives, justification and scope of your research, together with a clear definition of the topic being investigated. These elements will feature in the introductory part of your report. Similarly, the design stage will provide the research plan and methodology, both of which must feature in the final report. Also, you will have begun writing the literature review when you were formulating your research proposal. Thus, important components of your final report, in early draft form, will be available when you come to the point of writing the final draft of the complete project report. Therefore, writing is an activity that must be scheduled into every stage of the project life cycle.

Finally, it is important to reflect upon your research. This reflection must be a critical process. You should review all that you have done, from your initial idea, through topic choice and refinement, selection and use of research methods, capture, analysis and presentation of results, and reporting of the research. It is not common for time for reflection to be built into the research plan. However, some tutors suggest that their students should provide a critical evaluation of the research. This should be an important learning activity, since it can inform both your tutor and you of your research potential. This evaluation may suggest areas for further research that could be followed up either by you or by a student following on in the course. It may even provide a basis for postgraduate research. Thus, the outcomes of your research could start off another research cycle.

Advantages of a detailed project plan

Good planning can lead to a successful project, though not invariably so. Research is a general activity directed towards the achievement of prescribed outcomes. It is comprised of a number of specific activities, each of which is designed to achieve more specific objectives, both during and on completion of the project. Therefore, planning your project is concerned with establishing a particular, systematic and structured schedule of these activities that will lead to the prescribed outcomes. Planning includes establishing the pattern and schedule of work, determining procedures and resources required and their deployment, anticipating problems as far as possible and making decisions. It is important to clearly define the start and finish of your project and of each individual activity in your research. Also, build into the plan the provision for progress reports to your tutor and workplace supervisor, since reporting progress is a research activity and keeps all interested parties in touch with what is happening.

Planning is, therefore, more than identifying when specific elements of the project will start and finish; it is more than writing a list of deadlines. It should include careful determination of workflow, of the activities involved in that work, points at which specific procedures are initiated and terminated, points at which particular resources are to be phased in and out, identification of and provision for the interdependency of elements of the project and contingency planning. Your plan should also include the determination of the documentation and systems to record what is involved in your research.

There are several important advantages to be gained from careful preparation of your research plan. Bearing in mind that you will be doing other work in addition to the project work, a general advantage is that the plan will function as a desk reference tool. Used in conjunction with your research diary, this will help you to get back into the research frame of mind and remind you of the point you had reached when you last worked on the project if you have been away from it for some time. Other advantages are more specific.

You will clarify your thinking about your research and identify possible ambiguities and shortcomings in, for example, scope, aims and objectives. The requirement for clarity in the way that you present your ideas will bring out any weaknesses or errors in, for example, the methods that you propose to use. The time and work schedules that you have worked out may be recognised as unrealistic once they are presented in detail and in sequence. For example, students often under-estimate the time required for transcription of tape-recorded interviews. Also, they often make very optimistic assumptions of response rates within a specified time frame when using postal questionnaires. It is not possible to be accurate when estimating the times required for certain activities in a research project. Therefore, it is better to sensibly over-estimate times. It is not possible to add extra time on to particular activities once the plan is completed. There will be the danger of intruding into time allocated to other activities, probably resulting in your project getting out of phase, even risking becoming late. Conversely, if you have over-estimated any times and do not use all that you have allocated to particular activities, you can always make constructive use of that time. Equally important is the determination of precisely when particular activities start and finish. Your proposal probably contained a general indication of how long each individual activity would take and approximately when it would occur. In the plan, you will need to be precise. This is particularly important when individual activities are dependent upon others being completed before they can be carried out. Advice from your tutor plus reading of similar projects should significantly reduce the possibility of problems. Always keep in mind the submission date of your project.

The complete resource demands of your project will be set out in detail in the plan. This will enable you to review your estimates of what will be required and make such revisions as may appear necessary as your project progresses. This will be particularly significant when you have to use other people – for example, to conduct interviews – or use facilities that are controlled by others – for example, when distributing data capture instruments such as postal questionnaires. Also, students often under-estimate the quantities of stationery required for questionnaires and the cost of postage. Remember that, if your project requires resources, you must budget for them, show this budgeting in your plan and obtain approval for the budget. Never make assumptions about how costs will be met. For example, postage is often not considered by students yet many projects involve correspondence or even postal questionnaires. Correspondence and questionnaires are posted using the departmental postal system and 'costs are absorbed'. Do not assume that this is so. All expenditure is budgeted and must be approved, see Box 5.1.

Box 5.1: An embarrassing assumption about resources

A sandwich student prepared and distributed by first class post a four-page questionnaire; enclosed with it was a reply paid envelope. There were over 300 recipients. No estimate had been included for design and print or for stationery and postage. Working on rough estimates, the total cost of purchasing paper and envelopes, designing and printing the questionnaires, printing the return address on over 300 envelopes, filling and posting the envelopes to recipients, and sending reminders to those who did not return within the requested time, was well in excess of £500. The student had assumed that these costs would be absorbed in the general overheads of the sandwich placement organisation but had not cleared this with the workplace supervisor. The result was considerable embarrassment – to the student, to the workplace supervisor and to the department within which the project was done, as all expenditure was accountable.

If you set out the plan in a highly structured way, you will be able to use it as a checking chart, checking off each activity and stage of your research as you complete it. You can use this chart to monitor progress and, therefore, as the basis of the progress reports for your tutor. It can also be an alerting mechanism, for example, for you to confirm the availability of interviewees, or if you are falling behind schedule. It can also help you to keep track of resource commitment and utilisation.

Creating the project plan

Using the life cycle approach to our research enables us to break down the project into several clusters of related activities. These clusters may be further broken down into sub-clusters and, eventually, into individual activities. We can then determine which individual activities are independent, that is, they do not depend upon other activities being initiated or completed before they can be done, and plot these on our research plan at the appropriate times. This can also be done to identify which individual activities are dependent upon others, taking into account the extent of their dependencies. We can also note what resources and facilities will be needed to support each activity, to what extent and for how long. This method of showing the project work is sometimes known as *work breakdown structure*. Using this method of showing the work means that we are no longer managing a 'big project'; we are managing many small activities on an individual basis, perhaps no more than one or two at any one time.

It may appear that preparing the research plan is a complex and time-consuming business. However, if you adopt the work breakdown approach you will find that it is possible to complete the planning process for an undergraduate project in about two to three weeks. Remember that you are the only researcher involved, the time and size parameters of the project are prescribed and your tutor will keep in check any optimistic tendencies that you may have that will commit you to an excessively large project. It will be your job to do all the activities that are specified in your plan and there is a finite limit to the amount that you can do in the time allocated for your project. Indeed, if when inspecting your plan, there is any point at which you consider that there is too much to do, then your planning has served a purpose in that it has shown you a potential overload point which, in turn, may point to an over-ambitious piece of work. The work breakdown structure developed from the research project life cycle is shown in Figure 5.2. This figure is based upon Figure 5.1, *Research project life cycle*, and provides a clear indication of each area in which there is work to be done in undertaking your project. It shows a sample breakdown of the work and it is developed in detail for the literature review activities of the **doing the research** stage. Each of the other stages may be developed in greater detail than shown but do not provide more detail than is necessary for you and your tutors to understand what you will be doing during the project period.

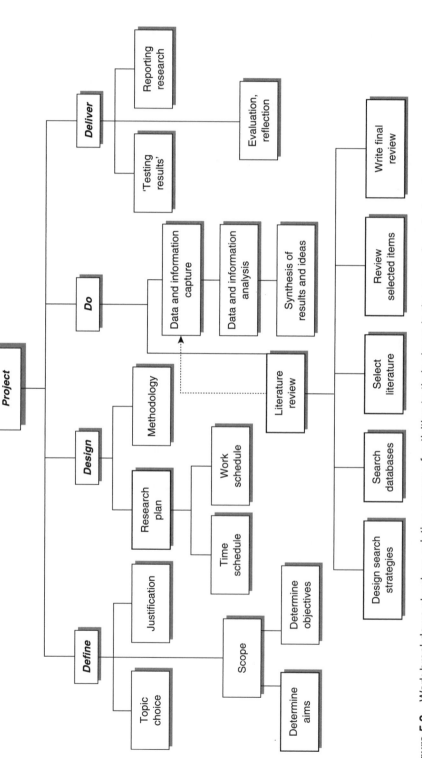

Figure 5.2 Work breakdown structure, relating groups of activities to their places in the research project cycle

How can this work breakdown structure be presented in a way that enables you to show precisely when each activity will start and end during the project period? One simple way is to use Gantt charts. These charts provide a picture of the time required for each activity plotted within the overall time period of the project. This period may be presented in increments of a month, a week or a day, depending upon the overall length of the project, its complexity, and the detail, number and length of each activity being plotted. Figure 5.3 provides a Gantt chart for an undergraduate project being done during a sandwich placement year. The activities have been given generic labels and are adaptable to many subject areas. Some of the activities listed are quite general and may be broken down into more specific activities. For example, the activity *prepare proposal* may be broken down into the following specific activities: generation of a research idea; selection and definition of topic; formulation of an hypothesis; development of the research question; preliminary literature search and review; selection of methods to be used; discussion with tutor; and writing the proposal.

Now that you have prepared your work breakdown structure and Gantt chart, it is possible for you to create an activity list in which you will show the dependencies between activities, their duration, the resources necessary for the activities to be pursued, and the risk assessment associated with each activity. The activity list is given in Figure 5.4. The dependency column shows what activities have to be either in progress or completed before a later activity can be initiated. Thus, the main literature search and review may not be started until the proposal has been prepared and approved, accepting that you will have done a preliminary, brief literature search and review to write your proposal. Methods to be used in your research cannot be selected until you have received approval for your proposal and have identified appropriate methods from the literature. Your proposal and the methods you have selected will indicate the sort of forms that you will have to design to record data and information captured in the research. Individual sections of the report may be drafted as the appropriate elements of your research are in progress or completed. The final report is obviously dependent upon these sections having been drafted.

The duration given is not a recommendation that the whole of each period should be devoted to any one activity. It will be clear that several activities may be underway concurrently. You will have to judge how to share your time among the various activities that may be concurrent. A relatively conservative statement of the resource requirements is given for each activity since it is assumed that the project will have been carefully thought through to create a sensible minimum demand. The finance mentioned for interviewing is to cover travel and subsistence costs if interviewees are remote from your workplace. However, there are costs implicit in the acquisition and use of stationery, the use of postage and IT facilities and of the design and print facilities of an organisation. Such costs may be absorbed into the general overheads but do

Activity	Month 1	Month 2	Month 3	Month 4	Month 5	Month 6	Month 7	Month 8	Month 9	Month 10	Month 11	Month 12
Research diary												
Tutorials	*				*			*				*
Prepare proposal												
Make research plan; include risk analysis				Review risk		Review risk		Review risk		Review risk		
Literature search										Ref check		
Critical analysis												
Write review				← Early draft→ ←Second and later drafts→ ←Final draft→								
Select methods												
Design forms, etc.												
Draft introduction												
Collect data, etc.												
Analyse data, etc.												
Interview subjects												
Analyse interviews												
Draft methods section												
Draft results section												
Draft discussion												
Write final report												
Submit report												*
Reflection												

Figure 5.3 Gantt chart for an undergraduate project, showing month-by-month schedule of work

No.	Activity	Duration	Dependency	Resources required	Risk assessment
1	Tutorials (minimum)	4 x 1 hour	Nil	Proposal; progress reports	Low
2	Research diary	12 months	Requirement for the project	Stationery; IT facilities	Medium
3	Prepare proposal	4 weeks	1; brief lit. review	Tutor; library; databases	Low
4	Literature search	3 x 2 months	1; 3	Library; databases	Low/medium
5	Critical analysis	8 months	4	Documents from lit. search	Low/medium
6	Write review	9 months	5	Notes on documents	Low
7	Select methods	1 month	1; 3; 4	Tutor; literature	Low
8	Design forms, etc.	2 months	3; 7	Design and print advice	Low
9	Draft report introduction	3 months	3; 1	Stationery; IT facilities	Low
10	Collect data, information	5 months	7; 8	Forms; IT facilities	Low/medium
11	Analyse data, information	6 months	1; 10	IT facilities; tutor	Low/medium
12	Interview subjects	3 months	8	Forms; tape recorder; finance	Medium
13	Analyse interviews	3 months	12	Stationery; IT facilities	Medium
14	Draft methods section	2 months	7	Stationery; IT facilities	Low
15	Draft results section	3 months	11; 13	Stationery; IT facilities	Low/medium
16	Draft discussion section	2 months	6; 15	Stationery; IT facilities; tutor	Low/medium
17	Write final report	3 months	2; 3; 6; 9; 14; 15; 16	IT facilities; results; proposal	Low/medium
18	Submit report	Half hour?	17	Nil	Low
19	Reflection on research	2 hours	17	Quiet time	Low/medium

Figure 5.4 Research project activity list, showing related dependencies, resource requirements and risk level assessment

not assume this; get confirmation in writing before committing yourself to the use of cost-generating facilities and services.

The risk assessments made for each activity are typical of many undergraduate projects. They are based upon the assumption that the topic is well chosen and defined and that the research is pursued in a systematic, logical and objective way and that the work was appropriately monitored and controlled. Why is the diary shown as having medium risk? Many students start their diaries with enthusiasm but this soon wanes and there is relatively little entered into it after about two or three months. The low/medium risks attached to the literature search and analysis reflect the possibility that some material that you need may not be easily accessible or be inaccessible though you may have identified that it exists from relevant information sources such as bibliographies or abstracts services. Similarly, the low/medium risk attached to the collection and analysis of data and information reflects the possibility that your data capture instruments may have been misinterpreted by those requested to complete them. Other possibilities may be that you are not skilled enough to use the analytical tools or that you misinterpret some of the returns. The medium risk is assigned to the interviews because it is not unusual for interview subjects to forget or be unavailable when their scheduled interview time arrives. It is very unlikely that any activity necessary for the completion of an undergraduate project should be judged of high risk. If there is such a case, reconsider that activity and the nature of the risk that you have identified with a view to at least transferring the risk or discuss with your tutor ways of reducing the likely occurrence and impact of the risk event.

There are certain little rules that you should try to observe when planning your research. First, do not try to estimate the length of time slots exactly. There is always the possibility that something will cause delays or interruptions. Second, remember that you are a normal human being and, as such, may suffer from influenza or the common cold during the project period, or you may have a sports injury or an unscheduled family event. Also, realise that other people upon whom you may be depending for assistance, advice or information may not be available when you need them and when you have budgeted to deal with them. Third, build in some slack time – known as slippage time – into your plan. Distribute it reasonably throughout the project period; do not concentrate it in one week or fortnight at what you judge to be an opportune time. Slippage time will enable you to catch up with your research if you fall behind for any reason. If you are fortunate enough not to have any delays or interruptions, or loss of availability of resources, including people, then you may use that time to add extra value to what you have already done. Fourth, do not rely on others for work that is critical to your project. It is your project and you are solely responsible for its satisfactory completion. Relying on others opens up the possibility of evading your responsibility, which is unacceptable and in an extreme case you may lose control of the project. You must keep control of your project; only you are responsible for what is done, what is not done and any variations to the approved proposal and to the research plan. Fifth, you must make sure that your tutor supervises you. Your tutor is appointed by your department to supervise you during the conduct of your research and the writing of the project report. Your tutor will have the necessary expertise to advise and pilot you on the subject matter of your project and with its management. However, do not expect your tutor to sit at your elbow throughout the project and nudge you whenever you stray off track. You should initiate tutorial contacts and provide an informal agenda for your meetings. Your university department may have a maximum number of hours allowed for tutorials during the project period. This may be from 10 to 20 hours. Many students make do with fewer hours since they consider that they are progressing well and do not need advice. Be careful not to fall into this way of thinking; you may delude yourself. A schedule of tutorials will at least ensure that you have prepared some work for your tutor to read. More important, if your department allocates 18 hours for project tutorials, then it had good reason for so doing. It is very likely that this time allowance is based upon the experience gained over many years and hundreds of projects. If the supervision time is there, use it.

A case study in project planning

Background

You are a student on an information management degree programme. You will begin your sandwich placement year on 31 August and complete it on 31 July the following year. You have been allocated a place in the special projects section of the County Council's Chief Executive's office. It has been agreed with you that you will be responsible for a substantial project during your year in placement.

The county has over 100 miles of coast and is mainly rural. There are seven main centres of population, a city and six large towns. The nominal population totals approximately one and a quarter million. There is significant population movement into and out from the county; young people moving out and older people moving in mainly from urban areas in the South East, Midlands and North East of England. A high proportion of the incomers are retired professional people in the middle and high-income brackets. Population growth has been between 1 per cent and 2 per cent for at least ten years. The main economic activity centres upon agriculture, fishing and tourism. The last includes extensive caravan and camping sites and holiday villages. The infrastructure and services of the county were established in their present form more than ten years ago. It is clear that there is significant dissatisfaction with all services, by ratepayers of the county and by tourists.

The county council has begun a comprehensive review of housing, industry, commerce, transport infrastructure and all the services provided by the county, with the intention of updating and improving these services. This will be done on a department-by-department, service-by-service basis with the overall management being the responsibility of the Chief Executive Officer (CEO), who has decided that the review of each service will be defined as a project. In Figure 5.5, *Genesis of the project*, an outline is given of the way in which the matter of the mobile library and information service became a project. The CEO has allocated you to the Information and Library Services (ILS) review. The Director of ILS will have the nominal role as Project Manager for your specific project but you will be the person responsible for most of the work. Your particular project brief is to review the mobile library and information service of the ILS. This is a very significant part of the ILS and serves the many small villages and hamlets in the county. The timing of your project is such that it will be one of the last components of the comprehensive review. This means that you will have up-to-date information on population profiles, distribution and movements, transport infrastructure, education, and care services. The existing ILS is comprised of the Headquarters library and two full-time branches in the city, one full-time and one part-time branch (two and a half days per week) in each of the large towns, and three mobile libraries, which call in at most villages no more than once per week and stay for about two hours each time. The ILS provides a service to schools throughout the county and the mobile libraries contribute to that service.

The project

The County Council has already agreed a general proposal for the comprehensive review and you have, as your first task, to produce a proposal specific to the mobile library and information service review and the project plan. The four stages of the research cycle are shown in Figures 5.6, 5.7, 5.8 and 5.9. The CEO requires that you complete the review, with conclusions and recommendations, including costings, so that he can present it for discussion at the preliminary budget meeting of the council, scheduled for 15 July. Therefore, your project plan must include completion of the project by no later than 1 July of your sandwich year. In other words, your project time line is 50 weeks long, with no possibility of extension. You will receive assistance from all relevant departments of the Council, including planning, highways, finance, social services, education, and management and support services. You will have a project steering group, the membership of which you must decide in consultation with the Director of ILS and your tutor.

A general picture is given here of the planning and proposed conduct of the research. This case study concentrates upon the planning aspect of the work and gives attention to the various influences on decision-making and on determining the profile of skills

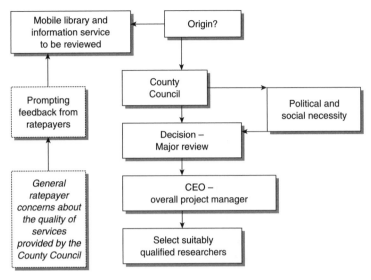

Figure 5.5 Genesis of the project

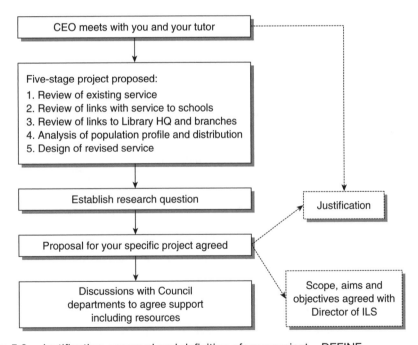

Figure 5.6 Justification, approval and definition of your project – DEFINE

necessary to do the work. For example, there would be significant constraints upon the work, including time – access to specialists within the County Council to assist by providing relevant data and information will be problematic as all departments are

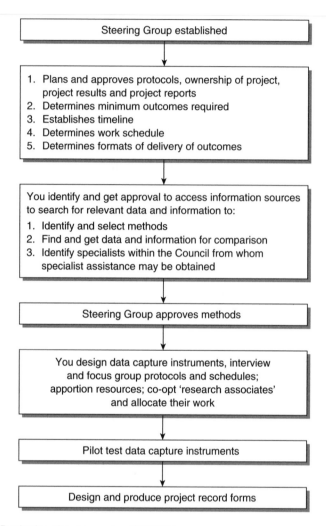

Figure 5.7 Designing the research – DESIGN

involved in the comprehensive review as well as doing their routine work. The availability of research associates to assist in the routine data and information gathering, finance and transport for travel and subsistence is limited.

Before committing to the research, it is useful to ask a few questions, the answers to which will give strong indications of the sort of knowledge, skills and abilities that will be necessary to conduct the research.

'What does the County Council want done – precisely?' The Council wants the effectiveness and efficiency of the current mobile library and information service assessed. It also

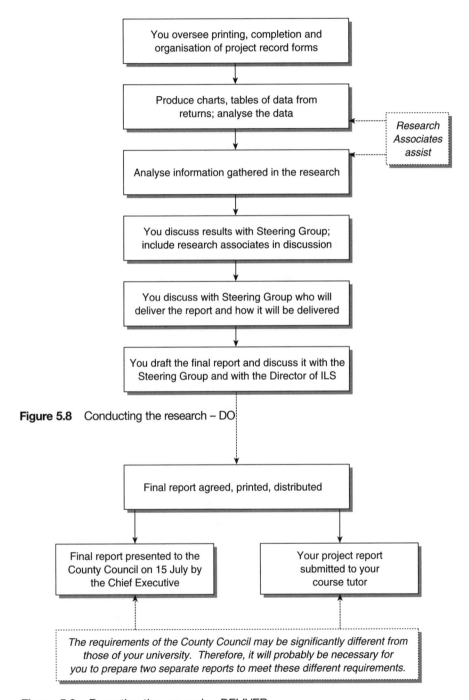

Figure 5.8   Conducting the research – DO

Figure 5.9   Reporting the research – DELIVER

wants a detailed picture of what the service should be providing, bearing in mind the substantial changes that have taken place in the county over the past 10 years or so. It wants to find out the expectations of the residents in the 200 or so villages and hamlets. To answer this first question, it will be necessary to build a profile of the population of each of the villages and hamlets. It will also be necessary to obtain detailed information on the transport infrastructure and geography of the county.

'*Why is the project being done?*' The reasons for doing the project are both political and social. Local councillors have been receiving substantial adverse feedback from ratepayers particularly those in the villages and hamlets, about the mobile library service. Inappropriate and poor quality stock, insufficient stock, visits of the mobile library too infrequent, and no access to services that are provided at the main library and the branches, such as social and health information, and the Internet. Local councillors are conscious that ratepayers are also voters and they perceive dissatisfaction as a threat, so there may be a political element in the initiative behind the review.

'*What, specifically, is the research intended to provide?*' The Council wants sound, reliable data and information to assist councillors and the ILS in providing an up-to-date, effective and efficient mobile library and information service that will genuinely benefit the ratepayers of the county.

'*Who should do the research?*' The employment of a sandwich student with a suitable academic qualification will enable the research to be done without having to divert a member of staff away from routine work. Where expertise beyond that held by the student is required, all departments of the Council have agreed to co-operate.

'*What is the size of the project?*' The Director of Information and Library Services will be able to estimate the number of locations that the mobile libraries have to service from the local gazetteer and county year book, the number of ratepayers from the electoral roll, and the routing of mobile libraries from a county map. Whether every location should be visited in the review would be determined after detailed financial and travel calculations have been done.

The time available to do the project is limited to 50 weeks. No extension is possible. The results and recommendations have to be available, tried and tested to meet a deadline determined by the scheduled County Council meetings, one of the most important of which is the preliminary budget meeting in July. Therefore, the project will have to be rigorously controlled.

Careful analysis of the answers to the questions and some informed extrapolation from the answers will give clear and precise indications of what you have to know or what you have to gain access to in order to do the research. It is clear that the range of knowledge and expertise needed is much wider than just the subject knowledge of librarianship and information management. For example, recognition of the political context involved suggests that you make contact with a member of the Council, perhaps the chair of the Leisure, Recreation and Arts Committee. Additionally, it will be useful to build contacts with important departments within the Council. These will serve as sources of advice and guidance, for example, on areas of interest that you should consider and the sort of data that would be useful for you to capture. The main categories of features that will be needed for the research may be deduced by analysing the project brief. These features are:

- **Political contacts and skills; understanding of the political process**

- **The County Council 'government' structure**

- **Knowledge of librarianship and information management**

- **Geography, size, economy and demography of the county**

- **Research skills and abilities, and project management skills**

- **Communication skills, including presentational and committee skills**

- **Mathematical and statistical knowledge and skills – for data analysis**

- **Information searching and retrieval knowledge and skills**

- **Report writing knowledge and skills.**

Summary

Planning is critical to the success of your project, yet it often receives relatively little attention from undergraduates. A good plan will demonstrate to your supervisors and assessors that you have the ability to identify and analyse the activities that make up your research, to determine and schedule these activities, to meet required outcomes and to recognise the importance of keeping to deadlines. One way of achieving this systematic approach is to utilise the idea that a research project has a life cycle. The life cycle approach has been used here to show how a detailed yet clear, uncomplicated project plan may be prepared. A brief consideration of some rules to observe when planning your research was followed by a case study that illustrated the use of the four components of the life cycle to shape a project plan, namely 'define, design, do, deliver'.

Further Reading

Heerkens, Gary R. (2002) *Project Management.* New York, NY: McGraw-Hill. (The Briefcase Book Series). (See particularly Chapters 3, 4, 6, 7 and 8.)

Project Management Institute (2004) *A Guide to the Project Management Body Of Knowledge: PMBOK Guide* (3rd edn). Pennsylvania: Project Management Institute.

6 Risk Assessment and Management

In order to assess the risks associated with your project and then to manage these risks, you must first accept that risks do exist and then you must identify and understand them. Your project will then be a vehicle to introduce you to the basics of risk assessment and management. In this chapter, therefore, we will begin by defining risk specifically for the purposes of your project. We will then examine risk in order to enable you to develop an understanding of how to analyse it. The chapter will end with ways of tabulating and charting your project risks for risk management purposes.

Project management in government, industry and commerce usually involves large-scale projects that extend over months or years and, at the same time, require the skills and knowledge of many people, possibly thousands of people and millions of pounds of finance. Such projects will encounter many risks during their lifetime and a critically important aspect of the planning of such projects is the assessment and management of these risks. Indeed, this part of the planning process may itself take time, weeks perhaps, and cost hundreds or thousands of pounds in a multi-million pound project such as the development of a drug for the treatment of cancer.

Projects are often described as being small, medium or large. These are very broad categories and are used very loosely. As a rough guide, the following person hours provides a parameter to indicate what the size of a project is. However, it is accepted that person hours is not the only indicator of project size. The resource demand of a project provides another guide.

Box 6.1: Guide to project size

Small project   →   up to 1,500 person hours for completion
Medium project   →   1,500–25,000 person hours
Large project   →   25,000 person hours and upwards

Your project is small, involving one project worker – you – and no more than about 800 hours over a period of no more than a year and probably less. Therefore, you may reasonably ask whether it is really necessary to assess and manage risk in something so small as an undergraduate project. Surely, there cannot be any risks of such significance as to adversely affect your project? Before answering these questions, let us explore what risk means to us.

Defining risk

The taking of risks in specific circumstances is something that humans have been doing for thousands of years. That is, actions have been taken that may have been accompanied by the chance that something unforeseen could have jeopardised the desired outcomes of those actions. Hunting, fishing and entering unknown territory all provide circumstances where risk, sometimes at a very high level, is present.

At a personal level, risk is a word that is used quite loosely in everyday conversation. People talk of risking a few pounds on a horse race, risking being photographed by a speed camera, risking a few extra calories when on a weight loss regime or risking driving home after a 'few drinks'. These are genuine risks but the chances of occurrence of the possible consequences are judged to be small, though, in all instances they may be very significant. Those who use the term risk in such situations would probably find it difficult to define precisely what it means. They would probably suggest that it is the chance of 'being caught', that is, of suffering the consequences of the occurrence of the risk event. This is not an unreasonable definition for the general social situations given. In two of the events mentioned, the consequences are prescribed by law and may be very significant. They may have a great impact upon the risk taker. In the other two events, the consequences will vary from person to person and will also depend upon the extent to which the few pounds or extra calories affect the well-being of the risk taker. Thus, the impact of these risk events is difficult to measure and will vary from person to person.

Taking the definition implicit here, it is clear that every activity in life involves risk. For example, travelling to work may be negatively affected by a random event such as a motor accident. 'Random' is used in the sense of being outside the control of the researcher. Completion of course work may be negatively affected by the sudden, catastrophic failure of the university information technology network due to a denial of service virus attack. Thus, risk is something that we all encounter and may, and often do, take account of consciously, subconsciously or unconsciously during daily life. Much experience has accrued on risk assessment and subsequent management of the environment and circumstances within which random events may occur, and this is widely reported in the literature of project management. In dealing with risk in the context of project management, it is important to define the term more precisely than it is implicitly defined for everyday activities and conversation. The following definition is used in this book.

Box 6.2:   Definition – Risk

The possibility that a random event will occur that will have a negative effect on the desired outcomes of the project.

Risk and your project

As the undergraduate project is a 'small' project, it is unlikely that all events that may constitute risks to the management of a commercial or industrial project will be encountered. However, risk assessment and management are important aspects no matter what the size of a project, and there will be risks associated with your project. Therefore, it is important to understand what is involved in the assessment and management of risk. The learning gains achieved by applying risk assessment and management to your undergraduate project will be transferable to other small projects directly or by logical and practical extension in the case of medium and large projects.

Undergraduate course work is carefully prescribed and defined by tutors acting within the limits of the course regulations and syllabi. In these documents, there is invariably some form of course work briefing that precisely sets out the terms and conditions of each piece of course work, including its parameters and assessment criteria. With such an apparently 'fine mesh safety net', it may seem excessive to consider risks in relation to an undergraduate project. However, careful thinking about what is involved in undertaking the project will show that even such a small project is likely to be exposed to quite a substantial number of risks, many, maybe all, of which will not be anticipated by the course work briefing given by tutors. For example, you may be ill and so lose substantial amounts of the time allocated for doing the project, or your briefcase containing your project files may be lost or stolen.

The aim of risk assessment and management in your planning is to protect the project against events that may have a negative or damaging effect upon it, which may reduce or eliminate the value of it. At the outset, it is important to clearly understand the difference between 'risk' and 'consequence'. 'Risk' is the chance that a negative random event will occur; 'consequence' is what happens *as a result of that event occurring* and relates to the impact of the risk event. The impact may vary from very low to very high depending upon the particular circumstances or the people involved. The above examples suggest a way of very generally categorising risk versus consequence, and this may be shown as four 'statements' relating the level of risk to the magnitude of consequences, shown in Figure 6.1. These relationships provide a useful, though very general, starting point for preparing to manage risk in any environment.

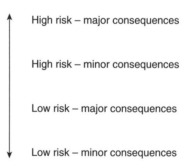

High risk – major consequences

High risk – minor consequences

Low risk – major consequences

Low risk – minor consequences

Figure 6.1   Risk related to consequences

Assessing risk

You should be alert to risk throughout the life of the project because the passage of time could bring changes in the risk profile. It is usually true that in a small project such as the undergraduate project, it is unlikely that there will be significant changes to the initial risk profile established for it. However, it is a valuable experience to continue risk assessment since this introduces you to a good practice. No one can foresee all possible risks at the project planning stage. For example, just as one of my students had reached the writing-up stage of his project, his briefcase, containing all his project notes and files of data, was stolen. This was a risk event with an impact bordering upon the catastrophic. Suitable security measures would have reduced the impact of this risk event to zero.

Continuous risk assessment and management is presented as the risk cycle, shown in Figure 6.2, which provides an analytical view of the combined processes. As risk is normally a relatively minor matter in a student project, surely there must be a limit to the time and effort you need to devote to risk? Here, common sense must govern your actions and this can be informed by advice that you should seek from your tutor. As with all other aspects of your work, you must strike a balance between the effort that you put in and the gain or saving that you obtain as a result of that effort. The balance is arrived at by estimating the effort and costs involved in the consequences of the risk event occurring, the contingencies provided against that occurrence and the value of the benefits obtained by implementing the contingencies when needed. This may be summed up in three short statements. Consider that a risk is recognised. The effort and costs of the consequences of that risk event occurring are assigned the value 'A'; the effort and costs of contingencies planned to deal with it are assigned the value 'B'; the benefits of dealing with the risk event are valued at 'C':

1. **If A + B < C then there is a good case for dealing with the risk.**

2. **If A + B = C then cost of doing something equals cost of doing nothing.**

3. **If A + B > C then you may decide to accept the risk.**

In equation 1, the value of the benefit outweighs the costs of gaining it; in equation 2, the value of the benefit equals the costs of gaining it; in equation 3, the value of the benefit is outweighed by the costs of gaining it. In the second and third cases, your decision will be based upon your knowledge and understanding of the significance of the risk to your project. Take advice from your tutor but only you can make the decision.

The overall assessment and management process may be broken down into a number of components, some of which are explicit in the risk cycle. The others are implicit. These components provide an analytical view of the risk assessment and management process for the undergraduate. The first four components are the processes that together make up the risk assessment phase of your project planning. Properly undertaken, they enable you to estimate the extent to which you are likely to encounter problems in doing your project.

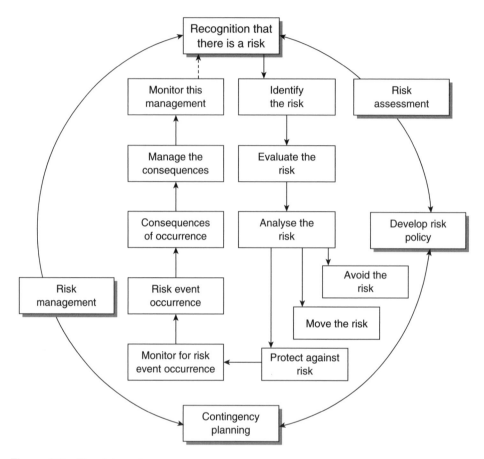

Figure 6.2 The risk cycle

Recognition that there is a risk

Every day-to-day activity involves some degree of risk. Undertaking a project is a formal and challenging process and will certainly bring with it a range of risks. If you analyse your proposal in detail for potential risks, the risk assessment and consequent management become an integral part of your operational thinking.

Evaluate the risk

Estimate the likelihood that each risk event will occur and when it is likely to occur in the lifetime of the project. Assess whether it will have a significant adverse effect on the project or even jeopardise it. Make contingency plans to enable you to cope with the risk.

For example, consider a project in which it is intended to interview senior officers in a large corporate enterprise. By agreement with the officers, you have scheduled the interviews for the 12th and 13th weeks of the project. You intend to remind the selected senior officers a fortnight before their arranged interviews. When certain officers are reminded, they are not available due to pressure of work. This should not be an unexpected occurrence since such senior officers are likely to be very busy with important organisational or operational matters and will have put your interview low down on their priorities list. Was your initial sample large enough to tolerate the omission of some of its members? Have you a reserve list of potential interviewees from which substitutes for the unavailable officers can be selected? Will the members of this reserve list be suitable substitutes? If the list has been properly compiled, they should be. Or can the interviews with the originally selected senior officers be rescheduled within the project time frame without adversely affecting other project activities? This is a situation in which slippage time becomes a valuable element in the project time line.

Analyse the risk

What are the components of the risk? Are they social, technological, organisational, financial, skills or materials oriented? What are its likely causes? Do they include lack of finance, lack of or failure of equipment, late delivery, non-availability of resources? Can you anticipate how it will affect the project? For example, will it affect the resources or services essential to the project, the time frames or deadlines established in the project, or the activities in the project, whether dependent or independent? Will it prevent particular equipment being available for use at a critical time in the project schedule? Will it affect the people associated with and important to the project, such as the researcher, supervisors, 'expert helpers', and subjects of study?

Having assessed the risks, it is now possible for you to develop a risk policy for your project. The remaining components in the risk cycle will assist in determining and carrying out that policy.

We cannot accurately predict the occurrence of a random event but we can make reasonable assumptions that some random event or events will occur during the life of the project that may have a negative impact on it. It is possible to plan in anticipation that some sort of random event will occur. Knowing this means that the planning must include contingencies to deal with the occurrence. How can this be done? For a start, you will have chosen the topic for your project. Much thought and discussion with tutors will have gone into choosing it. Overall, the topic will have been centred within a known and understood subject and working environment, with the intention to use particular methods, facilities, equipment and activities and involving particular people in that environment. Careful analysis of the topic, the subject and the environment will enable quite clear ideas to be formed on the types of risk to which the project may be subjected. We can explore the risks by asking and answering a series of five simple questions, shown in Box 6.3.

> ## Box 6.3: The five risk questions and your project
>
> 1. What is the risk?
> 2. What is the likelihood that the risk event will occur?
> 3. What needs to be done to reduce the chance of the risk event occurring?
> 4. What is the likely impact of the risk on the project?
> 5. What will be the consequences of the risk event occurring?

1. What is the risk?

Projects comprise a set of linked activities intended to produce particular outcomes, and every activity and outcome includes some degree of uncertainty that may involve a negative random event – a risk. Determining a risk is often a matter of common sense, which is an important quality for a researcher. However, common sense may be aided by some straightforward critical thinking about the project, what is involved in doing it, when, where and how it is being done and for whom or for what reason. For example, the task of assessing risks may be simplified by careful categorisation of the risks into types followed by identification of potential causes of these risks. The categories should be based upon significant components of the project, since the risks will involve or even stem from particular components. They should also recognise the context in which the project is being done. Typical categories might include methodology risks, facilities and equipment risks, people risks, and time-related risks. This categorisation of risks and identification of their possible causes will provide useful information for answering the remaining questions.

2. What is the likelihood that the risk event will occur?

The likelihood of occurrence will range from almost zero to almost 100 per cent. It cannot be zero since there would be no risk in such a case, and it cannot be 100 per cent since then it is not a random event but a fact, a certainty, or a constraint upon the project. Do not assume that, because you are an undergraduate, the risks potentially associated with your project will be minimal. For example, personal risks related to you or to people important to your project could be quite high.

3. What needs to be done in order to reduce the chance of the risk event occurring?

This is the core question in risk assessment and management. Answering it involves using the risk categorisation and analysis already done. The parallel question is '*Can a project be made risk-free?*' It is very unlikely, but risk can be minimised, planned for and managed. It is important to realise that something can be done to deal with risk. So much experience has accrued in risk assessment and management that there is a substantial body of knowledge recorded in the available literature of project management. Something can be done about risk. What is needed is for you to analyse very carefully what you are proposing to do in your project. The various sections of your proposal will provide you with a way of initially categorising areas within which risk events may occur. Take each section in turn and subject it to close scrutiny and try to anticipate all that could possibly go wrong. For example, in undertaking the literature search and review, can you be certain that you know and have allowed for searching all the appropriate databases and other sources of potentially relevant information? Are you sure that you understand and have the skills necessary to carry out efficient and effective searches? Are the search terms that you plan to use the most appropriate and do you know how to use them properly? Have you ensured that you will have access to all necessary internal documentation in the organisa-tion in which your project is centred, and is there any level of confidentiality given to some or all of it that may prevent you using much of it? Have you identified responsible members of staff who could give you clearance?

Suppose that your methods include interviewing selected subjects. How sure are you that your method of sampling is the appropriate one and that the selected subjects have the authority and knowledge to answer the questions that you intend to put to them? Were you aware of the need to obtain informed consent of the interviewees and have you obtained it? Can you be certain that the interviewees will be available at the appointed interview time? You may intend to distribute a questionnaire by post to several hundred recipients – have you a budget and have you included enough to cover a substantial reminder schedule? Or have you obtained written permission to use the departmental post to distribute it, and therefore received approval to incur substantial postal costs?

4. What is the likely impact of the risk on the project?

It is usual to assess the likely impact of a risk according to quite simple levels such as: acceptable, unacceptable, or catastrophic; or alternatively, low, medium, or high. If a risk is acceptable, it means that it is viewed as likely to have only a minor impact upon the project and may be managed at the time of occurrence. If it is unacceptable, this means that it will have a significant, though not 'life-threatening' effect on the project. Therefore, the circumstances likely to lead to its occurrence must be considered during the project planning stage and appropriate contingencies prepared in case of its occur-rence. If it is considered catastrophic, for example, resulting in probable termination or failure of the project, then the circumstances that are considered likely to cause the risk event must be remedied, with the intention of minimising or preferably getting rid of the possibility of its occurrence. The remedy may include significant redesign of the project even, for example, substantial changes in your methodology.

5. What will be the consequences of the risk event occurring?

The answer to this question will be dependent upon the answer to the previous question. It may be measured in terms of the likely effects of the risk event upon time planning, work scheduling, research methodology or availability of resources or even ultimate success or failure of the project. Consequences may range from very small to very large. It may be possible to accommodate small consequences and ignore the risk event if it occurs. However, judgement of what are small consequences must be carefully made since there may be occasions when a chain of unforeseen consequences may occur.

Managing risk

Avoid the risk

Eliminate the condition or potential event that is causing the risk. That is, if a part of your project has a high risk associated with it, then eliminate that part of the project. This may seem drastic but consider a project in which it is intended to make comparative use of data that another researcher is capturing at the same time as you are capturing data. This researcher is at another institution and you have only very limited opportunities to instruct this person in your data capture methods and instruments. You cannot guarantee that the methods and instruments will be applied correctly and so you cannot have high confidence in the quality of the data captured on your behalf. This could at least reduce the value of your research and at worst could invalidate it. Eliminate the use of that researcher and find some other way of capturing data for comparison, or redesign your project to avoid using other researchers of uncertain value.

Move the risk

You may do this by transferring the risk and, thus, transferring responsibility for managing it, to a party outside the boundary of your project.

For example, you may have the need to install and use sophisticated software for data analysis, yet do not have the necessary expertise to do so. It may be very time-consuming and expensive for you to acquire the expertise in the time available. Do not try to gain the expertise and do it yourself since the risk attendant upon this may be very high to the point that it is unacceptable and may result in catastrophe. You may find yourself using substantial amounts of time allocated to other, more important aspects of the project. However, if the understanding and use of the software are an integral part of the project, then the appropriate resources and time factor necessary for learning it should be built into the project plan. Otherwise, obtain the support of your faculty or university IT services. This will also ensure that your software is legal, licensed and conforms to the university's standards on information technology.

Categorising risk

Protection against risks and monitoring for risk occurrence require an understanding of the types of risk that can occur. Categorisation of risks helps to simplify understanding of the risks and formulation of protective measures against them. The following are some frequently encountered categories of risk that are directly applicable to undergraduate projects. The list is not exhaustive since it must be recognised that every project may have unique elements to it that may expose it to unique risks.

People risks

Every undergraduate project will normally have at least two people associated with it. These are the undergraduate doing the project and the university tutor. In the case of a work-based project, it is very likely that there will be a third person – the work-based supervisor.

People may be removed from availability to the project due to causes within their control and to causes beyond their control. Beyond their control is the obvious one of ill health, or relocation within the organisation at very short notice. Within their control are holidays, which may be taken at short notice to fit the requirements of an employer. Change of job within the employing organisation or a move to another employer is a fairly frequent occurrence. To these risks may be added lack of necessary skills, such as lack of project supervision skills or lack of communication skills. Individuals who may be affected by the project in some way, such as supplying data or information, may be defensive of their work. They may be proprietorial in respect of equipment, software, data or information. Thus, they may be relatively unco-operative, reducing their value to the project. In general, people bring risks to a project. These risks may stem from their attitudes to their work, to you or to the organisation in which they work. It is also sensible to recognise that you have attitudes or behavioural characteristics of which you may or may not be conscious. For example, your manner in an interpersonal event such as an interview may include certain behaviour that antagonises or confuses the interviewee.

Planning risks

As the project is the first over which you have management control, it is possible, even probable that there will be errors in some of your management decisions, for example, in estimation of time and work scheduling, and resource requirements. It may also become apparent that some of the dependencies that you have determined between activities are not satisfactory. Do not be put off by such an occurrence. Discovering your mistakes is part of the learning process in doing the project and should not be viewed as a disaster if and when such errors become apparent. It is only a disaster if you do not review and amend a faulty decision, that is, if you do not learn from it.

Resource risks

There is a range of factors that may affect the resource position of a project. These include: the unpredictable effect of inflation on prices; unexpected price increases (not due to inflation) of essential resources or travel; unexpected reduction of finance originally allocated; and failure of project-critical hardware or software coupled with delayed replacement. Also, remember that people are resources and so it is important to recognise risks, for example, the removal of essential collaboration due to unforeseen events such as job change by project-critical personnel; or lack of project-critical expertise – though, if known at the project planning stage, this is a constraint rather than a risk.

Project management risks

A common occurrence in undergraduate projects is failure to clearly and properly define the scope of a project. One reason for this is a lack of understanding of precisely what the desired outcomes of the project are. Another common error is the failure to understand the difference between and define clearly the aims and objectives. These elements – the scope, aims and objectives – are the foundations of a good project. Indeed, they are critical success factors in the project. If they are faulty, together they constitute a major, probably fatal, risk to the project. Establishing the scope, aims and objectives of the project is a critical activity early on in the project planning stage. Poorly established scope, aims and objectives usually reflect a poor understanding of the topic of investigation, with the consequent imprecision in the definition of the research question or questions to be addressed by the investigation.

A chain of inadequacy is often triggered by failure to define and establish objectives clearly. For example, the methods used in the investigation have a critical dependence on the objectives. Thus, a probable impact of the 'poor objectives risk' occurring is poor, even inappropriate, methods being used. Also, poor objectives make the accurate planning of the work schedules and time management of the project difficult. Imprecise or poorly defined objectives also lead to great difficulty in analysing and interpreting the results obtained in the project, since there are no clear pointers to the criteria to be used in analysis. With unsatisfactory analysis and interpretation of results, it becomes difficult to draw useful or meaningful conclusions, leading to an inability to make valid recommendations. Thus, the occurrence of the risk events of poor scope, aims and objectives have major impacts upon the project that could be sufficient to invalidate the work and result in failure of the project.

Risks related to methods

There are many risks associated with the selection and rejection of methods for use in the project. Appropriateness of methods, their proper use, and ensuring consistency in their use all contribute to satisfactory data and information collection. It is sometimes the case that the undergraduate is familiar with a particular method that is attractive and that method 'must be used' whatever the project topic. This 'method led' approach is very high risk since one certain consequence will be inadequate definition of the project topic resulting in poorly defined and established research questions. Fitting the topic to the method may also mean that any predisposition to a point of view about the desired outcomes will ultimately determine those outcomes. That is, the researcher may try to ensure that the research 'proves' the initial hypothesis or answers the research question in the way that the researcher desired. The occurrence of this risk event should lead to failure of the project.

Other, no less important, risks associated with methods are: incorrect choice of methods; lack of expertise in using chosen methods; lack of or poor testing of chosen methods; methods chosen for the wrong reason, e.g. 'I want to do a questionnaire survey'; or poor scheduling of particular methods. All these risks are generated by faults such as narrow thinking, lack of proper preparation, poor project planning, and inadequate search and review of the pertinent literature.

An example of poor scheduling of methods occurred in an undergraduate project in which a postal questionnaire survey was to be conducted on a number of academic institutions in England and Wales. There were 330 institutions and the questionnaire was posted on the last day of the Christmas term with the return date set in the first week of the Spring term, a time frame for responding of approximately three weeks including the holiday. The main reason for the short time scale was the intention to follow up the postal questionnaire with deep interviews of 10 per cent of the sample during a four-week period ending in mid-February. Each interview was scheduled for one hour and was to be tape-recorded for later transcription. The institutions in which the interviews were to take place would be distributed throughout England and Wales. The project report was due in at the end of April and the student had five other modules to study, each of which had assessed course work, and also final examinations in early June. The student did not seek advice of the supervising tutor and the workplace line manager until near the questionnaire distribution date and did not take the advice given. The problems created by the student, for the student, are clear and substantial. The project could have been very promising and could have produced some very useful results. In fact, had it been planned and carried out systematically and with realism, one of the outcomes might have been a paper for publication.

One of the most important methods to be used in all undergraduate projects is the search and review of the literature pertinent to the project topic. This is considered in detail in Chapter 8. If the search and review of literature is incomplete for any reason, there is the likelihood, possibly even certainty, that important ideas relating to the topic, to research methods appropriate to the project or to other factors relevant to the project (such as planning, problem-solving, data useful for comparison, and writing up) will be missed. This incomplete search and review may be due to poor topic definition leading to poor search formulation, poor refinement of searching and, thus, failure to identify pertinent literature. As well as the risk of failing to identify the most appropriate methods, you may well fail to capture a publication that reports on a project topic that is precisely the same as your chosen topic. Thus, your chosen topic is not 'new' and you will probably be reinventing the wheel.

There is another 'critical risk' linked to the literature review. That is the risk of plagiarism – briefly, the representation of the ideas of others as your own. The occurrence of this event may not be entirely conscious on your part. It may stem from a failure to record properly and precisely the sources from which you have obtained ideas, information and data during literature searching and reviewing and from communication with collaborators and other workers. Attribution is an important ethical responsibility for all scholars. It is important always to act in good faith and to behave with scholarly integrity. Carelessness in recording sources can put at risk your individual professional reputation at the start of your professional career. This is a major risk with dire consequences should it occur – having a reputation for lack of scholarly integrity due to apparent plagiarism will almost certainly exclude you from a very wide range of academic and professional employment opportunities. Good project records should reduce these risks.

External risks

There are some risks that are external to the project but which must be recognised since they may affect the project significantly. Such risks may reside in the university, or in the employing organisation if the project is work-based. These risks include changes in institutional management, bringing changes in supporting services and facilities, finance available, or staffing critical to project support.

Personal factors such as illness or changes in family circumstances are often not allowed for by students in their project planning. Illness of critical advisers such as the supervising tutor or the workplace line manager may have serious adverse effects upon the project. The university may be able to provide a substitute tutor; can the workplace provide a substitute for the line manager? Knowing the areas of expertise and availability of the staff of your academic department, and of the people in the workplace, can reduce the adverse effects of absence of such people by helping you to find a suitable replacement.

Weather may be important to the satisfactory use of certain methods such as street surveys or crowd studies. Weather forecasting is not an exact science. Therefore, it is wise to examine possible alternatives to any methods that involve being exposed to the weather for any length of time in order to capture data or information. Selection of the population to be studied, the sampling of that population and where it could be studied should be considered carefully. Are there any other methods or locations of samples that will be just as fruitful and objective yet will not be reliant upon the weather for successfully capturing sufficient and appropriate data or information?

Cultural attitudes to being studied may be important to understand if ethnic matters feature in the project. If you are planning a project that includes study of ethnic matters, it is essential for you to know enough about the ethnic groups to be studied to avoid causing any possible offence. The channels of communication into and within the ethnic groups may be complex and difficult for you to access. Gaining the confidence of the group may require time and the assistance of expert advisers but will be of benefit if contact with the particular group is essential for the success of your project. It will also reduce the chance of failure, that is, reduce the risk.

These days, recognition must always be given to the possibility (the risk) of loss or theft of intellectual property (e.g. your project notes); vandalism (e.g. destructive viruses in the university network); fire and flood, and equipment failure. Risk of loss of data and information may be reduced substantially by duplicating all paper-based and electronic project records such as results files, work in progress records, problems encountered and their solutions, decisions made and literature review, and storing the duplicates in a separate place.

Are there any risk-related regulations within or related to the field or environment within which you intend to do your project? Your university may have regulations that specify or limit subjects within which its undergraduates may research, or may specify methods that may or may not be used in undergraduate research. These regulations may be applicable to all undergraduates in the university or just to undergraduates in your faculty or degree course. Tutors should advise on these. An employer may have in-house regulations that determine what may be studied and used by students doing work-based projects. These may have been developed as a result of experience in providing opportunities to students over a period of years. The line manager should advise on these. Taking account of such regulations at the project planning stage will reduce the risk that significant parts of the project may be censored at a late stage.

Information and data capture risks

Many undergraduate projects suffer from the capture of inadequate or poor quality data and information. The risks that stem from this include putting in jeopardy the achievement of satisfactory outcomes in the project and may result in its failure. There are several causes of these risks. For example, the data capture instruments used may be inappropriate or inadequate for the chosen topic due to a failure to take appropriate advice. You may have prepared inadequately to use your chosen instruments, or do not understand them properly and so used them wrongly or imprecisely, again because you failed to seek advice.

If you are using collaborators, for example, to conduct a series of interviews or lead focus groups for you, you may not have prepared them properly to administer the questionnaire or lead the focus group. Such poor preparation may lead to inconsistencies in what is captured from the different groups, how it is recorded and reported to you. This will make integration, analysis, comparison and discussion of results very difficult and will diminish the value of your work. Therefore, ensure that instructions, guidance notes, and methods of recording data and information are clearly and objectively expressed and leave no room for individual interpretation. Never rely upon spoken instructions and advice. Keep exact copies of all that is given to collaborators.

Data and information from third parties may or may not be accurate. How can the accuracy be determined? Getting to know the third parties by personal contact, or by identifying their contributions to the literature and by doing a 'bio-check' (checking their professional and/or academic career) can provide enough information about them for you to form an opinion. From this, you can determine what level of confidence you can have in the value of their contributions to your project. Remember that they are not 'doing' your project with you; they are acting as your agents and carrying out activities designed by you to your instructions. Therefore, do not assume that they will correct errors that you may have 'built in' to what you provide them with to gain their assistance. Also, do not expect them to rearrange or restructure their data and information to fit your requirements.

Information and data analysis risks

Proper analysis of data and information is another critical activity in the project. If analysis is inadequate, the consequences for the project may be serious. For example, important inferences may be missed because the analysis of particular data has failed to bring out significant factors 'discoverable' from your research. Causes of poor quality in analysis include inadequate understanding of the analytical tools used such as statistical software; limited understanding of parameters used for measuring data; inconsistencies in data from different sample sets; incorrect categorisation of samples or data; insufficient data for meaningful analysis; or lack of skills necessary for analysing contents of text-based and graphics or image-based information vehicles.

Risk table and risk time line

When considering the risks to the project, it is useful to create a table in which the risks are shown in relation to their potential level of impact, the consequences of the risk event occurring and the actions that could be taken to reduce, minimise or remove the risk. A sample risk analysis table is presented in Table 6.1. The risks identified are typical of risks that have been encountered in undergraduate projects over the past 30 years. For example, poorly defined aims and objectives have been and still are quite common. It is registered as of 'medium level' only because there is always the opportunity to discuss and clarify these with tutors. If the opportunity is not taken, the risk moves to 'high level' with an even greater chance of failure of the project. It is worth noting that actions such as consultation with tutors, exchange of experience with fellow students and the reading of good project reports may all assist in reducing risks and their potential impact levels. The risk analysis table will be created at the project planning stage so the consequences shown are assumed or estimated consequences of the risk event occurring. Similarly, the actions are those that should be taken if the risk event occurs. However, it should not be assumed that every risk and every consequence has been identified in the planning stage of a project. The risk analysis table constitutes a ready reference should any risk event occur and should provide a good level of confidence in dealing with risk events if the risk analysis has been soundly conducted. It should be updated periodically during the project.

Risks occur throughout the lifetime of a project. Bearing this in mind, it is worthwhile preparing a time line of risk occurrence. This will provide a picture of the possible time and duration of occurrence of each identified risk. A sample risk time line is given in Figure 6.3. Six potential risks are identified and the time of possible initial occurrence is located on the line. An estimate of the level of the impact of the risk is also given. It will be noted that the level of impact is not necessarily constant during a project. A risk may be of low or medium impact at an early stage and if properly identified and assessed (and the appropriate contingency planning done in respect of it), the impact may stay as initially estimated. However, if no contingency is planned or if inappropriate or inadequate planning is done, the impact may increase as the project proceeds. Note that, if not dealt with effectively, a risk may have more serious impact upon some parts of the project than on others. For example, the impact of insufficient data is of medium risk early in the project life but, if nothing is done to rectify this, the risk becomes high. The effects of poor work scheduling may be overcome and the accompanying medium impact level may be reduced if appropriate action is taken soon enough. The impact of poor scope, aims and objectives is shown to become and remain high throughout the project life. This is quite common and reflects substantial experience during which it became clear that many students either failed to clarify these or failed to refer to them whilst doing their projects. Consequently, aims were often not fulfilled nor were objectives met.

Table 6.1 The risk analysis table

Risk	Level	Consequences	Actions
Computer failure	Low	Loss of processing time; loss of access to project notes; loss of project notes, data.	Keep copies of all files; revise time and work schedules; build in slippage time in project plan.
Network failure	Low	Loss of searching facility on Internet, databases; loss of access to stored data.	Build in slippage time in project plan; find alternative network or sources, e.g. the library at another university.
Tutor leaves university	Low	Loss of expert advice on subject and on project skills.	Identify other tutors with appropriate expertise.
Poorly defined aims and objectives	Medium	Poor, inappropriate methods chosen; lack of clarity in gathering and using data; possible failure of project.	Review and discuss with tutor; read appropriate texts on research; read examples of good projects.
Inability to use the chosen methods effectively	Medium	Poor, inadequate data and information gathering; failure to capture relevant data; failure to understand significance of results.	Review methods with tutor; review literature on research methods; consider changing to more easily understood but still appropriate methods; review topic.
Insufficient time for administration and analysis of survey instrument	Medium	Failure to obtain full value from responses; potential loss of significant results; less valuable project.	Review time and work schedule; recalculate time required for administration and analysis; consider reducing size of survey sample; review survey instrument.

Table 6.1 (Continued)

Risk	Level	Consequences	Actions
Insufficient time for transcription of tape-recorded interviews	High	Failure to obtain maximum value from important information sources; loss of significant input to the project; project value is seriously reduced.	Recalculate time required for transcription and analysis; revise time schedule; consider reducing number of interviews; consider change of method.
Personal illness; illness of project-critical people	Low	Loss of project working time; loss of 'subjects to study'; loss of expert advice.	Build in slippage time in the project plan; create reserve lists of 'subjects to study', expert advisers.
Insufficient data for the research to be meaningful	Medium	Loss of opportunity to develop useful discussion; cannot draw meaningful conclusions; cannot make recommendations; possible failure of project.	Review methods; review ability to use the chosen methods; review the topic of the project; review sample sizes.
Unskilled in use of sophisticated software	High	Inadequate handling of data; possible failure of project.	Move risk – use expert third party.
Ignorance of literature of topic, research methods	Medium	Missing significant published data and information; lack of knowledge and understanding of research methods.	Consult with library staff and tutor; search relevant secondary sources; enhance learning on reviewing literature.

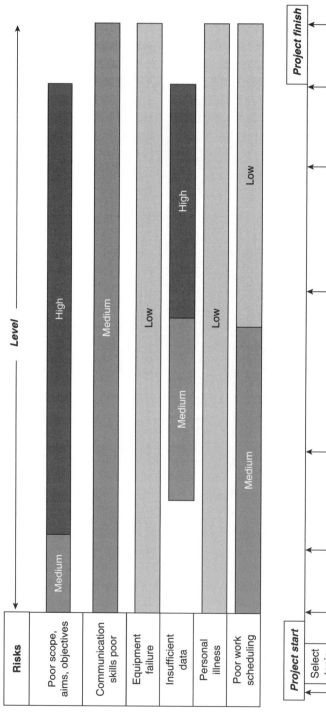

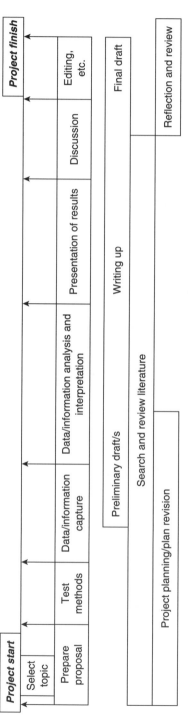

Figure 6.3 Sample risk time line

Summary

Experience has shown that the majority of undergraduates doing projects do not take into account the possibility that something unpredictable could affect their work. Yet there are risks associated with undergraduate projects. In this chapter, risk has been defined and examined in detail. The types of risks that are likely to be encountered when doing an undergraduate project have been categorised and explored by posing and answering five questions. Answering these questions in the specific context of your project will enable the risks to be tabulated in relation to their likely impact and consequences. Ways of assessing risks have been considered that will enable a risk management policy to be prepared with the purpose of minimising the effects of any risk events that occur.

Further Reading

Chapman, C.B. and Ward, S. (2003) *Project Risk Management: Process, Techniques and Insights* (2nd edn). Chichester: Wiley.

Project Risk Analysis and Management Guide (2004) (2nd edn). High Wycombe: APM Publishing.

7 Methodology

Finding out about methods

This chapter is intended to encourage you to think carefully about the methods that you will choose to do the research for your project. It is not meant to be a detailed description and explanation of each research method that is available for use in the subject areas in which undergraduate students do projects. Rather, it contains guidance on the various types of methods that are available and to which you should give consideration. It also provides suggestions as to the thinking that you ought to do before you settle on your methods. Do not 'rush in' with preconceived notions of the methods that you want to use. Give yourself time to make your selection.

Good research requires good, clear and justified methodology. The project is your first significant piece of research and so you may well have some difficulty in choosing the methods that will be appropriate to the work you will be doing. How do you know what methodology to use? You should have prepared at least a provisional proposal and discussed it with your tutor. It should include the aims, objectives and the research question, and your hypothesis or problem that you wish to study. These are essential elements in your preparation to select the methods to use in your project. For example, a research question will be a useful indicator of methodology. Analyse your question and determine precisely what data and information you will need to capture in order to answer the question and thus fulfil the aims and objectives of your research. You will have received lectures or seminars on research techniques before the start of your project period. These would certainly have included consideration of methods and so you will have an initial aid to choosing your methods. Figure 7.1, *Using the project life cycle to shape methodology,* is a modification of Figure 5.1, *Research project life cycle.* It illustrates the continuity that must exist between the various elements of the life cycle and how the methodology is related to and dependent upon several of them. It is important to recognise these links. Experience has shown that many students seem to think of each element in isolation and, in particular, often fail to realise the value of analysing the components of their proposal such as the aims and objectives, the hypothesis and their research question for indicators of possible methods.

After this, the next important point of reference should be the tutor appointed to supervise you, who, as well as discussing possible methods with you, will probably advise you to consult the literature of research methods. There are many general texts on research methods as well as texts devoted to research in specific subject fields. Your tutor will offer an opinion on which to consult. Remember that your university library and your department will have copies of theses and research reports. Examine those that deal with subjects similar to yours. Each will have a methodology section from which you will be able to gather useful information. Use all these sources to prepare a list of methods that you consider to be suitable for your research and discuss them with your tutor. Agree a provisional 'subset' from this list and study them to understand them. Take each aim and objective in turn and show what specific data and information you need. From this you will get strong pointers to what data and information collection methods, analytical methods, and interpretation are the most appropriate for achieving each aim and objective.

Something to bear in mind at this time is your capability in understanding and using research methods. When you were formulating the research question, you should have taken into account any strengths and weaknesses you and your tutor considered that you had in relation to the use of particular methods. As the research is yours and you are doing it to contribute to your degree result, you are responsible for gathering, analysing and synthesising data and information, and interpreting it in order, for example, to test your hypothesis, offer a solution to a problem, present a product, development or service design. If you have problems in understanding the methods

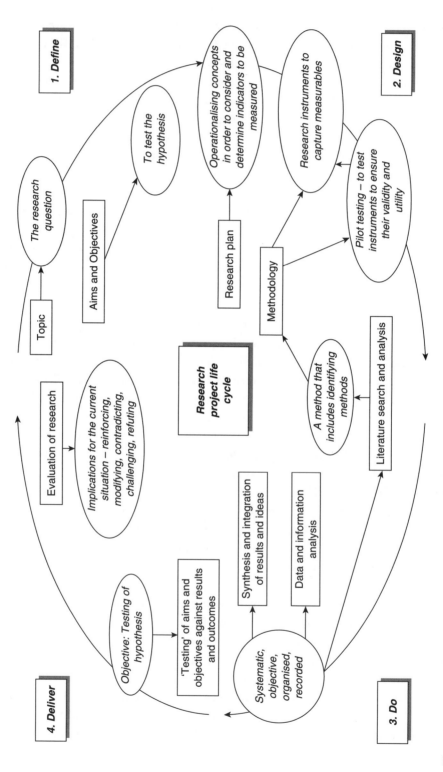

Figure 7.1 Using the project life cycle to shape methodology

1. Define

2. Design

3. Do

4. Deliver

Topic

The research question

To test the hypothesis

Aims and Objectives

Operationalising concepts in order to consider and determine indicators to be measured

Research instruments to capture measurables

Research plan

Methodology

Pilot testing – to test their instruments to ensure their validity and utility

Research project life cycle

A method that includes identifying methods

Literature search and analysis

Implications for the current situation – reinforcing, modifying, contradicting, challenging, refuting

Evaluation of research

Synthesis and integration of results and ideas

Data and information analysis

Objective: Testing of hypothesis

'Testing' of aims and objectives against results and outcomes

Systematic, objective, organised, recorded

that you have chosen, it is very likely that your work will be flawed and you will probably get a poor grade for your final report. This re-emphasises the importance of care in formulating your research question and your aims and objectives. Thus, there are two warnings here: first, if you have difficulties with particular methods, avoid a research question that requires use of these methods, otherwise your results may be lacking in value or usefulness; second, do not focus on using a particular method because it appeals to you and so you feel compelled to use it. Even though it appeals to you, you may not fully understand how to use it. This could result in a poorly framed research question that may lack real substance and so produce relatively meaningless results.

Whatever methods you choose and however many you choose, remember that the time frame for your research is prescribed by your course regulations. Also, within that time frame, the time available to you to do your research is quite limited since you will have other work or course commitments, depending upon whether you are a full-time or sandwich student. This time constraint on your project will have some influence on the methods that you can choose. For example, it is unlikely that you will be able to undertake a large-scale questionnaire-based survey since the conduct of the survey and the subsequent analysis of returns will require substantial time and effort. Similarly, an in-depth series of one-to-one interviews of all students in a university faculty will take considerable time to set up, do, transcribe and analyse.

When you have decided upon your methodology, ask yourself the questions in Appendix 7. If you are able to answer them positively, you will be able to have some confidence in your research design, including your methodology.

Relating the methods to the types of research

Library-based research

Library-based research has, as its major source of data and information, the published literature. The literature chosen will be determined by the topic of the research. It is important to realise that you define the topic. Do not use a dictionary definition just because it is convenient. Dictionary definitions tend to locate a topic within its discipline, yet many matters of great interest and significance are either interdisciplinary or transdisciplinary in nature. You will have chosen your topic because you have a particular view or interest in it, because you have encountered a problem or a gap in what is known about the topic and you seek to solve the problem or fill the gap. Your research will be primarily devoted to reviewing and analysing the published literature. Properly conducted, this will enable you to extract data and information from the published sources. You will then subject what you have extracted to quantitative or qualitative analysis or both. For example, you may use a form of quantitative content analysis to determine the frequency of occurrence of key terms in your topic and the rate of growth of the use of these terms in academic journals over specified time periods. Such an approach may enable you to identify when a particular topic began to feature as significant within its subject area and, possibly, when interest began to decline. Another possibility would be to apply content analysis to popular magazines published over a period of years, focusing on the advertisements in order to study changes in the ways that products such as motor cars, perfumes, clothes, holidays or household appliances have been promoted. In this instance, the analysis could be both quantitative and qualitative. Quantitative analysis would be obtained by counting the number and frequency of appearance of advertisements of a particular product, the numbers and types of features in each advertisement and the number of media in which they appear. Qualitative assessment of the advertisements could be obtained by opinion surveys of users and potential users of the product.

Qualitative analysis of content may be applied to literature in which opinions are the main focus of interest. For example, you may study journals devoted to art or literary criticism, or to radio and television drama. If you study a selection published over a period of a generation or more, you may be able to detect changing fashions in particular art, literature or drama. You will have to establish criteria for assessment of the opinions that you extract and these will have to be as objective as you can make them. Consultation with tutors will be very important.

Combining qualitative and quantitative methods in an undergraduate project is not recommended. Each category of method normally requires a reasonable level of expertise that will take time to acquire. The project will normally provide you with the opportunity to develop the necessary expertise for either qualitative or quantitative methods, but not both. It is important to seek advice from your tutor if you are convinced that you should use both types of methods. For example, in Chapter 3, *Choosing a topic*, the research question 'What is the distribution of specialist options choices made by students on the fine arts degree at my university in relation to their national and ethnic origins?' was examined. This question may be investigated using a combination of qualitative and quantitative methods. For example, quantitative data on the number of students, choice of options, national and ethnic affiliations, gender and age may be captured using a suitably designed questionnaire in which there are several closed questions – requiring box ticking or similar. Focus groups or one-to-one interviews could be used to gain opinions of, for example, the various national and ethnic groups on the modules offered and the reasons why particular ones were chosen.

Desk-based research

A very interesting form of desk-based research involves studying the internal documentation of an organisation as a critical source of information. The documentation of an organisation provides a very detailed history of that organisation. Studying it makes possible the identification of the thinking behind policies and decisions that have been made and the factors that have influenced them. Extraction and analysis of appropriate data and information will enable the story of specific decisions and the reasons for them to be told. It will also be possible to plot the changes that have taken place in the organisation, changes such as product shifts, trends in service operations, workforce requirements, and customer preferences.

The internal documentation forms the archive of an organisation and so will include reports such as the annual reports, auditors' reports, supplier, product and equipment assessments, marketing surveys, productivity, and health and safety reviews. Properly analysed, these can provide a picture of the changing performance and growth of the organisation. Data for many specific measures may be extracted from such documentation, including service outputs, service quality, costings, and productivity of individual workstations, factories or sites, equipment utilisation and downtime, and the changing provisions for staff development.

Survey-based research

Surveys constitute a useful method for gathering opinions of specified populations and are one of the more popular research methods used by undergraduates. Survey researchers will normally use a sample of the nominated population because it is not possible to include all of it. Generally, surveys may be categorised as either *cross-sectional* or *longitudinal*. Cross-sectional surveys are used to gather data or information on a population at a particular point in time. For example, television news organisations often gather opinions on matters that they believe concern the general public at a particular time. Recent matters have included the introduction of 24-hour licences for the sale of alcohol, involvement in the war in Iraq, and the amount of debt that individuals have incurred. Longitudinal surveys are used to gather data or information over a period of time, to discover changes in particular features and then to describe and explain them. There are three types worth considering: trend studies, cohort studies, and panel studies. Trend studies involve sampling the same population over a period.

One such study is an annual survey of the leisure expenditure of undergraduates. Cohort studies involve studying a group of people, the membership of which will be different each time it is studied. For example, a particular study may focus on first year students in a business studies degree course. The intention is to repeat the study over several years with each first year group in order to discover whether the different groups have similar or changing make-up and reasons for choosing their course. Panel studies use the same samples of people each time, perhaps each year. The same questions are asked each time with the purpose of seeking reasons for changes in habits or opinions, for example. Because the panel group being studied may disperse geographically, become difficult to contact or to communicate with, panel studies are expensive, time-consuming and have high attrition rates. A general point to bear in mind is that a survey is only as valid as the responses given, which it is not possible to guarantee.

Suppose you commit yourself to a survey of some kind. Your justification for the choice will have been spelled out in your project proposal. Your proposal has been approved. Now you have to do the survey. It is critically important that you plan your survey. The survey method must be carefully selected, questions to be asked must be objectively chosen and well framed. Remember that once you have started the survey, it will be very difficult for you to amend it in any way. For instance, you will not be able to change the substance of the survey questions since that will significantly reduce the validity of the data set obtained, nor will you be able to modify your research question. So you must specify precisely what you intend to survey. Next, develop the administrative plan that will ensure that you keep control of your research.

Let us assume that you wish to survey the students in your university faculty. The students will display between them a substantial number of characteristics. Suppose that there are several hundred students and that they come from overseas as well as the UK. The characteristics that may be used to categorise them will include national origin, ethnicity, religion, gender, age, marital status, physical condition, socio-economic group, mother tongue, pre-entry schooling and pre-entry qualifications, pre-course employment, political, leisure and sporting interests and activities, hobbies, career intentions, optional modules chosen from their course programmes. What is it that you wish to discover about these students? How many of these characteristics will be relevant to your research? How will they be related to your aims and objectives, or your research question? Will you use a sample or survey the whole population? Will your sample be randomly selected or will you select a specified percentage of the students on each course, in each year of the courses or in each school or department in the faculty? Be guided by your tutor.

Box 7.1:   Questions to ask yourself about your survey

Why am I doing it?
How much data do I want?
How useful will it be?
What method am I using?

  Questionnaire – numerical data; small sample: 30–50.
  Interview – intensive information from a few respondents (about 10).
  Case study – detailed analysis and evaluation of one 'situation'.

Why am I doing it this way?
What am I seeking, specifically – what data, what information?

  Numbers – use a questionnaire; limit to maximum of 20 questions.
  Comments, opinions, discussion – use interviews.
  Study of a context, problem, situation, development – use case study.

How useful will it be?
How will I present the results?
What uses will be made of the results?
What contribution will my survey make to the understanding of my topic?
What contribution will it make to the subject area in which my topic lies?
Am I satisfied with what I have done?

Will you use a questionnaire to gather the data and information that you need? You may think about using email as all students have a university email account and you think that this is more likely to guarantee a higher response rate than relying on contact in lectures. Other advantages of email surveys include speed of delivery and response, and relatively low cost. You may have to obtain the permission of your university authorities to carry out the survey. However, if you are sampling rather than surveying the complete population, how will you ensure that your sample is representative? How will you be sure that the email addressee is the one who has responded? It is not unusual for addressees to pass on email questionnaires to others. You must also realise that some recipients may dislike unsolicited email – spam – and ignore your questionnaire. Recognise that anonymity of respondents is not ensured in email surveys. A point to bear in mind is that you will be surveying a special population and so you will not be able to generalise your results.

An alternative would be to seek approval to use the documentation that the university has on file for each student. This latter method will require that you gain the informed consent of each student and that you must explain every aspect of what you will be doing with the information. You may consider that one-to-one or group interviews will be appropriate ways of gathering what you require. Remember that you may encounter language problems with overseas students and a reticence when it comes to the disclosure of certain types of information. Also, there may be occasions when you have to rely on interpreters to try to ensure that those whom you are studying completely understand what it is that you are doing and require from them.

You may feel tempted to include questions in your survey instrument that will elicit as much information on the students as possible. Resist the temptation. It is possible that you will breach research ethics and probably encounter considerable difficulty in getting certain information that individual students may consider to be too sensitive to declare. Add to this the problems that you will have in making sense of the resultant data and you may well find that you are unable to present a coherent story and so will not be able to draw worthwhile conclusions from your work. Thus, your research will have been wasted. A useful piece of work could be concerned with discovering why students of particular backgrounds – educational, national, ethnic, socio-economic, employment – chose the module packages to which they committed themselves. It may be useful to add gender and age to these characteristics.

Whatever methods you use, justify them. Make sure that you convince yourself and your readers that the methods you used were necessary to elicit sufficient data and information, to meet your aims and objectives. Some years ago, I had to assess a project in which a student reported a survey. It was an interesting survey and had some relevance to the topic of the report. However, it was not clear how the survey results contributed to the research. There was not a link to any of the aims or objectives of the research. When the survey results and the discussion of them were ignored, the remaining 'report' continued to make sense and was more coherent. It later became apparent that the survey had been added because the project was running significantly short of words; it would have been 20 per cent or more short.

So, how do you choose a survey method? First, remember that you have a time constraint because you must complete your project within the time frame allowed by your course regulations. Second, the different methods available involve substantially different levels of cost. For example, an email questionnaire is quite cheap; face-to-face interviewing will be relatively expensive, particularly if the interviewees are widely distributed geographically. Third, remember ethics and sensitivities. If you are intending to survey a multi-ethnic population, be aware that there may be a range of sensitivities to the disclosure of certain types of information. Fourth, in certain social groups, there may be significant literacy problems, either because of lack of knowledge of English or because the educational level of some recipients could result in poor responses – if they do respond.

Laboratory-based research and fieldwork

Originally, a laboratory was a building or a part of a building designed for scientific or technical experiments. However, for many years, the term has been used to describe an environment in which something is studied experimentally. For example, social scientists may regard a community as constituting a laboratory for certain studies; a university librarian may regard an Internet facility in the library as a laboratory. Thus, there is something of an overlap between laboratory research and 'fieldwork' – a term frequently encountered in social science, archaeology and environmental work.

The social scientist may observe the range of interactions between members of the community being studied, over an extended period of time. The librarian may study the users of both Internet and available specialised databases to discover whether users from different courses, or academic disciplines exhibit differing skill levels and capabilities when using them, and what the differing demands of these groups are.

In these cases, an important method is observation, though it will not necessarily be the only method used. The observation may be obtrusive – that is, the users know that they are being observed, or unobtrusive – the users are not aware that they are being observed. Observation is a valuable method for the study of crowds and crowd behaviour. The observation may be conducted in person by the researcher, who may become a member of the crowd being studied, or may observe from an observation point overlooking the crowd. Television and film may also be used to study and to record crowd behaviour, making more considered assessments possible. Remember that the observations must be conducted ethically.

Case studies

A case study is a method of study in which a particular organisation or situation is used to explore an occurrence, for instance, and to examine it as a possible indicator or typifier of potentially similar occurrences in other organisations or situations. You may wish to study the reactions of a group of skilled manual workers in a particular industry to a proposed change in employment law certain to affect industry generally, and to use the outcomes as indicators of the possible reactions of skilled manual workers in other industries. In your opinion, the case study method is the best means of doing this study. Be aware that a case study is complex and time-consuming to design, set up and manage. Considerable contextual knowledge and research expertise are needed to do it properly. Also, it provides you with a research environment over which you will have relatively little control. It is mentioned here since it is a research method but you are recommended to avoid using it in your project since you should accept that, as an undergraduate, you will not have either the necessary contextual knowledge or the research expertise.

Operationalising a concept

Box 7.2:   Definition – Operationalising

Operationlising is transforming a theoretical concept into something that can be measured.

Research normally involves instruments to measure something, so define what it is you intend to measure in your project. Define the theoretical concept. Analyse it and break it down into its different dimensions and indicators. For example, suicide – self-killing – is often studied and is expressed as a theoretical concept. Dimensions that may be identified that are relevant to studying suicide include the person who died, indicators for whom could include age, gender, ethnicity, religion, marital status, physical or health condition, and socio-economic status. Another dimension could be the means by which suicide is effected, with associated indicators including the individual weapons used. The location of the event is a relevant dimension and associated indicators would include the locations at which the act took place. Finally, the time of suicide may be a relevant dimension and this would include the time of day, the particular day of the year and the time in the year. Such an analysis will enable you to construct questions that will gather the appropriate data and information. Your questions would have to be designed to collect data or information for all indicators, which are the variables in your study.

Data and information capture instruments

All researchers need the means to gather and record the data and information that will be obtained during their research. These means are referred to as data and information capture instruments or, more simply, research instruments. It is important for you to know and understand precisely what you need so that your research is appropriate, rigorous and objective, and enables you to obtain the data and information that you need to test your hypothesis or fulfil your aims and achieve your objectives.

What are these instruments?

They are the devices, mechanisms and other means by which data and information necessary to the furtherance of the research embodied in the project are 'discovered and recorded'. There are many published sources on research methods. In these sources, there will be chapters or sections on the design of data and information capture instruments. They may not be referred to as 'instruments'. They may be referred to as, for example, questionnaires, logs or diaries, tally sheets, record sheets, transfer sheets, observation sheets, literature review records, progress reports or charts. They may be equipment for recording visual images or sound, or for automatically counting and logging transactions on Internet or database facilities. The nature of the research and, specifically, the methods to be used will suggest the instruments most likely to be suitable.

Who decides what instruments are needed?

You do, in consultation with your tutor and, possibly, with your workplace supervisor. It must also be borne in mind that the proper search and review of the pertinent literature will, almost invariably, enable suitable instruments to be identified. It may become apparent from the literature that there are certain instruments that you ought to use since they are accepted for the sort of investigation that you intend to do. Conversely, literature sources may set out arguments suggesting that certain instruments should not be used. Ensure that you explain clearly how the instruments that you intend to use relate to your hypothesis, research question or matter to be investigated and how they will contribute to the fulfilment of specific aims and achievement of objectives. As the project is your first significant piece of research, it is useful to use instruments that are tried and tested. This will preclude the necessity for you to provide a justification for your choice in terms of validity and reliability.

What is the difference between choosing and designing the instruments?

You may choose instruments that already exist and are reported in the literature pertinent to the subject of the research, and use them exactly as reported in that literature. Indeed, such an exact use may be appropriate and fruitful in that it will often give opportunities for comparison or aggregation of results obtained with published results of other research.

However, it may be that your research cannot be pursued with the known existing instruments reported in the appropriate literature. For example, it may be that the proposed research is centred upon a new area, a new phenomenon or, perhaps, a new population of instances of a unique nature. Existing instruments may not provide the means by which relevant data or information may be captured and recorded. In circumstances such as this, it becomes necessary to design new instruments or substantially modify existing instruments. There may be existing instruments that you can use as a guide when designing new instruments.

Are there any criteria that can assist in the choice or design of instruments?

Yes. The first thing to do is to examine the aims and objectives of your proposed research. If this examination is careful and thorough, it will become apparent just what is necessary to realise the intended outcomes of the research. For example, you may seek to determine the ethnic and religious make-up of a local authority to gather information and data to assist in the provision of appropriate services. You will need quantitative and qualitative data and information. Some of these you will obtain by using surveys of the local population. Other data and information will be obtained from the electoral roll, from the national census, and from the local authority documentary records. The methods that you propose to use in your research must give sharp indications of the information and data that must be obtained if the research is to be completed successfully. Remember that success in a piece of research means correct use of appropriate procedures to, for example, test an hypothesis, examine a problem, undertake a feasibility study, or study a phenomenon. The substantiation of a theory or point of view, or the establishment of the definitive explanation of a 'mystery' may be an outcome of a piece of research. If it happens, it will be a 'natural outcome' because the essential objectivity applied in gathering data or information appropriately and analysing and interpreting it objectively make it so.

Second, refer to authoritative published sources on research methods, particularly but not exclusively those in the subject area or discipline in which your proposed research nominally resides. Such texts are usually the result of detailed examination and assessment of the research literature of the subject area. Thus, methods will have been identified that have been used. Additionally, the relative merits of these methods in terms of, for example, ease of use, applicability in specific situations, or limitations in value, almost certainly will have been explored. Any particular problems or disadvantages identified will have been considered and possible solutions to these may be offered.

What instruments should be used in your investigation?

The type of research, the nature of the 'target' situation, environment, population, phenomenon, or problem, for instance, will be the major determinant of the instruments to be used. If the intention of a particular piece of research is to replicate the work of another researcher, then the methods and instruments used must be identical to those used by the first researcher and they must be used in exactly the same way. If the intention of the proposed work is to provide comparative data or information to that already published, again, as far as is possible, the same methods and instruments should be used in the same way.

If the proposed research is new and has some 'unique' feature to it, then it may be necessary to design new instruments. Think about importing methods from another subject area. On examination, you may consider them to be more appropriate than those available in your nominal field of enquiry. You may need to modify the methods. Your careful analysis of the *aims* and *objectives* of the proposed research will enable you to infer appropriate methods. In turn, these methods will lead, naturally, to inferences about instruments suitable for the research. It is important to ask yourself the question '*What do I need to capture in order to satisfy my research needs?*' Be specific, objective and clear in your answer. Then ask the question '*Will any of the existing methods enable me to get what I need?*' If your answer is 'no', then you need to determine whether you can modify existing instruments or whether you will have to design new instruments. Designing a research instrument can be a significant project. At undergraduate level research, it is unlikely that you will struggle to find suitable instruments already existing.

How many instruments should be used?

As many should be used as are necessary to pursue the aims and objectives of the proposed research. It is not an uncommon mistake for students to focus on one type of instrument and exclude consideration of any other. There are possibly several reasons for this. One reason may be that a student understands and knows how to use one particular instrument but is not aware of any other that might be more appropriate or useful. Alternatively, it may be that a student is fearful of using other than a well-understood, tried and tested instrument. It has been known for a student to be persuaded to use a particular instrument because its use has been reported in the literature so widely that 'it must be the thing to use'. Such attitudes may be limiting on the proposed research and may make it relatively sterile or worthless.

Let the proposed research, through its aims and objectives, be the prime determinant of the methods and instruments to be used, not whims, likes, dislikes, fears or undue confidence. Thus, it may be that a particular piece of research requires several instruments to be used at different stages or in different elements of the research. For example, you may be studying the lifestyle and behaviour of students at a university. Lifestyle is a complex combination of many interesting and diverse features. These will require information and data that will be obtainable using questionnaires, one-to-one and group interviews, observation of social behaviour, discussions with tutors and academic administrators, and analysis of student union and local leisure and sporting opportunities.

What guidance is there on selection and design of data and information capture instruments?

There are many published sources devoted to research methodology (see *Bibliography*). Each subject field or discipline has several such sources and your tutor will be familiar with most of them. However, one body of sources that is often neglected by student researchers is the research report literature and theses. These sources are, by definition, reports of research undertaken. Some of this reported research work is unique; it has to be to fulfil the requirements of, for example, a university in the case of a PhD thesis. Such a body of literature constitutes a very fertile source of ideas to aid in the selection of methods and in the selection and design of instruments.

Data and information collection and organisation

Making records

It is important to keep records of all that you do whilst engaged in the project. The records should be clear and detailed enough for them to act as good memory aids when 'picking up' the project again after being away from it. The types of records that you make will vary with the type of project that you are doing. However, there are some fairly standard records that should be mentioned. Since you will be making many records of similar activities, events and features, it is worth spending some time designing forms on which you will be recording information and data. You may find it necessary to have several designs even with a relatively straightforward project. It will not be enough to have one fairly broad, simply structured form to act as a 'project record sheet'. Plan and design as many forms as possible, within the limits of common sense, at the outset of the project. As the project develops, you may find a need to design more.

Progress record

This is to record project progress at regular intervals, e.g. every four to six weeks. It can be brief. Date and time each record. Include achievements such as completion of significant phases of your project, problems encountered and solutions as appropriate, and summaries and analyses of interim results. Your university may have a standard form for progress reporting.

Interview record

Have a separate form for each interviewee. Include provision for recording the interviewee's name, interview location, date and time of interview, topic and purpose of the interview. Outline the approach you will take in the interview. Provide a summary of the questions you intend to ask or attach a copy of your script. It would also be useful to describe the extent to which you prepare and guide the interviewee for and during interview.

Correspondence

Experience has shown that many students do not regard correspondence connected with their research as information sources, yet emails and letters may contain useful advice, guidance, opinion or data that is of value to the work. Therefore, examine all correspondence and highlight that which may be significant to your research. Also include copies of letters, emails and faxes sent to and received from tutors and a copy of your situation paper, if one has been required of you, since it is a relevant communication from you. Internal documentation received from an employer should also be kept. This may include a contract of employment, training programme, health and safety information, security, benefits and use of certain 'controlled' facilities. Make sure you keep records of correspondence (see Appendix 1).

Data sheets

Data sheets are designed for recording raw data such as numbers or occurrences relating to particular instances. For example, if you are intending to survey undergraduates to establish reasons behind their choice of course and modules, and to discover whether there are any detectable trends in or correlations between their choices and their ethnicity, nationality or precourse experience, then you will have a data sheet for each undergraduate studied and will record the particular characteristics of each student. This will comprise information such as ethnic group, nationality, age, gender, precourse experience (education, type of employment, type of employer), country of origin, marital status, and socio-economic group. When all students have been interviewed, you will use a summary sheet to enter totals for each characteristic. Thus, the data sheets will be of two kinds for this study – a sheet for each individual studied and a summary sheet for the group. You should make provision for noting the date and time of completion on each sheet.

Documentation review sheet

All documentation that you have read and from which you have obtained information or data relevant to your research should be noted. Each document used should result in generation of a record. The documentation will comprise the published literature that you have used as well as unpublished material such as the internal documentation of an organisation. The records of published literature are so useful and important to your research that a sample of a literature item review record sheet is given in Appendix 3.

Questionnaires

Many projects quite naturally require the use of questionnaires to capture data and information. Many undergraduates choose topics that lend themselves to the use of questionnaires. This is acceptable since much learning about research can be gained from suitably designed and conducted surveys. However, questionnaire design requires great care. You may require specialist help to produce a satisfactory design. Consult a suitable authority such as your academic tutor.

Exercise close control over the administration, distribution and completion of a questionnaire. This control should range from a well-written, concise guide to recipients on how to complete it to a detailed set of notes for guiding the person or persons, including yourself, who will be distributing and explaining it to recipients. Other parts of the control will be the recording of distribution and return, using a controlled distribution list to keep clear, precise notes. Also prepare transfer sheets on which to accumulate data from the individual questionnaires and summary sheets on which the data from the transfer sheets are to be summarised. It will be useful to create a comments summary sheet to record comments made by respondents that do not lend themselves to counting since they are qualitative not quantitative. An additional useful record will contain your justification and explanation of the design and nature of the questionnaire, the reasons for its use, comment on problems in its administration and use, results from the pilot testing of it, and feedback about it from respondents. Also, record your thinking in respect of the structure, form and content of each question.

Designing a questionnaire

Where do you start? The social sciences section of a good academic or public library will carry many books that have sections devoted to questionnaire design. Your university library will have treatises on the design of research instruments. You should be able to find out from these sources if there already exists a questionnaire that fits your requirements and seek permission to use it. This will mean obvious saving in time and will have the added advantage that it will have been tried and tested. It may also have been used to produce data that you could use for comparative purposes. However, bearing in mind the project management aspect of your research, it will be a better learning experience for you to design your own questionnaire. What sort of questions are you going to ask? Will the questionnaire be used in conjunction with interviews, will you issue it to assembled groups of respondents and provide an explanation and an opportunity for discussion at the time? Answers to these questions will have an influence on the type of questions that you ask.

There are two main types of question. The first type is the closed or closed-ended question. These require a respondent to tick boxes or circle numbers following each question. A very common use of these is in student satisfaction surveys undertaken to determine students' reaction to courses at university. Respondents tick boxes corresponding to their ethnic group, age range, pre-entry qualifications and other relevant features. Opinions may be sorted as to the perceived quality of particular modules or lecturers by circling a number on a five- or seven-point scale. One advantage of this type of question is that the questionnaire is relatively simple to analyse. A disadvantage is that the respondent is constrained by your 'definition' of specific answers. Also, this system is subjective since it is very likely that the value attached to a particular number will differ from student to student. The second type of question is the open or open-ended question. These are intended to give the respondent the opportunity to write a statement giving an opinion about a matter or situation briefly described in the question. An advantage is that the respondents are not constrained in what they can write. A possible disadvantage is that respondents may be put off by having to be creative, particularly if you leave what may appear to be quite large spaces in which to answer. By their nature, they are time-consuming to complete, another daunting feature, which may further dissuade respondents. Finally, analysing and interpreting the responses take much time and effort and, as your time is limited, you should think carefully and take advice before committing yourself to a questionnaire that relies on a substantial number of open questions.

Piloting a questionnaire

Your questionnaire is not a simple document to design. You have expended considerable time and thought in designing it because you want your research to be of good standard and achieve sound outputs. You are very close to it, you know what you want and are convinced that what you have prepared will get it. But when we are too close to something, we are very likely to miss something of importance, or to take for granted that what we have produced is exactly what is required. So, put your questionnaire to the test. Pilot it with a small but meaningful number of the population that you intend to survey. Yes, you want to pick out the spelling and grammatical errors, the repetitions and the vagaries. More important, you need to find out whether any of the questions are difficult to understand. Will they prompt recipients to avoid answering them because they do not understand what you want from them? Also pilot the covering letter that you will send with the questionnaire. In this, you will explain the purpose of your survey and make clear that the response of each recipient will provide valuable data to be used in the research, the outcome of which will, itself, be valuable.

What do you want from the pilot test? You want to be able to answer at least the following questions about your questionnaire. You want comment and opinion of the format – does it lead or encourage the recipients to respond? Is the understanding shown by the pilot recipients of your questions the same as your intended understanding? Should you categorise the questions to assist recipients to structure their thoughts when responding? Are any questions too complex, too long or too vague? For example, you may have framed some questions in such a way that they seek response to two or more points. You may have asked business studies degree students 'Did you choose the project Management module because it was unusual or because you seek a career in project management?' How will you interpret a 'Yes' answer? How long should it take to complete the questionnaire? Is the purpose of your questionnaire clear and acceptable to your population? Do they think that what you are seeking is realistic?

Experience has shown that many students consider that piloting a questionnaire is a waste of time; that it prevents them from 'getting their research done'. Do not adopt this attitude. Piloting your questionnaire may result in you detecting a glaring error in it, which, if not corrected, could have a catastrophic effect on your research, and possibly result in failure in your project.

In Box 7.3 are some questions that you are recommended to answer before you start your survey. It is very possible that you have been asked to take part in a survey of some kind and it will be useful and informative for you to reflect on your attitude to it. It will be useful because you will refresh your memory on what it is like to be a respondent and this will help you when preparing your survey instruments; informative because you will begin to realise what is involved in administering a survey. You will also realise how important it is to convey the purpose of the survey and to ensure that recipients understand the questions.

Box 7.3: Consider one type of research – social surveys

Have you ever responded to a survey?

How was it conducted – by post, email, or interview?

Was the purpose of the survey clearly explained to you?

Were you fully informed of the ethical aspects of the survey?

Was your consent to being studied informed, i.e. were you made aware by the researcher of all the implications of being a subject of the study, such as the uses to which your responses and personal information would be put?

Box 7.3:   (Continued)

Were you guaranteed anonymity?

Were you guaranteed confidentiality?

What did you have to do in responding?

Did you complete a questionnaire on your own, or did an interviewer write your responses on a form? Were you able to see what was written?

What sorts of data and information were you asked to disclose?

Were there any questions that you did not want to answer?

If so, why? Was any pressure put on you to answer these questions?

Were you told where the results would be published or what they would 'influence'?

What did you think of the survey and the survey instrument?

One point to highlight from Box 7.3 is the matter of informed consent. It is unusual for undergraduates to consider the need to obtain the informed consent of their subjects. Many may not even be aware of what informed consent is. It is the agreement of people to be subjects of study in a project that involves research. The consent only comes after these people have had the full implications of their participation fully explained to them. Tutors should make a point of explaining it to those whom they supervise. Certainly, much of undergraduate research will not create a need for such consent, but you should always clarify this with your tutor. Some research may involve populations in which there are literacy problems or in which there is a range of different mother tongues spoken. Do not consider that it is unusual. Supposing you are studying public library usage in a major city in the UK. There are many multi-ethnic and multinational communities in the UK and their members have the use of the public library system. Also in such cities there may be many local people with special educational needs. All these people may have attitudes and sensitivities that must be taken into account in your study. You may have to develop special informed consent procedures if you wish to pursue your study in such groups of people. Another problem to be aware of is that, with language difficulties among the population being surveyed, you may have to rely on translators to assist you in administering your research instruments. Professional translators are expensive, local people acting as translators on a good will basis may not have the expertise to give exact translations/interpretations and may 'interpret' what your respondents tell them. You are recommended to avoid these problems, though you need to recognise that they exist. Remember that you are learning about research as much as doing research.

Box 7.4: Some 'products' of surveys

Quantitative values:

- Numbers of people using museums and libraries, related to purposes of use
- Size of demographic, ethnic, religious groups
- Average spend by consumers on, for example, cinema, motor cars and sport
- Use of scientific periodicals in a university library
- Public library usage by mothers of primary school age children
- Average cost of book processing in public libraries.

Qualitative values:

Explanations of 'social phenomena':

- Why women are more likely than men to watch soap operas
- Why there has been an increase in cheating at universities
- How people choose their career pathways
- Why people indulge in 'binge drinking'
- Why people entitled to vote choose not to vote at general elections
- Why people use or do not use their public library.

In Box 7.4 are listed some of the categories of data that can be obtained by surveys. The list is not exhaustive but includes categories of data that have been gathered in undergraduate projects over the past 35 years.

Organising records

Date, time and number all your project records, including your notes of the activities and interactions in the project work and notes from internal and external documentation reviewed to prepare and undertake the project. You may have quite a large range of record types and so it is unlikely that there will be only one way in which you may organise them. Remember that you are not just organising the completed records of interviews, reviews of individual items of the literature, or completed questionnaires. You will have the records of what you are doing in your research and how you are doing it. For example, you will have to keep a record of the distribution of your questionnaire and the receipt of completed copies. From this, you will know how many reminders are needed and you will have to record this. The procedures for administering questionnaires, for interviewing and for dealing with problems should also be recorded. In Box 7.5, several ways are given of how you may record the distribution of your questionnaire.

Box 7.5:   Ways of recording distribution of questionnaires

- Alphabetically by recipient
- Chronologically by date of distribution
- Categorically by, for example, type of organisation, or type of employment of recipient
- Alphabetically by interviewer
- Quantitatively by size of organisation
- Alphabetically by nature of business, business sector or product type
- By social, cultural or ethnic grouping
- By age of recipient.

The ways chosen will depend upon the nature and purpose of the survey.

Why go to so much effort in designing your project record forms? Because this sort of effort expended at the initiation of the project will enable time to be used more effectively. Also, by providing the means to monitor the progress of the project, it will help you to ensure that sufficient data and information are collected for the outcomes of the project to be meaningful. Also, you will have the means by which you will be able to 'tell the whole story' of your project.

Summary

Think very carefully about the methods that you choose to use in your project. The starting point for choice should be a detailed analysis of what you wish to discover by your research. Analyse your research question, the aims and objectives of your project. This will give you strong indicators of possible methods since you will be identifying precisely what you want to find out. Operationalising the concepts that form the research focus of your topic will enable you to identify measurables and this will help you to determine the research instruments that you will need. A series of questions has been provided and discussed to help you to finalise your instrument choices. Particular attention was paid to the design and use of questionnaires since these constitute a research tool favoured by undergraduates. There are several sources of assistance that you must consult before settling on particular methods. These include lecture notes, texts on research methods, and reports and theses in your university library. Make sure that you discuss your possible choices with your tutor.

Further Reading

Orna, Elizabeth with Stevens, Graham (1995) *Managing Information for Research*. Buckingham: Open University Press. (See particularly Chapter 4, pp. 59–73.)

Wilkinson, David and Birmingham, Peter (2003) *Using Research Instruments: A Guide for Students*. London: RoutledgeFalmer.

8 The Literature Review

All research has a link to something that has already been done, however tenuous that link may be. It is very unlikely that you will be involved in 'blue sky' research for your project since you have not yet proved yourself as a researcher. Also, the saying 'there is nothing new under the sun' may not be absolutely accurate since the literature of human endeavour frequently contains reports of new inventions, new phenomena, new discoveries or brief mentions of unexplained occurrences or situations. Nevertheless, however 'new' something is, there will almost certainly be a trail back in the literature to a related idea, proposition, theory, suggestion, or similar. Somewhere, someone will have reported something that has some relationship to, similarity to or has features in common with what is 'new'.

As a researcher, you have a responsibility to find what has gone before for many reasons. These reasons are presented in this chapter. They will help you to understand how important it is to discover all that has been reported about your topic or in some way related to it in order to ensure that your research is properly informed and has the necessary authority. Also, you will understand the value of reviewing the literature, and how to do it. The exploration of the literature review in this chapter is detailed since there is much to learn about what is possibly the most important component of the research and of the subsequent project report.

Research normally starts from an idea born from inspiration, serendipity, reflection, or problem analysis, from lack of knowledge in a specific topic area or by the prescription of a desired future position. A classic case of a prescribed future position resulted from a decision by US President John F. Kennedy, at the beginning of the 1960s, that the USA would put an astronaut on the moon by the end of that decade. Contemporary knowledge was not sufficient to enable that objective to be achieved. It would demand much research and many discoveries and developments in many disciplines including science, technology, engineering, medicine, behavioural sciences, and project and human resources management. However, this did not mean that the researchers and developers in these fields would be working in an entirely new field; they were not starting from scratch. Work had been done or was in progress in all these fields including much that would be of potential usefulness, and that had previously been written about.

There may be a slight similarity between your project and the moon project in that you may have your research topic prescribed for you by your tutor and the time frame will be prescribed by your course regulations. Whether your topic is prescribed or freely chosen, you will start by discussing it with your tutor. From these discussions, you will formulate an hypothesis to test and develop a research question or questions to answer. Your tutor may recommend some readings that will help you to clarify your thinking about research generally and to refine your ideas on your topic. Your tutor will also make clear to you that your research must have authority, be credible and its aims and objectives must be achievable in the time available. At this stage, you may know and understand very little about your topic. This is normal so do not worry. However, you must relatively quickly expand your knowledge and understanding. This is where the literature makes a major contribution because it is in the available literature of a subject that the establishment of the authority and credibility of research is founded and from which your knowledge is gained. Completion within the permitted time is achieved if your project management is satisfactory. There is a substantial literature on project management and it forms part of the body of literature essential to researchers.

So much importance is attached to the literature of a subject and its effective and efficient review in furthering research that it is considered separately from the main methodology and report writing chapters. There is not a single text that provides guidance on literature reviewing to undergraduates generally. There are sources that are devoted to reviewing the literature in specific subjects; a notable example is the book by Hart (1998), and there is a section in the book by Bell (2005). Though the book by Hart is written for postgraduate research students in the social sciences, undergraduate students in many disciplines will find it useful. By intention, the undergraduate project is not so demanding of research preparation as a higher degree is and so such detailed guidance is not needed. However, by design, it tests a student's use of research methods including reviewing the literature. Undergraduates ask many questions about the literature review when they begin their projects and this chapter is designed to provide answers to them.

The purpose of a literature review

What is a literature review?

In essence, it is a demonstration vehicle. It demonstrates three main things. First, that you, the researcher, have made yourself fully familiar with what exists in the subject area within which your chosen topic resides. You have identified and understood it in terms of, for example, the theoretical and practical concepts, the current and past research contexts and directions, and the subject boundaries. Second, you show the extent to which you have the capabilities to be a researcher by the quality of your review in terms of your pursuit of relevant material and the insights and arguments that you deploy in it. Third, the clarity, fluency, precision, accuracy, and the systematic and logical way in which you present it will demonstrate your ability as a research communicator, which is integral to the research process.

Your review will cover published and unpublished but available documents, such as journal articles, papers, reports and books, emails on relevant lists, Internet publications, discussion groups and bulletin boards, and non-textual materials. In fact, anything that could reasonably contain information and data relevant to the topic or matter that is the subject of study should be included. Be aware that caution is essential when using email lists and the Internet since such sources may not be refereed or editorially controlled and thus their quality may be open to question. Similarly, unpublished sources may not be editorially controlled. For instance, your project may be work based and include the need to review internal documentation, such as correspondence, memoranda and reports produced in the organisation.

Why review the literature?

The general answer to this question is 'to find out what has already been done and thus gain a good understanding of the subject of interest and to recognise the key features and communicators in that subject'. A subsidiary answer is 'to gain information on appropriate research methods and how to use them'. That is, reviewing the literature is an intellectually fruitful part of the overall research process. Your review will have a critical influence on your study. Without it, you cannot proceed with confidence.

Returning to President Kennedy's prescription, the value of finding out what already exists becomes clear. Most of the disciplines that became involved in the research programmes to put an American on the moon were already well established at the time. This meant that considerable amounts of information and data already existed that would prove to be useful. These would form the starting point for new research and would be reported in both published and unpublished documents. Your situation as an undergraduate will be similar in that it is unlikely that tutors will allow you to do research in a topic in which the literature is very sparse or non-existent. Recognise this and use your discussions with tutors and the readings that they have recommended to inform your search for pertinent literature. The claim that there was no literature pertinent to your topic is very unlikely to gain a sympathetic hearing when you discuss a failed project.

A thorough and systematic search for the available material will enable you to discover and retrieve what has been written and where it is located. Successful completion of the search will result in a body of material in which there may be significant amounts of potentially useful information and data. This documentary material will have to be critically reviewed to extract from it any authoritative data and information that might prove useful. The critical reviewing will ensure that you identify a range of ideas on which you will be able to build your knowledge and understanding of your topic and should significantly reduce the chance of duplicating previous work with the consequent waste of your efforts. This is one important reason why you must review the literature and begin the search and review at the start of the project period. How do you know that you have 'captured' all relevant literature? You cannot be certain. For example, there will be publications in many languages including your own, some of which may not be covered by secondary services available to you, either in the original languages or in translation. However, if you have formulated good search strategies and used them systematically, it is unlikely that you will have missed significant items.

Reviewing the literature of a subject provides an academically enriching experience if properly done. It should be regarded as a process that is fundamental to any worthwhile piece of research or development work. A scholar has a duty to find out what already exists in a proposed area of study before embarking on the so-called 'research proper'. Indeed, the literature review is the foundation of the research proper, since knowledge of the contributions of others in your chosen subject area is critical. At the simplest level, it is important to discover the ideas of others in order to avoid claiming them as your own. More significantly, you may find that the solution to your research problem or the answer to your research question already exists. Alternatively, you may find literature that proves your proposed work to be totally lacking in feasibility yet other ideas that appear to be very promising are suggested. This is another important reason why you must begin your literature review at the start of the project period.

Box 8.1: Danger in the late literature review

Students often leave the literature review to late in the project period. They prefer to 'get on with their research'. I have been involved in the assessment of projects for which the students had begun the literature review when writing up the final report. Consider the implications of this. At worst, the topic may have been thoroughly investigated and reported in the literature. In such an instance, the project must normally fail, as it is no more than a replication of work satisfactorily completed.

Also, the student might have failed to identify more appropriate research methods than those used. Interesting and possibly supportive or challenging results might be found too late to have a significant, possibly enriching effect upon the work done. Similarly, there would be too little time to digest, assimilate and integrate, as appropriate, the ideas available in the literature retrieved. At best, the report might gain a pass. In one of the instances with which I was associated, the student's writing skills were better than average and so the project gained a reasonable pass grade. However, the literature review still had clear evidence of being 'bolted on at the last minute'.

Realise that much may be overlooked in respect of subject knowledge and research skills if the literature search and review is neglected or regarded as a necessary but time-consuming inconvenience that may be left until the 'real work' has been done.

The general answer to 'why do a literature review?' may be developed into a series of reasons that are more detailed and specific. If you examine these reasons carefully in relation to the topic in which you are researching, you will be able to develop the search strategies that you will need to begin your literature search. You will also be able to extract ideas from them that can be used for categorising the items that are produced by your searches. Finally, you will be able to use many of the concepts present or implied in these reasons to analyse each item for ideas that you may extract and use in your review.

Planning and management. One practical product of your literature search is that the planning and management of similar projects may feature in some of the literature, as may useful advice on how to provide for and cope with the unexpected as well as the expected. Thus, you do more than build your research on the subject ideas of others; you capitalise on their project management experience. Also, it may be possible to link up informally with some researchers for the exchange of ideas, data and information, insights and advice – on methods, theories, and interpretation of results. You may even be given pointers to possible topics worth researching. At a simple level, these people may prove useful in locating and obtaining relatively inaccessible documents. These gains provide substantial justification for thoroughness in your search for relevant literature.

History. It is a basic requirement that you should understand the history of the subject area in which your investigation is centred. This will serve the general purpose of raising your subject awareness and understanding. Also, it will provide you with a perspective on how your chosen subject has become established and is developing, and assist in the development of the appropriate vocabulary; good knowledge and understanding of the vocabulary of your subject is important. Additionally, it will ensure that features such as names, concepts, events, and methods significant in the development of the subject are identified and understood, both in terms of their meaning and their roles in and contributions to the subject.

Current situation. Searching, reading and critically reviewing the literature must ensure that you will be made aware of the current general situation in the subject. This will make it possible to identify general areas of concern that might give pointers to specific matters worth studying – research questions. Areas of concentrated, current interest and, possibly, areas of relative neglect will become apparent. You will also gain an understanding of the interrelationships between the topic being considered for study and the other parts of the general subject area. Thus, you will be able to recognise and define the context in which your subject resides. If you discover and review properly the appropriate literature, an important outcome will be the provision of authority for the work that you propose to do. This will help you to avoid investigating marginal, insubstantial or unrealistic topics.

Mapping the literature. Initially, the literature search will provide the current leading concepts and topics attracting most interest. It will enable the theories of interest to be discovered, considered and understood together with the matters that feature most significantly in debate. Proper analysis and review will enable the literature to be mapped in terms of, for example, its definitions, its historical development, key theories, methodologies, key thinkers and experimentalists and organisations, bodies of evidence, notable themes and arguments. Another key feature stemming from the review is the determination of the range of publication types – the form spectrum – and the main languages in which pertinent material is published – the language spectrum. This will help you to decide whether you have captured enough of the relevant literature.

Identification of subject gaps. If the map of your field of interest is carefully done, it may be possible for you to identify gaps of some kind. These gaps may be conceptual in that there is a lack of acceptable theoretical explanation of phenomena. There may be a methodological gap in that there is apparently no acceptable method for investigation of particular observed phenomena, conditions, events or problems. It may be that particular matters have never been investigated or explained. It is in such gaps that there may be fertile areas for investigation. Remember, also, that the boundaries of a subject are defined by those who work in and write about it, not by a classification scheme, catalogue or index or by a disciplinary categorisation. These are devices of convenience for organising documentary material for access by readers.

People and organisations. It is necessary to become familiar with the names of those people and organisations that are working in the area of your proposed study. In other words, you must know who is doing what that is of interest and relevance to your study. Within the literature covered by your review, there will be people, organisations and possibly even research programmes worth noting as being possible sources of ideas or even for use as components in search strategies when furthering the literature search. It may also prove possible to identify people and organisations with whom or with which some degree of co-operation may be fruitful. Their views and opinions on suitable research strategies could prove useful. They may suggest specific topics, problems or situations in which research is necessary.

Identification of peers with whom to discuss ideas. Although the final report is entirely your responsibility, there is obvious value to be added to it by the discussion of research methods and results with other like-minded workers such as those identified by the literature search. Among these there may be some who may prove to be useful sounding boards for explanations of the unexplained, or sources of help in solving the unsolved. Your final, written discussion of results in your project report, of which the review of literature forms an early part, will be more rounded and informed if you have taken the opportunity to gain the opinions of other workers in the field. Such opinions, however, must be used cautiously and must be attributed when they have been influential on or have contributed significantly to the discussion.

Subject biographical information. Remember that the review is critical. That is, you must adopt an objective, analytical and evaluative approach to the work being reviewed and to the people who are doing and reporting that work. Thus, it will be useful to discover subject biographical information about the authors whose work you are reviewing. They will have particular ideologies or points of view. They may follow one particular school of thought rather than another. They may have made specific assumptions when beginning their work or when interpreting, explaining or discussing their results. Always be prepared to challenge assumptions. It is one of the norms of scholarly practice. They may have used methods of investigation that could, and perhaps, should be challenged. No matter what the status of the author whose work is being reviewed, always adopt a critical attitude to it. At a relatively simple level, check whether the journal or other publication in which a particular contribution appears is refereed. Peer review is normally a rigorous process that tests whether an article should be published, yet even this should not be taken as proof that a particular contribution to the literature is above criticism. Remember, also, that criticism must be a constructive process.

Identification of research methods. The identification of research methods you may consider using will be one of the more important outcomes of the literature search unless there is a generally accepted methodology or you have been prescribed one. Even in this last instance, you should still challenge the methods prescribed. When reviewing methods, the determination of their appropriateness will be assisted by the description and explanation of their use by other workers. The relative merits of different methods, their advantages and disadvantages and reasons for use may be explicitly or implicitly disclosed. Particular modifications made by a researcher to a specific method may prove to be suitable for your proposed work. Reasons may be given why some and not other particular methods were used. Other researchers may offer views and advice on tactics worth using in particular circumstances. Always remember that each researcher will have a point of view and that it may be idiosyncratic.

Identification of research instruments. In many subjects, there are certain research instruments that are recognised as generally appropriate for particular types of investigation. These may include questionnaires, interviews, focus groups, filming or audio recording, or categories for the selection or organisation of populations or samples. It may be possible, even advantageous to adopt or adapt these instruments for your investigation. They will be familiar to and accepted by those working in the field and will enable you to produce results that will be suitable for comparison with the results of others.

Results for comparison. Results reported by other researchers in your field will be of importance for several reasons, not least of which is that they may provide useful data and ideas for comparison with your results. The fact that your results correspond and correlate with those of other researchers may provide support for your hypothesis. The use of the results of others is a legitimate practice provided that appropriate attribution is made and that use is proper. Results of others normally must have been obtained in similar or parallel situations, using similar or comparable methods and must be used cautiously. Normally, it should be a matter of comparing like with like. Otherwise, you must have objective reasons for using the results of others when significantly different methods have been used in obtaining those results. Again, always exercise caution in considering the results of other workers.

Table 8.1 Gains from doing a literature search

Key ideas	Key concepts
Themes	Characteristics
Opinions	Arguments
Issues	Controversies
Theses	Hypotheses
Problems	Ways of thinking
The research mind	Other researchers
Motives	Research programmes
Research teams	Organisations
Places	Significant events
Development	Reading skills

Thus, the end product of a properly undertaken review of the literature of a subject is fundamental to satisfactory research in that subject. However, at the time that the project has to be started, undergraduates will not usually have fully understood and developed the scholarly practice of gathering and understanding evidence before embarking on discussion of ideas. Discussions thus founded are almost invariably insubstantial because they lack richness in ideas. Yet there is a temptation to spend little time and effort on the literature search and review in order to give more time for the often-called 'real research' – getting data, getting results. This is a false economy in time since there is so much to learn from the literature. In Table 8.1, the categories of concepts listed suggest what should be targeted in a properly prepared and conducted literature search and show just how much there is to learn from the literature. These categories would also be suitable for use at least as a provisional system for arranging the material that you capture in your search, much of which you will include in your review.

Figure 8.1, *The literature review underpins research* on page 163 identifies the most important ideas that you must discover by doing the literature search and these must be discussed in your review. If you have done your work properly, you will find that they lead to the answers to the most important questions that you must ask of the literature. Thus, it is clear just how thorough and detailed your search and review must be. Naturally, as your project is a small one, the size of your review will be of an appropriate number of words, within the overall word allowance for the project as a whole. The subject and the nature of your investigation will also have an influence on the size. However, experience has show that the literature review section of many undergraduate projects accounts for between 20 and 30 per cent of the word allowance for the project. Appendix 8 contains a method of working on the literature review that I have been recommending to students for several years. It comprises a set of simple, practical suggestions that should enable you to manage the review process relatively effectively.

What a literature review is not

This is not directly a question asked by undergraduates. However, it is clear from reading and assessing many project reports that a question based upon it should be asked. Many of the early attempts by students to produce their reviews result in assemblies of words and sentences that bear little if any relationship to what should have been produced. Sometimes, tutors have to make considerable and repeated efforts to draw from students a product that has the required form and style. Yes, a literature review is a demanding document to prepare and write. By its very nature, it is very demanding in its preparation and presentation but there is much help readily available. An excellent way to become familiar with the literature reviewing process and how to write the review is to read reviews published in a variety of refereed sources. Select a few of these, no more than three or four, making sure that they deal with subjects that you can understand, and read them to perceive the way that the content in each is developed. Also, your university will have the project work and higher degree dissertations and theses of many former students. As a member of the university, you are entitled to read these. Every one of them is likely to have a literature review. You are strongly recommended to read some.

Determine how the sources of the ideas in each review are used and referenced. Try to establish what the structure is and how the reviewer has woven together ideas of the authors of the works cited in the review. Do you find a review easy to read? Is there progressive development of the argument? Can you detect a reviewer's style? Is the vocabulary intensely technical? Are the sentences and paragraphs simple or complex? Does the subject, by its nature, lead to simplicity or complexity? In finding answers to these questions yourself, you will be developing an understanding of how to write your review.

Because students often have problems with reviewing and with what they produce as their reviews, it is important to recognise what *is not* a review of the literature of a subject. Analysis of many projects provides examples of the sorts of 'reviews' that have been offered by undergraduates who have clearly not grasped what was required. Sometimes students convince themselves that they cannot write a review and so they make do with a mechanical assembly of bits and pieces culled from apparently relevant literature sources.

It is not an exhaustive, critical or selective annotated bibliography

Bibliographies are very useful as search tools but are inappropriate as literature reviews as they are selections of items containing information about a subject, not a critical analysis of that subject. The critical aspect is implicit in the principles used to select items for inclusion in them. But is the average undergraduate student aware of the principles that he or she has applied in selecting the items listed? There is not any overall analytical or critical coherence; the coherence that is achieved is more apparent than real and results from the selection of items for a list dedicated to a particular subject. The critical element stems from the presence of an item in the bibliography, not from an evaluation of its content leading to establishment of its relevance.

It is not a list of unconnected, critical evaluations of individual documents in the subject area

It is not uncommon for undergraduates to be required to produce critical evaluations early on their courses. The purpose of this is to encourage them to learn how to assess individual literature items. As such, it is a valuable piece of work. It is apparent that many students regard a compilation of such evaluations as a suitable review of the literature. However, such evaluations are not appropriate for a literature review because the ideas given in each evaluation will be detached from those in the other items and critically considered separately. Such a list does not satisfy the requirement of a review, namely that it be a coherent analysis and synthesis of the ideas extracted from the items.

It is not a combination, compilation or list of extracts carefully selected from relevant documents

Such combinations and compilations will contain many different styles reflecting the many sources from which the content has been extracted. There will be little overall coherence and true development of themes or arguments. Again, the critical and analytical elements are implied only in the selection of items, to the exclusion of others and not in the evaluation and synthesis of ideas from the range of items.

It is not a selection of judiciously chosen quotations linked by some hopefully acceptable phrases in an attempt to 'tell the story' in the words of key communicators

Again, there will be little overall coherence in spite of the care with which the linking phrases have been crafted. The joins will be obvious to the tutored reader. Also, there will not be a clear picture of the reviewer's level of knowledge and understanding of the subject since there is no true synthesis of ideas. Do not think that the use of many words of published workers in your subject field will lend scholarly quality to your review. One certain result will be that your reader will react adversely to having to wade through endless quotations. This is not a way of holding your reader's attention since you are not showing clearly what you know, you are showing only that you found some documents apparently relevant to your subject by authors who *do* know something relevant to your subject. You must show your understanding by weaving together the ideas of others with your own ideas and building a foundation for your research. Sometimes individual students have presented these 'quotations' without indicating sources, creating the impression that they are their own work, intentionally or unintentionally. This may be taken as plagiarism by those of your readers who recognise the sources of 'your words'.

It is not a set of carefully arranged and categorised abstracts of relevant items

This is one of the more dangerous substitutes for the real literature review. First, if you have extracted the abstracts from secondary sources, they may not be the work of the authors who wrote the items that the abstracts represent. Second, there is no indication that you, the reviewer, have read the original work, suggesting that there is no certainty that the content is entirely relevant since abstracts are often justifiably slanted to meet the needs of particular readerships. Third, there is no certainty that abstracts are always accurate or of good quality. Fourth, abstracts may have been taken from several different sources that may have different abstracting policies.

What should be reviewed?

The range of information sources available in terms of format is wide and has been referred to elsewhere in this manual. It is not possible to provide a very precise definition of what should be reviewed. One reason for this is that authors do not necessarily write with the publication structure of their subjects in mind. They obviously seek publication for a range of reasons, one of which is to let their peers know what they are doing. Some authors publish articles in specialist academically oriented journals to present a scholarly perspective on a particular matter and also publish in a professionally oriented journal to present a practical perspective on the same matter. Conference papers are not always published concurrently with or even within many months of the conference. Also, much information is often published in information sources that do not fall within the nominal or apparently natural literature outlets of a topic of investigation. This is particularly the case when the topic is of an interdisciplinary or transdisciplinary nature. Do not forget that audio, video and electronic formats are now quite common in some subject areas. This nature should be evident to the reviewer at the outset and so the approach to the literature search should be governed accordingly. Faced with such a wide range of information sources, the citation index becomes a valuable search tool (Box 8.2).

Box 8.2:   Citation indexes

The citation index is based upon the use of the items that authors cite in their publications. Each reference at the end of a paper, article or thesis, for example, is used as an entry point in an index. The authors of the cited items are listed alphabetically. There is an entry for each item written by the cited author. Under each entry is listed each of the sources in which that particular item has been cited. Thus, the citation index is not dependent upon a subject arrangement of entries, although the most widely used and available citation indexes – Science Citation Index, Social Sciences Citation Index, and the Arts & Humanities Citation Index – are broad subject areas though not mutually exclusive in their subject coverage.

Recognise that, if the investigation that will stem from the literature review is centred upon or within an organisation, then the literature to be searched will include the internal documentation of that organisation. It is important that the literature cited in the review should normally be accessible to anyone reading it. You may become aware that some of the internal documentation is classified as confidential by the organisation and you may not be permitted to cite it, though you may have been allowed to read it to familiarise yourself with ongoing work. You should not use any classified material in your project unless you have been given explicit, written permission by the responsible authority within the organisation.

How much literature is there in your subject?

You may have concerns about the size of the literature in your chosen topic – the initial experience of many students shows that there is either not enough or far too much. Logical thinking, careful planning and seeking help should solve this 'problem'. You will be able to estimate the approximate size if your search is well prepared and thoroughly done. Seek the help of bibliographic specialists in your university library; they are skilled subject searchers. They will help you to develop appropriate search strategies that will enable you to achieve sensible and manageable limits. Knowing the size of the literature helps you to determine the level of confidence that you can have in the thoroughness of your search. Also, some indication of the dynamism of the chosen subject area may be gained, that is, the parts where there is relatively intense research and development activity. This is reflected in the nature and rate of growth in the number of certain types of publications, such as reports, conference papers and journal articles. The parts of the subject in which there is considerable dynamism can be good indicators of topics with research potential. 'Dynamic subjects' and 'emerging subjects' usually have relatively high growth rates in their literature, yet the amount of that literature is often relatively small if these subjects are identified early in their life.

Doing the literature review

How is the review done?

This is, for the student, the crucial question. Reviewing the literature requires many of the skills of the researcher that are considered in Chapter 1. As an undergraduate you will have already begun to develop many of these skills, most evidently through successful completion of course work in the earlier stages of your course. Yet many undergraduates lack confidence in their ability to do a review. This may have something to do with the fact that much of the practical side of reviewing, finding and retrieving the literature requires working for long periods of time in the library or using databases and on-line information sources and subsequent reading of the products of the searches. Students consider that there is certain tedium in searching and also in the subsequent reading and re-reading, and writing and re-writing. The great majority of researchers probably experience this. Yet discovering what other researchers have done can be a fascinating activity if you get yourself into the right frame of mind. Careful time planning and management of the search and review processes can limit or even eliminate the tedium. Accept that there may be tedium in such 'desk work' and plan it sensibly. For example, avoid spending periods of several hours at a time searching, reading and reviewing. Schedule the literature search and review for periods of about two hours at a time with at least 30 minutes break afterwards. Try to avoid more than two sessions consecutively. Yes, there will be times when you are in exactly the right frame of mind to spend a long and continuous period of time in the library. If you are in such a mood, capitalise on it. Plan to use it profitably, map out how you will use that time. Such times will compensate for the occasions when you just 'cannot face another journal or book'. Conversely, do not work on the review when you are 'too tired to do anything else'.

The review process includes an analysis of each document to establish its validity in and relevance to the work envisaged. This analysis must be constructive, critical and objective. Its purpose is to identify ideas that will be of specific interest in your chosen topic. As the reviewer, you will weave together these ideas in a piece of scholarly writing to convey a clear, well-structured picture of the current situation in the proposed field of investigation. Your review will be a progressive development of ideas that will demonstrate the authority for research in the topic chosen. It will lead the reader to the key features you have identified in the literature that will underpin your research, as indicated in Figure 8.1.

It is in the selection, consideration, analysis, synthesis and ordering of the ideas of others and in the development of argument that you make your scholarly contribution. It should

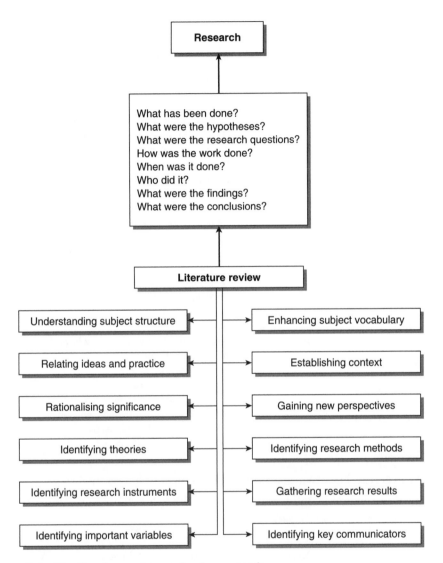

Figure 8.1   The literature review underpins research

be realised that there is no one correct or standard way in which to review literature and write the review. However, notable features of a good review will include coherence, continuity, clarity and fluency in the expression and development of ideas and argument. You will have recognised these features in reviews that you have read to 'learn about reviewing'.

How do you choose the literature to be reviewed?

Before beginning your searches, ask yourself what your specific information needs are. Careful thinking will cause you to realise that these needs fall into several clear and

Table 8.2 Relationship of category of need to information and information source

Category of Need	Information/Information Source
Research	General critiques on research
	Reviews of research methodology
Subject knowledge	Critiques on research in the subject
	Reviews of research in the topic area
	Topic information sources
	Related topics
	Similar projects
Environments	Similar – for comparison, transfer of ideas
	Different – for contrast, comparison,
	(to encourage serendipity)
Other researchers	On your topic
	On related topics
	Using appropriate methodology
Methodology	What is available?
	What should *not* be used and *why not*?
	What should be used?
	Why should it be used?
	Where has it been used?
	Any other suggested uses?
	Any shortcomings in the chosen methods?
	How can or should it be used?

logical categories. These will suggest to you the types of information sources that you should use in your searching. These are listed in Table 8.2, *Relationship of category of need to information and information source.*

Next, you should develop the search strategies that you will use to find pertinent literature. What are these search strategies and how do you develop them? Search strategies are formulations of terms that succinctly describe the topic on which you want to find literature. The terms may be simple subjects, names of people, organisations, places, events, theories, phenomena, products, equipment and similar. You may use them as individual terms or in combinations of any, even all such terms. It is often wise to start with simple terms even though this will result in the production of large numbers of hits, that is, items apparently pertinent to your topic.

Where do you get the terms for your strategies? When you discussed your project with your tutor, you began the thinking necessary to do the literature review. You will have discussed some books and, possibly, journals and reports that your tutor considered useful for you to read. The discussions will have resulted in you beginning to form a picture of your topic in your mind. You may draw this in the form of a mind map, see Buzan (2003). This will help in the provisional definition of your topic. Adding your mind map and provisional topic definition to ideas gleaned from the initial readings recommended by your tutor will enable you to formulate some search strategies that you can use to begin searching for relevant literature. Depending upon the nature of your topic, you may consider it useful to examine the subject entries related to it in your university library catalogue. Additionally, you will gain useful ideas on the structure of the topic by examining how it is arranged and structured in a suitable classification scheme and in a thesaurus devoted to a subject that includes your topic. These will be useful sources of potential search terms. What do you search with the strategies? Once you have prepared your search strategies, use them to search the secondary information sources available in the subject areas of interest. These secondary sources are the bibliographies, indexes, abstracts, bulletins and databases in which the journal articles, theses, reports, conference papers and other primary documents are listed and organised. You may find that there is a book devoted specifically to your subject, suggesting that the subject has been investigated in some detail. If the book is an advanced treatise on the subject, then it will prove to be a valuable source of search terms. You may find an opportunity for research in an aspect of your subject that may be suggested explicitly or implicitly by something that you read in the book. Check the index of the book – there will be many potentially useful terms from which you can choose.

Your search will produce a large quantity of material from which items that are clearly relevant to your topic must be selected using appropriate criteria. What are appropriate criteria? You can answer this by thinking of precisely what you were looking for in the literature. The ideas that you were looking for, such as specific theories, methods or phenomena will be appropriate for selecting and grouping the items that are produced by your search. These criteria should be established at the start of the investigation by detailed analysis of your topic. It is a strong possibility that the criteria will be amended, perhaps very substantially as your review of the literature progresses, due to your increasing knowledge and understanding of your subject. This requires the development of a particular frame of mind. This is achieved by carefully analysing the situation within which the topic for research has arisen, the environment within which it is located, the potential and actual influences on the topic, and the specific context in which it resides. Selection and definition of your topic are considered in Chapter 3, *Choosing a Topic*.

What should be searched?

If the preparation of the search questions has been good, the secondary sources for the general subject area should be among the first to be consulted. It is important to become familiar with secondary sources since these, in effect, form the gateways or approach materials to a subject for the new researcher. Certainly, the project topic that your tutor has agreed with you will be covered by some of these tools, though there may not be one dedicated specifically to your subject. Your university library will have secondary sources suitable for your search, and the subject librarians or bibliographic specialists will be able to provide advice and guidance on the choice and use of these. They may offer tutorials in their use and in the development of some suitable search terms. There is a substantial number of secondary sources that will prove valuable to researchers in the arts, humanities, social sciences, business and commerce (see Appendix 9: Databases).

Secondary sources will lead to identification of leading primary sources in the field and will give a clear idea of what may be called, for example, the form spectrum of the literature of the subject. Recognise that published sources appear in many forms – books, journals, reports, theses, for example. Papers appear in many guises, such as conference, working, occasional, and position papers. Useful, perhaps essential, information may also be held in non-textual formats such as video and audio forms, films – ciné and still, graphical and real forms. Remember that information is increasingly being released in electronic form only, on the Internet, in electronic journals and in intranets of particular organisations. Where is the balance, is one particular form dominant? Also, what language is dominant in the subject literature? English is recognised as the dominant language of publication in many sciences and technologies. However, in the humanities, social sciences and arts, disciplines that are more culturally specific, the range of languages of publication is very wide.

It is important to understand this since it will help to ensure that the search coverage is appropriate. Significant authors or workers, institutions, apparent complexity, organisations and company or university research teams in the chosen field may be identified. Do not limit searching to those literature sources that are familiar and readily accessible. For undergraduate students, the literature of a subject is largely undiscovered territory. Searching is a voyage of discovery and what is being sought is more than the content of the sources. It is necessary to discover and map the range of published and, if possible, unpublished but available material in your subject.

Box 8.3:   Useful review skills

- The ability to use technology such as computers, on-line databases and the Internet, and multi-media.
- Subject understanding and English language skills such as the ability to analyse what is written, to understand meanings and the effects of context on meaning, to use properly both general and subject-specific dictionaries and thesauri, and to understand the basic principles of grammar.
- Communication and problem-solving skills.
- Time management and work scheduling.
- Appropriate, good preparation.

What limits a review?

There are many factors that may limit your review, some of which are directly within your control and some are not. Those within your control include personal skills, many of which you will have begun to develop in the earlier years of your course and some you will have brought to the course. You may need to refresh skills that you have not been required to use since being introduced to them in early modules. These days, information and communications technology skills are essential to the researcher since there are many important databases available via most university libraries. Also, the Internet may provide access to valuable sources of pertinent information and data not readily available from your university library. However, you should not forget the limitations of the Internet. Much of the material available on the Internet is not peer reviewed or editorially controlled. Thus, research data and information reported may not be proven.

The availability of and access to facilities and resources such as on-line databases, libraries, finance to promote accessibility to literature, such as by translation of non-English material, or the time frame for working, may be outside your control. Your university or workplace may limit or exclude access to some external information sources such as certain online databases and electronic journals due to the costs involved in their use.

How should the boundaries of the search be set?

There are several factors that will shape the search. Time available for searching is one of the most obvious. Proper time management will enable the maximum amount of time to be allocated within the limits of the work programme. Availability of search facilities and the ability to use them will also be limiting factors. With many subjects, a natural limit seems to develop. This may be determined by the way that interim outputs of search suggest things, since they will aid in the continuing development of the subject map. Also, you will develop a greater understanding of the subject as the search progresses and will begin to recognise apparently natural clusters of ideas that may lend themselves to investigation. It may be that a time-limited search is appropriate because of the nature of the subject, because of the way that it is developing or because there has been a 'breakthrough' type of occurrence that has formed the subject. Or it may be that some important items have been translated that have triggered an increase in interest in the subject. Lack of facility in or access to foreign languages is very often a limiting factor. Your university library bibliographic specialists may be able to help by directing you to indexes of translations. Do not expect that everything of interest to you has been translated or that translation indexes are comprehensive.

A problem may be caused by the fact that the literature of some subjects may include substantial and possibly significant proportions of unpublished or ephemeral material.

It is in such cases that the services of bibliographic specialists become essential. It may be impossible to capture relevant material of this type. If your project is work-based, you may find that the organisation within which you are working has contacts whom you may be able to exploit in tracking this type of material. If such ephemeral material lies within the area of interest of the organisation, its library or information department may hold copies of the items that you discover you need.

If you are researching into some aspect of local government, local history or tourism, or indigenous industry, for example, you may reasonably limit your search mainly to publications in the UK. However, recognise that research in other countries may have some value, if only for comparative purposes, in such cases. Also, realise that papers written in the UK but read at international conferences may be published in the country in which the conference took place, or in the country of the organising body. A possible justification for limiting a search by country of origin of publication is that publications by public institutions such as local government agencies and local authorities are often very specific to a country and have no clear comparison abroad. However, do not assume that this is the rule. There may be useful ideas on methodology, for example, that you could consider.

What should you look for in the literature?

Reading for literature reviewing is a cyclic process when first entering a field of enquiry. Initial learning gained from the literature feeds back ideas that provide the reviewer with the means to make more, and better planned journeys into the literature of the topic. Thus, the process of reading is critical. Do not scan, skim or speed read. Be prepared to actively read. Read with a clearly defined purpose. Read to gain meaning and understanding. Read for sense, for ideas.

Box 8.4:   Definition – Reading

Reading is the general process by which information is gained from the printed word, leading to the development of knowledge and understanding.

Reading for your literature review has a two-fold value that demands that you have a purpose in doing it and that you prepare systematically to do it. First, the item that is read informs you whether you are prepared. Second, assimilation and understanding of what is read transform this information into knowledge. The explanation of 'reading' may be extrapolated to include visually, aurally and intellectually assessing non-textual material.

When reading is done in order to review the literature of a subject, it has the purpose of interpreting the meaning of what is written in order to understand the work reported and also to understand its significance and contribution to the subject. So the reading must be done in the context of the purpose of your literature review. Is it a stand-alone contribution to establish the state-of-the-art in some subject? This is unlikely, although your tutor may have approved of a proposal where you provide a state-of-the-art review because you have chosen a topic that demands the provision of a coherent and complete statement of its current position and how it arrived at that position. It may be many years since the topic was last reviewed and its state of dynamism may be persuasive of the need for a state-of-the-art review. This type of review will be a more extensive and detailed consideration of the literature, with substantial structure. It will be reasonable to limit the search for pertinent material to the period since the last review in the same subject area. You will have to review a wider subject area than if you were dealing with a topic for a specific research project. Normally, a reviewer of the state-of-the-art will be a significant worker and writer in the subject field and will have the necessary subject expertise to provide the appropriate critical evaluation of what is published. Therefore, if you are contemplating a review of this type, be sure to agree a detailed and precise project brief with your tutor. Your review may identify implicitly or explicitly, topics that could be suitable for research. Indeed, this may be one of the reasons why your tutor agreed to you doing it. Your work could then benefit students who follow you on your course. It is also an implied compliment to you since such reviewing requires skills and abilities above those normally expected of an undergraduate.

Is your review intended to provide the ground base from which research subsequently will be undertaken? This would normally be the case for undergraduates. Such a review will require a different strategy. First, in addition to being the reviewer, you will be the person who is to do the research work. In some circumstances in academic and commercial organisations, senior researchers sometimes get their juniors to prepare a literature review. The specific subject area for research will be new to you and so one important reason why you are to do the review is to learn about the subject. Your subject area will usually be quite narrow and your available learning time quite limited. Hence the need for careful preparation. It is here that the thorough analysis of the topic of investigation begins to pay off.

There is a useful reading rule that you should keep in mind when you are reviewing literature.

Box 8.5:   Reading rule

Identify the purpose in reading each item and write it down!

The main purpose of the review is to gain the necessary subject knowledge and understanding to ensure that your research is well informed and worth doing. This purpose has been summarised graphically in Figure 8.2 *Key stages in reviewing the literature* on page 172, in which the important questions that you should bear in mind when doing your review are given. If you conduct a well-ordered and thorough search and review, you will have ensured a sound exploration of the literature from which you will be able to identify and develop understanding of many significant features of your subject. In so doing, you will have accumulated a substantial body of knowledge that will answer the questions. This knowledge is the foundation upon which you will build your research.

There are other gains that you can make from reading the research literature and these are identified in Table 8.1 on page 157. This table is included to demonstrate that effective reading and reviewing of the literature should enable you to 'grow' as a researcher by, for example, extending your knowledge of the specialist vocabulary of your subject, understand the importance of knowing the hypotheses and theses, problems, arguments, controversies and opinions current in your subject. In seeking these features, you should certainly extend your potential as a researcher. You will improve your reading skills and begin to develop the research mind necessary to satisfactorily complete your work.

Also, it is necessary to develop a certain way of thinking when undertaking research and in reviewing the literature of a subject. Listed in Box 8.6 are the thought processes involved. Reflection is an important process that must not be neglected, though often is. It can, at times, lead to interesting and possibly quite significant insights.

Box 8.6:   Thought processes important to the research mind

Induction	Deduction	Intuition
Reason	Interpretation	Conclusion
Analysis	Synthesis	Insight
	Reflection	

If this approach to reviewing the literature is adopted, then it should be possible to define needs and categorise them, and then to identify what kinds of information and information sources will be needed to satisfy them.

How should the review be written?

The review is a piece of academic writing. As such and, in common with any other piece of writing, it must have a clear and logical structure that is easy to follow. It is important to realise that the review is not a continuous piece in the manner of an essay. This should already be clear since the review may well cover several quite distinct elements including ideas, theories, methods and results of others. The writing must be fluent, leading the reader smoothly on from one set of ideas to the next.

Box 8.7:   Elements to consider when doing a literature review

Preparation	Fluency
Content	Attribution
Structure	Evaluation

These elements are all interrelated and also have varying degrees of dependency. These dependencies and relationships are shown diagrammatically in Figure 8.2.

Preparation. Every stage of a research study should involve preparation and this is no less important when writing the literature review than with any other stage. Just as it is important to define the purpose of the study, so it is to define the purpose of the review. You should establish clearly and precisely why the review is being written and what it is to cover. When these have been established, it becomes possible to determine the broad structure of the review and, thus, where and how to use the ideas, results, data, and theories that you have culled from the literature. The notes containing the products of the literature search should be organised into categories that correspond to the overall structure that you have determined for the review. It may be necessary to reconsider locations of some ideas several times before the final, seemingly best place for each is settled.

What form do the notes take, what should their content be and how detailed should they be? These are some of the questions that cause concern to most reviewers when reviewing for the first time. If the definition and explanation given earlier are understood, then the answers to these questions are simply determined. The crucial thing to keep in mind is the reason for selecting each of the items to be considered for the review. In preparing for the review, it is helpful to create a rudimentary set of categories to which each item can be assigned as it is obtained and read. You could base these, initially, on your search criteria. An item may have been selected because it was produced when you were searching for information on theories or conceptual frameworks in the subject; if so, then categorise it thus. Again, if items were selected when searching for methods of investigation, then the category is obvious.

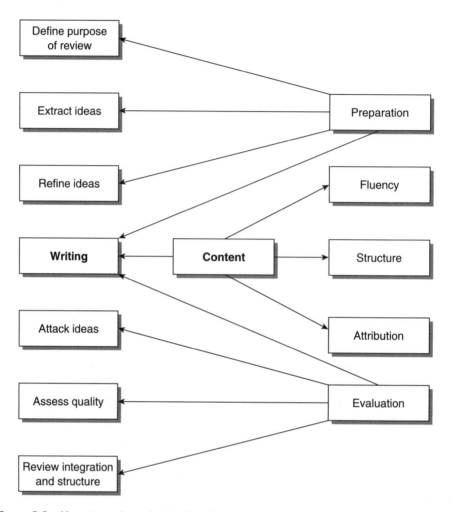

Figure 8.2 Key stages in reviewing the literature

There is a range of forms that the notes could take. Some reviewers create a separate file for each category of information sought from the literature. Within these files, the information may be recorded on cards, paper or audiotapes, for example. Increasingly, reviewers are using computer databases. Make sure that the organisation and indexing of entries is planned at the set-up stage of the database. Returning to entries to re-index them for improved retrieval is wasteful of time and effort. 'Maximum effort at input, minimum effort at output' is an old but applicable adage to bear in mind at this point but common sense is essential.

Content. The notes that you make on reading a document should be more than just reworded key ideas picked out from it. Each document has its relevant content and you should identify and briefly note this in your own words. A format is recommended for your notes on individual items and is given in Appendix 3.

Box 8.8:   Suggested content for the notes on an individual document that you have read

1. Full bibliographic citation for the item; use a standard such as the Harvard system, or the British Standard for Bibliographical References. Some standards are given in the reading list.
2. Ideas and other content selected – some of these may support your ideas, some may conflict with yours or may have a contrary perspective.

   Note the contents of the documents that you have read are the intellectual property of the authors.

3. Comment on the reason for selecting the document and reading it.
4. Give your opinion on the relevance of the document to your research.
5. Give your opinion on the value of the document to your research.
6. Note the thoughts you had that were triggered when reading it.

7. Location of the document – library, personal collection, database, and other sources of the documents that you have used.

   Note the contents of the third, fourth, fifth and sixth sections are your intellectual property.

The detail of your notes may vary from brief telegraphic phrases to several hundred words. When reading each document, you should seek to understand the ideas being communicated, making every attempt to identify the purposes of the author. The notes made should cover those elements of the document that are clearly relevant to the matter being reviewed. The words used to represent this essence should be yours not those of the document's author. Using the words of the author may lead to problems of understanding and to the danger of failing to attribute sources. The chance of this happening is greater if the notes on individual items extend to several hundred words. The process of presenting the ideas of the author in your words should help you to understand those ideas, making it easier for you to comment on their value or contribution to your research

Structure. Your note-taking will probably result in several batches of notes within which there seems to be no clear order or linkage between ideas. The first thing to recognise in such an instance is that this may be due to nothing more than a difference in the way that the individual notes have been made. Or it may reflect a poor understanding of the structure of the subject being investigated. Alternatively, it may be an indication that you have not built up an appropriate command of the vocabulary essential to the understanding of the subject. Such lack of understanding can cause discontinuities between ideas because you have expressed them in non-subject specific, tangential or incorrect terms. This should be only a temporary setback which can and should be rectified quickly by consulting with your tutor and by reading appropriate advanced and review texts in your chosen subject field. It is useful to bear in mind that, in subjects that may be described as relatively dynamic and which are often the most interesting in which to research, the vocabulary will probably not have settled since it will be developing in parallel with the subject.

Fluency. There may be occasions when vocabulary differences will result from you staying too close to the words used in original sources. Notes made from sources should be in the words of the note-taker. They should not be gained by what amounts to copying sentences, paragraphs and sections from the original. This fault, staying too close to sources, may show itself in the final version of the review when changes in the style of paragraphs could cause the reader problems in following the theme or argument because of a lack of continuity in the expression of ideas.

Another cause of apparent lack of linkage is that there may not be any conceptual links. In such a case, it may be necessary for you to redefine the subject, or the scope of the review. It may be that careful reconsideration of the sources and content of the information in these notes is required. The information may be of debatable relevance or the notes may be poor representations of what was in the original information source. When this occurs, it is important to go back to the original document to check. This emphasises the need for careful, accurate recording of each source and its location.

Attribution. The proper extraction of ideas and their representation in the review will make a considerable contribution to the structuring and development of your research and your project report. The relating of the review to its clearly established purpose should ensure that what has to be presented to the reader will be fluent, clear and easy to follow. The review is a document that, by its very nature, depends for its existence on the reported work of other people, published or unpublished but available.

Therefore, it is essential to meet the scholarly requirement of giving recognition to those from whom you have obtained ideas. This attribution has the purpose and effect of declaring to readers what has been gathered from the work of others. It is legitimate to use the work of others but it must always be acknowledged. The contribution that you, the writer of the review makes is in the critical selection of sources, the critical selection and use of information from those sources, its organisation, integration and synthesis, and its presentation and use in argument. Also, it is reasonable for the reader to make the assumption that, if an idea is not attributed to another researcher, then it must be the intellectual property of the writer of the review. Attribution – recognition of the 'help' of others – is a feature of scholarly integrity. It is an essential ethical requirement and is a sign of information literacy in the researcher. It is the payment of your intellectual debt.

Evaluation – attack ideas The evaluation of the review is expressed in Figure 8.2 as a combination of 'attacking' the ideas presented in the review, reviewing the integration of the ideas, that is, how you have related and developed them, the structure or order in which you have presented these ideas, and assessing the quality of writing and argument. The evaluation is the essential final step in writing the review. If the evaluation is properly undertaken, you can have confidence in what you have written. There will probably be several rewrites before the final version is completed. This is usual and reflects the need for you to be as sure as possible of the relevance, value and importance of the ideas of others to your work and of the clarity and precision with which they are presented.

It must be recognised as a scholarly requirement that what is written has been checked as thoroughly as possible within the limits of reason in the period of the project and that due acknowledgement has been given. This establishes some of the bases for the attack on the ideas. In this context, attack means challenging the validity of the ideas that have been taken from sources, challenging the way that the ideas have been used in those sources, and challenging whether these were the only appropriate or most appropriate ideas. You should also challenge the way that you have used the ideas.

Evaluation – review integration and structure. The order of ideas is equally important. There may be a natural progression in which to present the ideas that you have culled from the literature. This will convey to you a 'natural order' for the review and, therefore, suggest a 'natural' structure. It may be that a useful order is suggested for some of what has been found in the literature. The specific information can then be related to the 'order of events' in the project – the project management plan should prove to be useful here – to provide a reasonable overall order for the review. Order within the specific categories of ideas will depend upon the nature of the categories. For example, if there is substantial information gathered on methods of investigation, it could be useful to start with two subcategories – methods considered and rejected, methods selected and used with or without modification. A category of theories could be arranged in chronological order or in some order related to the parts of the subject to which they are applicable. Whatever the overall structure or order within categories, question whether it is the best. As the work on the project progresses, it may be that the initial ideas on the order of things are changed. This is quite reasonable because working on the project is an informing process that must normally lead to greater understanding of the subject by you.

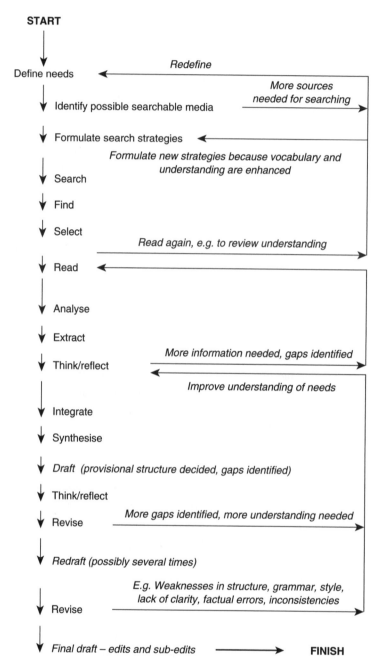

Figure 8.3 Reviewing the literature

Evaluation – assess quality. Attention must also be given to the quality of presentation of ideas. This is to ensure that what is presented is in good style, using the appropriate vocabulary and with objectivity. Style is a combination of several elements and it is worth giving these some consideration. The way the review is written is important. Lack of attention to quality of writing may, and often does, result in lack of clarity of understanding by the reader. It is good and important to have ideas and it is just as good and important to be able to express them in a clear and intelligible way.

The style features that should receive particular attention are accuracy, brevity and clarity. They are essential to any worthwhile piece of writing. It is worth noting that 'borrowing' the words of other writers may impair the continuity and flow of ideas and will almost certainly result in a lack of uniformity and clarity in their presentation. The discontinuities may reduce the readability of the review, thus substantially reducing its value. Also, words and phrases borrowed from others may introduce vagaries and inconsistencies in the 'technical' vocabulary used.

The effort and resources that you will have invested in reviewing the literature of your subject are considerable. If the quality of your grammar, the construction of sentences and paragraphs and the style of language are poor, these investments will be devalued, even wasted. Thus, poor English means a poor review. Because of its importance, your review must have the highest level of quality consistent with the aims and objectives of the research being undertaken. Reviewing literature may be represented as a series of specific and consequential procedures with feedback loops adding up to a critical learning process. These procedures, which are set out in Figure 8.3, provide a systematic way in which to achieve a good quality review. There may be several interations in each feedback loop. This is to be expected.

Summary

You have a responsibility to demonstrate a good understanding of the subject area within which you are researching. This is achieved by thorough, careful and objective reading of the available literature on the subject. The literature review must feature in the project report because it is the means by which you establish the authority upon which you base your research. The nature, importance and value of the literature search and review to your research have been explored in detail in this chapter by posing a series of questions that have frequently been asked by undergraduates. The answers lead to an understanding of what the review is, why it must be done and how to do it. This last question leads, in turn, to further questions concerned with how to choose the literature to be reviewed, how to search it and how to limit the search. Your academic responsibility in writing the review has been considered in some detail. Finally, and critically, detailed attention has been given to explaining what a literature review is not. This has been included because it has become so apparent over the years that many students have poor understanding of how to review literature and how to present the review. The consequence for the project is usually a poor grade.

Further Reading

Bell, Judith (2005) *Doing Your Research Project* (4th edn). Buckingham: Open University Press.

Buzan, Tony (2003) *Use Your Head*. London: BBC Books. (See particularly, *Mind maps*, pp. 80–139.)

Hart, Chris (1998) *Doing a Literature Review: Releasing the Social Science Research Imagination*. London: Sage Publications.

9 Using Results

You have completed your research and you have your results. These may be in the form of data, textual material containing information of importance to your work, fine arts materials, and even realia. Undergraduate projects do not normally produce large amounts of primary data and information directly from the research. However, your literature search and review may have provided relatively substantial amounts of useful and usable secondary data and information. You have to use the results to determine the extent to which the aims and objectives of your research have been fulfilled. Are there enough results to fulfil the aims and objectives? What do you do with them? What story do they tell? What do they mean? How can you interpret them? How good are they? You will be able to answer all these questions satisfactorily if you prepared your results analysis strategy when you prepared your proposal because the aims and objectives of your research provide strong indicators for the shape of the strategy.

Results analysis strategy

Reviewing your aims and objectives at this point will refresh your ideas, as some time will have elapsed since you used them to determine what methods to use and thus, exactly what data and information to collect. Each method selected will require you to develop a strategy specifically for analysing the results obtained by it. Therefore, the data and information must be recorded in ways that lend themselves to analysis, evaluation and interpretation. In fact, your analysis strategy will give you clear pointers to the types of records that you should create.

Examine your aims and objectives in detail. Precisely why did you formulate them as they are presented in the proposal? Why did you decide to look for the particular features that form the data and information that are your results? Note the reasons down and use them to form the tools that you will use to analyse and evaluate your results. The categorisation of questions in your questionnaire, for example, will suggest what you need to focus upon. You may have quantitative data and some qualitative information. Similarly, you will need to conceptually analyse, evaluate and interpret the content of documents such as published material or opinion-seeking reports of personal interviews as well as the content of interview reports. You should have categorised the concepts for which you will be studying the documents and reports and so have the criteria for analysis.

Questionnaire results analysis

Suppose that your questionnaire does provide both quantitative and qualitative answers. If the quantitative values obtained relate to a particular sample of a population, and you need to show proportions, trends and confidence levels, you will perform statistical analyses on your data. If, for example, you have studied the growth of students in higher education over a period of years, you will need to determine annual enrolments over the period and, possibly, the spread of enrolments over the higher education institutions and across the range of degree subjects. Other criteria that you may consider could include age, gender, pre-course qualifications and experience, and ethnicity. You will use descriptive statistics and present the results graphically; using xy plots to illustrate, for example, the take-up of specific subjects by particular ethnic groups, or the pre-course qualifications or experience against module choices in the degrees. Such plots will help you to determine whether there are any relationships between any two of the features chosen. If you have any problems with statistics, consult your tutor and remember that there is a large number of texts on using statistics available in your university library. Seek out a relatively straightforward one (such as *Statistics at Square One* by Swinscow (2002)). There are also statistical packages that you may decide to use; again, consult your tutor before choosing and using one.

If you have used multiple-choice questions in your survey, realise that you are asking respondents to make subjective judgements, no matter how refined you think you have made your questionnaire. You may have offered respondents the opportunity to mark on a point scale. A three-point scale may seem attractive, but 'very useful', 'useful', and 'rarely useful', or 'certain to vote', 'may vote', 'never vote' are not particularly discriminatory. Student and customer satisfaction surveys often use a five- or seven-point scale for respondents to register their degree of satisfaction with a course, product or service. These larger spans do not necessarily mean that more precise and, therefore, possibly more meaningful results are obtained. Some respondents may be confused or rather overwhelmed by a wide span or they may not be inclined to take the necessary time to think out their responses.

I recollect that, some years ago, a student satisfaction survey required answers on a five-point scale, in respect of equipment and facilities provision for specific classes, of opinions on lecture content, handouts and lecture delivery. The great majority of approximately 60 student responding circled the number 3 – the centre of the scale range – even when, for example, some classes were entirely theory based and did not require equipment. It suggested that the opinion of the majority of the students was that 'everything was about average'; but upon what basis did they determine what average meant? Was it average compared with other classes or courses within their particular school, department or university? A possibly reliable conclusion might have been that most students were of the same opinion and thought that 'things were not bad'. Such a conclusion may be of value but leaves much to be desired. The shape and form of that particular survey was used for several years in succession. Yet, as each group responding was different, with different pre-entry qualifications and experience, even if their responses had been about the same, the value of the results for year-by-year comparison would be doubtful.

Interview results analysis

Interviews can be difficult sources of data and information, and the extent of the difficulty depends upon the mode of interviewing. If you have used the telephone, you will not have been able to 'read' the body language – the non-verbal communication that can be very useful when interpreting responses – though vocal variations may help if you know how to make sense of them. The personal or face-to-face interview is the best mode of interviewing to use in your project. You will have the advantage of seeing the body language and linking it to the vocal variations. You should take detailed notes. Even if you record the interviews, still make notes. Write up the notes as soon as possible after each interview; the memory fades and plays tricks, so do not take chances. Build time into the interview schedule for writing up. Some years ago, I was contracted to interview a person who featured in the national news for some weeks. The interview lasted a little over an hour and was recorded, though I did take quite detailed notes. Transcribing, including using the notes, and producing an article from it, took more than two working days. The notes sometimes helped to decide the importance of particular comments. During the interview or when transcribing it, be alert to words, phrases or comments that may prove to be useful quotes. If you have recorded these verbatim, you should be able to give the source of each in your final report. Make a point of counting and recording the occurrence of particular themes that may occur in several interviews. Tabulate these and represent them in bar charts. This will enable you to indicate the extent to which these themes are common in the sample population interviewed.

Product results analysis

If your research has resulted in a product or service, how will you evaluate it? In a scientific or technological project, there will normally be standard testing procedures and performance standards to meet. What is the situation in other disciplines? If your project brought about the redesign of a service, such as a company information service or an office-cleaning service, there would have been reasons why the service was studied. It is very likely that, as part of the project aims and objectives, performance standards were agreed that the redesigned service would have to meet. These standards would probably have been developed 'in house' rather than have been taken from a published source, though there may have been some regulatory requirements to meet. The redesigned service would be monitored using the agreed standards and this will determine one of the elements of your results evaluation and subsequent presentation. The evaluation may also include the opinions of the customers using the service.

As one outcome of your project, you may have been required to produce a saleable item, such as a garment for use in specific circumstances such as extreme weather. Again, it is very likely that there will be performance standards established by the appropriate trade body and the British Standards Institution. These will include properties of materials used, such as strength, durability and resistance to the extreme conditions in which the garment is to be used. The impact on potential retailers and customers should form a part of the evaluation. They will be able to offer opinions on the style, material, visual impact and pricing policy. Thus, the evaluation of a retail product will depend upon both objective and subjective criteria.

Realia results analysis

If your research product results include, or are based upon, realia produced or studied by you, your evaluation may include a dimensional analysis to form an opinion on proportions, for instance. You may also consider origin – national, ethnic, cultural, religious – age, materials, colours, and style. You may have, as part of your evaluation of a work of art, taken the views of significant people – academics and professional practitioners – as to the quality, value and utility of it. These views form part of your 'results', though they may be regarded as anecdotal evidence about the work. You should incorporate all such views, even those that are less favourable than you like. Just as favourable views will not guarantee a well-graded project, so these less favourable views will not necessarily invalidate your work or lead to a failed project. However, they should prompt you to subject your work to a careful re-examination enabling you to determine reasons for your 'underperformance'. You may disagree with these views. That is your right, but you will have to provide sound arguments to challenge them. This, itself, is a good thing since it will require objective principles of argument from you. Conversely, you may agree with the adverse views, partially if not wholly.

Document analysis

There will be other subject areas in which projects do not result in 'hard data' or objective evidence. The humanities and social sciences are areas in which subjective judgements and opinions are important and often dominate interpretation and evaluation. Therefore, your analysis, interpretation and evaluation must be critical and clear. The criteria you are using in analysis must be explained and must be justifiable. You may be concentrating your study on textual material such as journal articles. These could be analysed for content such as theories, opinions and critiques of the work of other authors, subject concepts, events, people, flora, fauna, place and period. Technicalities such as the number and nature of citations made, the institutional or national affiliation of the authors, grammar and syntax, the structure and layout of the articles and the use of illustrations may also feature in your analysis.

Suppose you have studied a selection of works of fiction. You may have had several reasons for your study. For example, you may compare the way that characters are developed, the use of particular idioms or vernacular to create atmosphere in a text, the author involved in the plot, the occurrence of common themes, interpretation and use of real events or people, writing style and quality of language, and nominal target readership. Many of these 'results' will be based upon subjective judgements, which you should discuss with your tutor. Provided that you have sound arguments to support your judgements, your project will be valid.

Case study analysis

The case study is a way of transferring classroom learning – both theory and practice – into a real or 'near-real' life situation. A major advantage in using real case studies is that theory is put into practice and the real consequences of that application are available to study. However, the method is not as easy as many students who used it in their projects seemed to think. Some have presented what amounted to no more than a critical description of a circumstance or an organisation without making clear the purpose of their work. Others had merely presented a commentary on the perceived purpose of an organisation. Therefore, it is important to establish the type of case study so that your analysis is properly informed. It is also important to explain why you have chosen to use the case study method.

There are three main types of case study:

1. **analytical**

2. **illustrative or exemplary**

3. **hybrid – a combination of analytical and illustrative.**

The *analytical method* is concerned with problem-identification and problem-solving. It recognises that problems are universal and usually independent of time, whereas solutions are dependent upon people, time and environment. Thus, it is possible for a given case study to have different and satisfactory resolutions recommended at different times. For example, a local authority has decided to decentralise its social services department, establishing a local office in each ward. The immediately identified problems are extent of need in each ward, staffing mismatches with office locations, all records are centralised and computerised and finance for development is very limited. The context of these problems, such as staffing levels, client base and finance, will change with time. The *illustrative or exemplary method* is intended to open up points, ideas or situations for discussion and understanding. For example, a given illustrative case may be used to enable discussion of the restructuring of a business organisation, or re-alignment of a company into a new business sector. In the *hybrid method*, the case will be used to explore a problem or problems and, at the same time, to illustrate other matters possibly connected with the problem or problems. For example, in addition to dealing with a problem and arriving at a solution, the opportunity is taken to discuss the selection and use of appropriate solving methods or external factors that influenced the choice of solution from a prioritised schedule of solutions.

So which type of case study did you choose to do for your project? Or did you choose to study in detail a case study already reported? Whichever type of case study you chose, it is essential that you adopted an objective and analytical approach from the outset and avoided the descriptive approach often used by undergraduates. The simplest way to deal with a case study is to adopt a step-by-step approach. Consider an analytical case study. The first step is to identify the problems and then to determine the external and internal environment. This should lead to the steps of identifying the causes of the problems, possible solutions, implications of solutions, proposals or recommendations, implications of these, implementations of the proposals or recommendations, monitoring of these, and costing the implementation. A useful and important next step would be an after-action review, or careful reflection on what you did. These steps give you the criteria for judging your case study or for judging a case study that you have decided to use as a focus of study in your project.

Problems and errors in research

The project is your first significant piece of research. Therefore, it is very likely that some things will go wrong, that you will make errors. What could have gone wrong, if anything did? There are several simple questions that you could ask yourself. For example, were there faults in your selection or use of particular methods? Did you draw conclusions and make decisions with insufficient data? Did you generalise without logical justification? Did you make deductions or draw conclusions with inadequate information or data; because 'it was so obvious' you saw no need to gather more? Were your notes of interviews accurate and complete or did you occasionally fill in later what you thought you heard? Maybe you did this when the interviewees were no longer available and you found gaps in your notes and so made a guess as to what was said. Have you used secondary data in combination with your data without carefully checking that it was appropriate and so could be used? If you used a sample of a population, was it sufficiently representative of the particular population that you were studying? One project I had to assess was concerned with the information gathering and using habits of mathematicians. The report was illustrated with interesting and eye-catching charts of various kinds, in which, for instance, usage of sources by percentages of the sample were displayed. Conclusions were drawn based upon the work and these could have influenced the purchasing decisions of library staff. Unfortunately, the sample size was five. Was your sample biased? Did you choose members of the sample because you thought that they would be more likely to co-operate in your survey? Was your study concerned with students in general in your university yet you sampled only those in your faculty because you were located in a site geographically distant from other faculties? If you studied use of your local public baths, it would not have been wise to sample only those who used them during the mornings or afternoons from Monday to Friday since you would have missed working people and might have had unduly high proportions of school pupils, unemployed people, and housewives/husbands.

Did your personal views or preconceptions colour some of your decision-making? Did others influence you, possibly unduly – such as your tutor or your workplace line manager – in some or all of your conclusions and decision-making? This sort of thing does happen and it is not always possible to recognise it or to oppose it as it happens.

The project is yours, you should make the decisions and so you should learn to defend these provided that they are well founded. This ability to defend a position is an important part of the learning experience of project work.

There may have been problems with people, software or hardware involved in your work and these problems may have been beyond your control. These problems may have been such that you could not vary your project sufficiently to remove their adverse effects in the time available. Do not leave out mention of these problems. Describe them and explain how you tried to work around them or to minimise them. Always keep in mind that project work provides learning experiences, not just in research design and methodology, but also in contextual matters such as the everyday concerns related to people's behaviour, economics, organisational politics, and resource constraints. Did you anticipate the possibility of any such problems in your risk assessment? You should have anticipated them and you should have prepared a contingency plan.

Your data and information will have to be presented and evaluated. They will not speak for themselves – you are the interpreter. Your evaluation must be objective and rigorous. There will be data and information that, in your opinion, apparently do not make a positive contribution to your results or to answering your research question. Do not let this give you excessive concern. Also, do not omit them from your results and do not omit to discuss them. You should regard them as a test of your academic ability to argue a case and to 'tease out' the relevance or usefulness of these particular results. Remember that negative results can also make a contribution to thinking and to development of ideas for future research.

If you are using secondary sources of data and information, be sure to determine and understand the people or organisation behind each source. How authoritative is the author? is there a particular agenda being pursued by the author or the organisation? In other words, you need to judge – as far as possible – the objectives of each source. If you have concerns about certain data, for instance, but you cannot 'put your finger on' precisely why you are concerned, express them as clearly as you can and indicate the nature of these concerns. Discuss them with your tutor before committing them to the final version of your project report. Do not leave them out; use them cautiously. In drawing attention to your uncertainties and their apparent relationship to the work that you have done, you will be extending consideration of the results and thus making a contribution in your subject area that may be of some value to other workers.

What do you do if you cannot find evidence to pursue your aims and objectives, either by your investigation or from secondary sources? First, ask why you cannot find evidence. Is it that your methods are inappropriate? This should not be the case if you have consulted with your tutor and used the methodology literature properly. Is it because you have not used the methods properly? Again, your tutor's advice should have prevented this, if you took it. At this stage in your project, it is too late to redesign your research and revise your methodology. Experience over many years has shown that there are students who ignore the advice both of their tutors and the literature. Sometimes it is because they have had fixations about particular methods, either being determined to use a method that appeals to them or to avoid a method which fellow students have tended to condemn. At other times, methods have been used in an attempt to emulate work that has received favourable reviews in the research or professional literature, or that have been used with success by other students. In such cases, insufficient consideration has been given to the context of that other work, discovery of which might have made clear the inappropriateness of the methodology in the student's research context.

However, you have to deal with this lack of sufficient evidence. So think logically and laterally. Up to this point, have you focused too narrowly and with 'tunnel vision' on one particular sample, one area, one specific environment, one set of circumstances, and ignored any that are complementary or adjacent to that which you chose for your research? Now think constructively about each adjacent and complementary area, but obviously not with the depth or intensity with which your main research was undertaken, because of the time constraints. You may be able to infer from them the type and nature of evidence that could be 'discovered', if you were to research them, that would provide some help in explaining your results. You would not have these results, you would be suggesting that such results could be obtained and that, if obtained, may possibly contribute positively to your work. Presenting this in your discussion would demonstrate to your tutors and assessors that you had gained more from your research than just a set of data and explained it. You will be demonstrating an academic approach in the making.

Summary

A key requirement in using your results is 'care'. When you chose your research methods, you took care and discussed possibilities with your tutor before making a final choice. The choice was determined by the need to fulfil your aims and objectives, which you had formulated very carefully. At the time that you chose your methods, you should have developed the results analysis strategy that you intended to use. In this chapter, the basic thinking that you need to do to develop strategies applicable to the main methods used by undergraduates has been introduced and discussed. One of the seeming inevitabilities of undergraduate work is that there will be problems or errors in some of the results, possibly all of the results. All need not be lost provided that some objective thinking is applied in such a situation and suggestions are given.

Further Reading

Blaxter, Loraine, Hughes, Christina and Tight, Malcolm (2001) *How to Research* (2nd edn). Buckingham: Open University Press.

Fink, Arlene (2003) *How to Manage, Analyze, and Interpret Survey Data* (2nd edn). London and Thousand Oaks: Sage Publications.

Swinscow, T.D.U. (2002) *Statistics at Square One* (9th edn). edited by Michael J. Campbell. London: BMJ Books.

10 Writing the Project Report

A good project deserves to be well reported yet many good students have difficulty starting to write up their work. Indeed, many experienced writers admit to having problems getting started. The report is probably the first substantial piece of writing that has been required of most undergraduate students and this, coupled with its great importance as a major contributor to the final degree, seems to create fear when having to write it. Do not worry; thousands of students conquer this fear every year and write good reports. We will dispel the fear of writing by concentrating on the elements of good preparation and good writing.

The briefing that you will have been given by tutors to prepare you for the project will contain a specification of the length of the report that you have to write. Usually, an undergraduate report is of the order of 10,000 to 12,000 words. The specification given to you may also include guidance as to the structure and layout, reference style, use of graphics and tables and detail on the font size, spacing, title page, indexes, and binding. If you are fortunate enough to have been given such a guide, you will find it useful whilst doing your project since it effectively consists of a series of reference points on the various stages of the project. For example, the structure will normally follow the order in which the project develops from topic choice through selection and justification of research methods, data capture and discussion to conclusions.

In this chapter, you will be introduced to the report writing process. A search of a university library catalogue will reveal a substantial literature on writing and, more specifically, on report writing. It will quickly become apparent to you that there is not one standard way of writing a report. Indeed, reports are such a common way of communicating information that most organisations, including universities, have their own style guides for report writing. You may well find that each of the courses in your university will have its own report style guide. Therefore, you should make sure that you familiarise yourself with the guide for your course.

The recommendations and advice given here may seem to be very formal and disciplined. One important reason for this is that the project report tells at least two stories and you must get both of them right. The first and more obvious story is that of the research undertaken. The second is the story of the researcher. This is embedded in the quality evident in the use of the English language, grammar, syntax and vocabulary, and in how you designed and accomplished your work. The report is a communication device and is used to inform readers about the particular matter that was investigated. If the language – the basic communication mechanism – is used effectively and properly in terms of grammar, syntax and vocabulary, then there will be a greater likelihood that the readers will be well informed by the report. Add to this a well-thought-out, logical structure that leads the readers clearly and directly to what they want to know, and you will convey an impression of a researcher who is systematic and precise in all aspects of the investigation. Thus, the readers will be more likely to have confidence in the work reported.

What a report is

The definition of a report is clear from its primary purpose, which is to furnish information to one or more people who, on the basis of that information, can make a decision, form an opinion or simply become enlightened. Facts, figures, data and information are put into perspective, arguments are weighed, conclusions are drawn, and recommendations may be made in a report.

Box 10.1:   Definition – Report

A formal statement of the results of an investigation, or of any matter on which definite information is required, made by some person or body instructed or required to do so.

Shorter Oxford English Dictionary

From this formal definition you will realise that you are to investigate a matter – your topic – on which definite information is required. The topic may be specified for you or you may choose and agree it after discussion with a tutor or a workplace manager. There is only one major difference between your situation and that in a business, professional or industrial concern and that is that you are being tested primarily on your project management skills and will have direct and relatively easy access to your project supervisor. In a large organisation such as a bank, media company, cosmetics manufacturer, public library, hospital, college, or government department, it is not usually possible for the decision-makers and policy formulators to see and speak to everyone who has information to communicate that could assist in their decision-making. These people must rely upon written reports, which they may have requested, for that information. For them the report is, therefore, an important communication vehicle. In such an environment, as a project manager, you will be the person responsible for seeing the project through and are not likely to have significant supervision.

Written reports form the basis for decision-making in most organisations. They also permit the creation of an archive – a recorded history of decision-making in an organisation. The reports become an important foundation for decisions about the future of, for example, a company or its products or services, departments and processes, contractual commitments, and its staff. They also become an important source of information about what decisions were made, when they were made, who made them and why they were made. Such information may be critical when contractual, regulatory or legal matters are in dispute.

With the passage of time, your project report is likely to be the only evidence, the only record that the project – your work – has been done. One implication of this is that the report will be the only public place in which you are acknowledged as the person who carried out the project. It will probably be the only way in which you feature in an organisation's memory. Therefore, the report is a crucial document; crucial to you and your professional development and image and, if you were employed during the project period, crucial to your employer since the work was to support some aspect of decision-making in an organisation for which you worked, if only as a sandwich placement student.

Something else that you should bear in mind is that the great majority of those who read your report will know you only as a name on a title page. They will form their opinions of you on the basis of what they read in the report. If the report is clear, well written, well structured, easy to read; if the arguments are easy to follow and understand and the answers to the readers' questions are clearly evident, then the impression the readers will have of you will be good. The converse is also true. Therefore, it is worthwhile investing effort in planning the writing of the report.

The writing plan

If you are systematic in the way you prepare to write your project report, you will develop confidence in what you are doing because you will have a pattern to your work. This pattern will reflect the way in which you have conducted your research. So prepare a plan before you start writing and make sure that you stick to it. Circumstances may occur that cause you to modify the plan but you can minimize this possibility by sensible risk assessment and scheduling of the work involved, and ensuring that you have allowed enough time to complete it. Most of your tutors will have had to plan writing schedules for their own work and will have provided advice to other students, so capitalise on their experience, consult with them on writing strategies before you start writing. Always bear in mind that planning to write a substantial document such as a project report is not as simple and straightforward a process as many students think. There are significant differences between the processes that you will have used when writing your essays and term papers and those to be used in writing a report.

The writer's five questions

As the writer of a report, you should ask questions of yourself when planning it. The answers to these questions will help to inform the writing process and give you confidence in what you have done in your research. The writer should ask and answer these questions before beginning to write the report. The questions are:

1. **Who is to read the report?**

2. **What do the readers want to know?**

3. **What do the readers already know?**

4. How can I add to the readers' knowledge?

5. How will the readers use the report?

1. Who is to read the report?

In the first instance, you and tutors from your academic department and, possibly, your work-based supervisor will read your report. Your examiners will also read it. Therefore, you may make certain positive assumptions about these readers' knowledge and understanding of the topic of your report. You have to convince yourself that you know and understand the work that you have done and that you have represented it accurately and concisely in your report, which is why you must read the finished report before any one else does. You also have to convince your tutors and examiners that you have carried out a good, acceptable piece of work and written it well in report form. Additionally, you will have to convince your examiners that you have satisfied the requirements of the course in respect of the project. You may consider that you have only to satisfy your tutors and examiners and, as appropriate, a work-based supervisor with the report. However, remember that copies of your report will be held in your academic school or department and in your university library. If your work was well done, it will probably be listed in the library catalogue, so students and staff of your university will be potential readers. It may even be made available via inter-library loan, giving it a much wider potential readership. If you did a work-based project, you will have to convince your work-based supervisor and, possibly, more senior managers about the value and usefulness of the work done. Also, in addition to being held in an organisation's information department, copies of a work-based project may be circulated throughout the organisation in which it was prepared. This means that the great majority of your potential readers will be unknown to you. You cannot make the same assumptions about the knowledge and understanding that these 'unknown readers' have as you made in respect of your tutors and examiners, only that they may not all be qualified in the subject area of your project. Thus, for most readers, your report will be a stand-alone document with the necessary demands that makes on clarity and conciseness.

When writing a report for people other than your tutors at university, an understanding of who is to read the report will enable you to judge the degree of specialisation of vocabulary that you can use and the extent to which you will have to define technical terms. Normally, it is worth finding out whether the readers for whom your report is mainly intended will be, for example, technical people seeking technical updating or advice prior to selection of processes or equipment, or financial people who may need convincing that particular services, technical facilities or equipment are worth the expenditure requested. Financial and administrative decision-makers may not have the technical expertise necessary to understand a report loaded with technical jargon.

Conversely, technical people may not have the expertise or need for understanding the financial vocabulary used in an argument for funding of, for example, a development project, but they will require the related technical argument to be set out clearly in their terms.

2. What do the readers want to know?

Your tutors will be marking your project report to determine what contribution it will make to your final degree result. They will also be expecting you to be able to use it to make useful contributions to the class discussions that you will be involved in when you study the modules that follow the project period. Therefore, they will want to be convinced that you have:

- **Worked to the project scope**

- **Reviewed the literature relevant to the topic and to potentially appropriate method-ology with thoroughness and objectivity**

- **Chosen appropriate methodology and used it properly and ethically**

- **Gathered information and data objectively, and ensured its accuracy, relevance and completeness, and used it ethically**

- **Analysed the information and data objectively, appropriately and completely**

- **Worked towards achieving the aims and objectives stated**

- **Reported the work in a satisfactory way.**

If you satisfy these requirements, you will have demonstrated that you can do research and can manage a project.

The approach of work-based readers will be different. They will want to know what the work that you have been doing has contributed to the organisation, whether it is credible, and how the organisation will benefit from it. Your 'unknown readers' will have some obvious reasons for reading the report, such as the methods that you chose, why you chose them and how you used them, or the results obtained, the argument in which they are used and the conclusions drawn. If they are students, they may have an interest in the particular form, structure and style as they may be at the project stage in their courses. They may want access to your literature review and references as they may intend to work on a similar topic.

3. What do the readers already know?

When you are able to answer this – when working in a professional environment after graduation – you will avoid annoying the reader with material of which he or she is already aware and will ensure that your report is not excessively long. However, as an undergraduate, recognise that your tutors and examiners will be expecting to find much that they know in depth since they have the responsibility of determining from your report the extent of your knowledge of the chosen topic. They will have been chosen to supervise and assess your project because they have the relevant subject and professional knowledge. You report will inform your tutors and examiners of your abilities as a researcher and of your potential as a project manager in embryo. You may have to convince workplace supervisors that your investigation has made a valuable contribution and that you were worth your sandwich placement. Therefore, recognise that your report may have several different purposes and target readerships and be careful to ensure that you take account of all possible readers in determining content, approach and style. Do not be unduly influenced by the opinions, sought or unsought, offered by any other potential readers of your report.

Since the main readers of your report will be the tutors and examiners, and their primary purpose in reading it will be to assess it and, therefore, you, a clear and precise understanding of what they need to know will help you to define and keep to the terms of reference of the project. These will be clear from the aims and objectives that you established for your project and from your discussion with your tutor of the assessment criteria. However, recognise that other readers may want different things, so do not forget the staff of your workplace, who may have provided the means and the environment for your work, but always keep in mind the main readers. For example, you may have done your project in a local authority department or a hospital trust. The report that you submit to the local authority chief officers' committee, or to the management board of the trust, will have a very wide range of professional and technical competence to inform. This will influence, to some extent, the way that you express your ideas and present your argument. You may have to be careful in the selection and use of technical vocabulary and, in places, may have to adopt relatively simple language in explaining certain matters because specialists are not necessarily familiar with the vocabulary of specialisms other than their own. This may mean that the report for a sandwich placement provider will have considerable differences from that for the university though there will be substantial overlap in content. In an extreme case, you may have to produce two parallel reports if the differences in demand of your course and of your workplace are very significant. For example, your workplace may not be interested in a substantial literature review or in the detailed description of the methods used and their justification, yet these are very important requirements of your university department.

4. How can I add to the readers' knowledge?

If you have dealt effectively with the previous three questions, then you will have good ideas on the answer to this question. The scope, aims and objectives will be strong indicators of the knowledge that you hope to gain from your research. The conclusions will suggest what you have learned. Also, remember that the structure of a report contributes substantially to the ease with which the reader can gain access to and understand the information in it. A well-structured report will lead the reader to the section that contains the knowledge of particular interest. It will also add to your tutors' and examiners' knowledge of your project management skills. In essence, your report should inform your readers of how much you know and understand about the subject of your investigation as defined by the aims and objectives and conclusions, and how much you know and understand about research and project management. Thus, it is *knowledge about you* that you will communicate to your readers rather than anything fundamentally new about the subject of your research. This is why you must regard yourself as an important reader – the first reader – of your report.

5. How will the readers use the report?

You may have ideas on the potential uses to which the information in your report can be put. No doubt these will be valid. However, you cannot be expected to know all possible uses. For example, your project may have been undertaken with the intention of proving the value and cost effectiveness of a particular service and recommendations in your report may include maintained or increased funding for the service. You have the impression that a decision about the service will be dependent only upon your work. However, the reality may be that your report will be discussed by a committee which is considering a dozen or more reports, each of which makes a different case for maintained or increased funding for different parts of an organisation. This is quite common in local and national government and in other large organisations. Therefore, in such a situation, your report is in competition for money from a budget which may be fixed or even declining; something that you may not have been able to take into account. It may even be the case that your project, if specified for you, was deliberately intended to provoke and test the competition for funding.

Another possibility may be that you have evaluated some equipment parts for inclusion in a product that you employer is supplying to a major customer. You have researched the complete market place without constraint. You may not be aware, for reasons of business confidentiality, that your employer has a sole supplier agreement with one particular parts' manufacturer. You may consider that this makes your work valueless but there may have been good in-house reasons for letting you go ahead with your project, not the least of which was to preserve the confidential nature, or even the existence of the sole supplier agreement. It may be that your employer is using your research to put pressure on the sole supplier. Alternatively, your manager may be using your work to assess your potential for movement or advancement in your organisation. This is yet another way in which the realities of the workplace project provide real-life learning to the undergraduate.

This process of challenging your report will help you to anticipate questions that may be put to you or that the examiners may ask of the report when they assess it. You will be able to prepare answers before the questions are put, which will serve to put you in a more comfortable frame of mind about your work. A further benefit of the challenge process is that you will be able to prepare a commentary on the report. Prepare this as if you were going to have to speak to the report and defend it at a meeting, which you may have to do if your university includes assessment by viva.

The basic structure of a report

You have the general outline of a writing plan, what next? You have to build the report from the plan. So, now we come to the question of what the structure of the report should be. There are many structures suggested in the literature of report writing, all of which are appropriate for the situations for which they were first designed and many have subsequently proved applicable beyond their initial environment. As this is the first major report that you will have had to write, it is worth keeping to a relatively simple structure. In Box 10.2, a structure is suggested as being straightforward and easy to follow. It has been recommended and used for some 30 years, with modifications, in an undergraduate course at a UK university. It is based on the accepted idea that an academic document should have a beginning, a middle and an end. The beginning of a document should normally establish the reason for its existence and set the scene for what is to follow. The middle will contain the main substance of the document, the data and information, the ideas and theories, and the discussions in which these are employed. Finally, the end normally provides outcomes, conclusions, recommendations if requested and indications of source material. If there are substantial tables or graphical representations of data, diagrams, charts or similar displays, these should be presented in appendices, which will be included at the end of the report. In essence, these contain support for the main part of your document. It is unlikely that all these sections will be required in most undergraduate reports; different subjects may need some particular elements and not others. Some university departments may specify a more limited set of elements, for example, it is not usual to require an executive summary. However, it is a standard report element in many business organisations, including those that provide sandwich placements.

Box 10.2:   A suggested structure for an undergraduate project report

*Executive summary	OVERVIEW
Title page	
Acknowledgements	
Abstract	BEGINNING
Contents list	
List of diagrams, charts, tables, and illustrations	
Introduction	
Methodology	
Literature review	MIDDLE
Results	
Discussion	
Conclusions	
Recommendations	
References	
Bibliography	END
Appendices	
Glossary	
Index	

*A business organisation may request an Executive summary.

Although each section should stand alone, there must be an overall smooth thematic development or flow of ideas from the introduction section to the conclusions section. The arches linking each section represent this symbolically in Figure 10.1, *The report structure plan*, which provides a general indication of the sections of a report, their content, and the dependencies between sections. Under each of the section headings is an indication of the type of content that should be written into it. For example, in some organisations, house style requires that the introduction section includes a summary of conclusions and recommendations. One reason for this is that a busy manager will have, together in one place, a succinct statement of what the project was designed to do and what it achieved. In such a case, it is unlikely that an executive summary would be required.

The terms in italics immediately under the conclusions and recommendations sections are intended to stress the point that these sections are entirely dependent upon what has gone before in the report. If new material is introduced into either of these sections, it will jeopardise the validity of the report since it will not have been through the intellectual processes to which the other project material has been subjected in the

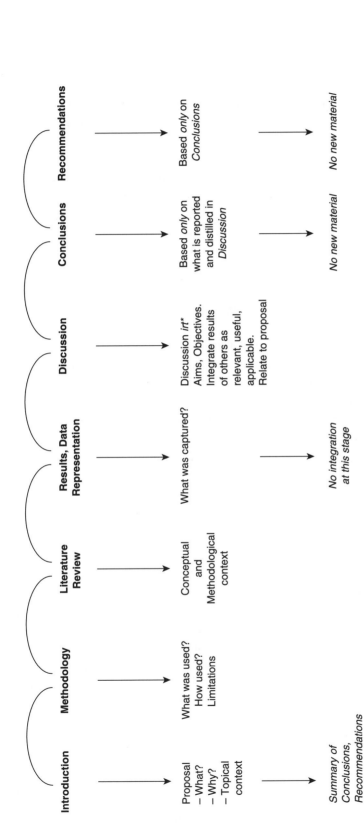

Figure 10.1 The report structure plan

discussion section. It is also possible that it will not have been produced by the selected and tested methods reported in the methodology section. It may even suggest to some readers that the researcher had a pre-determined viewpoint or conclusion before doing the research or was intending from the outset to make a particular recommendation. Such a reader would question the worth of the project as a whole.

Within this overall structure, it helps to clarify your thinking about the report if you view it as having two facets to its structure; that is, two different perspectives from which it may be viewed, the *Intellectual facet* and the *Physical facet.* The intellectual facet is concerned with the substance or content of the report. It contains the analyses, evaluations, syntheses, opinions, discussions, conclusions and recommendations that make up your work. These are what may be called the outputs of your mind. The order in which these are presented, and the logical, objective way in which you develop your argument, will also be critical outputs of the mind.

The physical facet defines the make-up of the report in terms of structure and layout, illustrations, footnotes, inserts, format, appendices, and fonts used. In essence, it is the physical image of your report. Selection of these features deserves careful consideration since readers are certain to be impressed, positively or negatively, by the initial visual impact that your report makes upon them and so the better the package the better disposed the readers may be towards your ideas. The physical and intellectual facets are integrated within a report, though the main physical features do enable the intellectual structure to be made evident if properly used.

Executive summary

It is unlikely that your course regulations will require an executive summary but, if you are doing a work-based project whilst on your course, your employer may want one. It is a summary of the salient features of the work reported and is intended to give an executive the key points, including conclusions and recommendations. Its value is particularly evident when a report is very long. Some commercial, social and governmental reports are hundreds of pages long. A busy executive does not have the time to read full reports of this length and so the executive summary has developed as an effective briefing tool on the work reported. There is no fixed relationship between report size and summary size. However, from one to four pages, 200 to 1,000 words, depending on the size, nature and substance of the report is a guide.

Title page

This is a very important part of the report. It serves as the source of details that will be used to identify your report. It will contain the title of your report – its 'name' – and your name as author. Other information should include the name of your university and department, your course, the relationship of the project to the course – for example, '... submitted in partial fulfilment of the requirements of the BA (Hons) Business Studies', the date of submission, the name of an employer if appropriate and a copyright statement.

Acknowledgements

People and organisations may have provided advice and guidance to you, funding and other resources for some part of your work and may have acted as 'sounding boards' for your ideas. It is a matter of courtesy to acknowledge the help that you have received by naming these people and organisations early in your report, often on the page following the title page, though there is no standard for this.

Abstract

What is an abstract? It is an informative statement of the essence of your report. It is not a précis, nor is it a summary, yet students often provide one or other but call it an abstract. The main purpose of the abstract is to enable readers other than your tutors and examiners to determine whether they need to read your report. It must provide a clear indication of what you did; what knowledge your work has added to the topic; what are the main ideas introduced; and what are the conclusions drawn. It should be a short, succinct and accurate piece of text, grammatically sound and smoothly presented. It can only be written after the report is complete. Do not use sentences extracted from what you may consider to be the more important sections of the report. An abstract is not the same as an extract. The abstracts in most undergraduate reports are between 150 and 300 words presented in one paragraph. Longer abstracts would be unusual.

An abstract is a work of scholarship in its own right and so, to ensure that your abstract is well constructed, examine some publications and databases that contain abstracts. Familiarise yourself with abstracts so that what you write conforms to what readers will expect. In particular, consult abstracts sources that state that they provide informative abstracts. It is this type of abstract that you should write. An informative abstract contains core content of an item, such as results and conclusions, whereas an indicative abstract consists of pointers to what will be found in the report; for example, the reader has to read the item to find what the results and conclusions are.

Contents list

You must provide a list of the contents of your report. This list will provide your readers with an outline of the main sections of the report, leading through them in a logical manner. The sections listed will enable them to identify where they might find their questions answered by directing them to the page on which each element of the report starts. Make sure that the chapter and section headings on the list correspond exactly with the corresponding heading in the text. The title page, abstract and contents list may be regarded as 'approach elements' to what you have done in that they provide a lead in to the report.

List of diagrams, tables, charts, and illustrations

Undergraduate research usually produces data and information that may be presented in graphical and/or tabular form. Often, tutors will suggest topics that will inevitably result in useful amounts of data being produced as they may wish to determine the extent to which the students have mastered the techniques of gathering, analysing and presenting data. Thus, projects often contain figures and tables that have been provided to help the reader to accept the relationships or trends, for example, which the student has identified. Tables can also help to clarify or emphasise comparisons that the student has drawn from data and information gathered, either from experiments or from the reported work of others, or both. The figures and tables play an important role in clarifying the results and the student's thoughts presented in the discussion section. A table of data or a graphical image of a perceived trend or relationship may be more easily understood than the 200 or more words that may be needed to explain the same thing in the absence of the table or figure.

Box 10.3:   Some simple rules when using diagrams, tables, charts, and illustrations

Keep them as simple as possible and in perspective in terms of size, number and sophistication. Tutors have been known to describe complex, beautifully drawn, multi-coloured graphics adorned with esoteric symbols as immaculate rubbish.

Do not break up text excessively with illustrations. Put those essential to a specific point in the most logical and convenient place in the main text, put large ones in appendices or, if you are convinced that they belong in the text, put them on pages facing the relevant text. Recognise that an illustration within the text almost inevitably interrupts the smoothness of reading and so its location and the extent of its intrusion should be carefully assessed. This is not a case for never locating an illustration within the text, it is a case for care in choosing the location and determining exactly how the illustration is displayed at that location. Does it illuminate a specific matter at that point? Conversely, does it do little more than break the reader's train of thought?

Ensure consistency in style, numbering, and legends.

Introduction

You will be expected to provide a definition of the subject of the report, state the scope, aims, objectives and terms of reference, and provide the background that leads to the report being prepared. Also, it is useful to summarise a long report and outline its structure. If the subject is technical, it is helpful to define unusual terms and phrases. In essence, the introduction sets the scene for the reader.

Methodology

The methods you chose and how you used them must be spelled out in detail. Among other things, this is to enable others to replicate your work using only what you have reported. Replication of research work is not so common in the arts and humanities as it is in science and technology, for example. However, if you follow the tradition of clearly and precisely setting out research methods, you will enable readers, including your tutors and examiners, to assess the quality and validity of your research practice. Research methods are considered in Chapter 7.

Literature review

You will provide the authoritative foundation upon which your project is built by reviewing all pertinent documentation, internal and external, that you have captured in your literature searches. The literature review is explained and discussed in detail in Chapter 8. It is important for two main reasons. First, because it is from your preliminary search and review of the literature that you will develop understanding of the topic or even find your topic. The literature review will also provide you with the methods of research and, probably, with techniques of analysis and synthesis applicable to your results, and with other skills and knowledge needed to do your research. In other words, it will help you with your preparation as well as with the core research. Thus, the literature review is important because it enables you to prepare for your research and it is also one of the most important research methods available for your core research. In fulfilling this major role, it belongs in the *MIDDLE* section of the report. This bridging effect of the literature review emphasises how important it is for you to know and understand what has been published on your chosen topic.

Results

Conventions vary as to what precisely should be included in this section. Some project guides require inclusion of the results and discussion of them in this section. The recommendation here is to present only the results without offering opinions about them or discussion of them. If the results are very substantial in terms of the size and number of tables of data, charts, drawings or similar illustrations, it may be advisable to place these in appendices, and include summary tables in the main text, making references to the main results tables and other illustrations. This will enable you to avoid fragmenting text with large graphical interruptions since that could make it difficult for readers to follow your arguments.

Discussion

This is the place where you demonstrate very clearly your intellectual capabilities, your critical, analytical and synthetical thinking and objectivity, and where you move strongly away from description. Here, you will consider issues and problems that have been identified and examined in your investigation and for which you propose answers or show that answers are not possible or feasible. Note that a discussion is an examination by argument and an argument is a reasoning process in which evidence gathered is evaluated objectively in order to determine the extent to which the aims and objectives of the research have been achieved. Bear in mind that, in addition to using the data and information that you have captured by doing your research, you should include information and data that you have gathered from the literature that you reviewed, provided that it is relevant and appropriate. It is evidence. Such inclusions may significantly strengthen your argument or enable you to challenge, even refute arguments that you have discovered in the literature. They may enable you to make deductions or draw inferences that were previously not possible due to insufficient evidence.

Conclusions

This is, for many readers, the most influential part of the report. It is very often here that the greatest impact is made. Therefore, it is important to ensure that your conclusions are credible. You will do this by making sure that your conclusions draw logically and objectively and only on the evidence, arguments and facts presented earlier in the report, and are not excessive in number; sometimes it may be that there are very few conclusions that may logically be drawn. Use simple, direct language, and itemise the conclusions – it helps in scanning. Do not introduce new evidence or arguments.

Recommendations

These are not always required. Normally, you should only provide them if they are asked for, or if they flow naturally and obviously from conclusions. They should follow logically and only from the conclusions, stating what should or should not be done, what is or is not so, and should be brief, direct and clearly set out. Itemise them in an order that corresponds to the order of conclusions. Do not introduce new material or arguments.

References

These are the items that you have used and from which you have obtained and used information useful to your research. They must include all documentation, both that which is internal to your workplace or university and that which is external but possibly not published. Include in this list appropriate entries for all sources that you have consulted and which have aided your work. These sources may include journal articles, conference papers, books, newspapers, lecture notes and handouts, correspondence, conversations, advertisements, and electronic sources such as emails, electronic journals and items on the Internet. Also include non-textual items such as films, audiotapes and videotapes, maps, and paintings. In some subject areas, realia such as models, globes, sculptures and equipment may have been used as sources of information and so should be entered. How do you describe the sources? There are many authoritative guides to citing practice for all media forms. First, consult with your tutor as your university department may issue a referencing standard to which you are required to conform. Make sure that the guide that you use is current. The latest guides include practice for citing electronic sources, including Internet sources.

Bibliography

What is a bibliography and how does it differ from the references? In the sense in which the word is used here, a bibliography is a list of items devoted to a particular subject, in this case, perhaps slightly more broadly defined, but including the topic of your research as presented in your report. It is intended to provide a systematic and an authoritative listing of the material, including non-textual material, that covers the subject. It will include the items that you have entered in the list of references. Additionally, it will include other items that are significantly informative of the topic and which you used for general awareness and acquiring background knowledge on your topic. State of the art reviews, reviews of recent research, theories or developments, advanced treatises and general texts are some of the items that may be included.

Appendices

Your course regulations may specify that you present illustrations that occupy more than a small proportion of a page in appendices. Include copies of questionnaires, interview schedules and scripts, pertinent correspondence and extensive calculations, unless the calculations are a special focus of your research. You may also find it useful to include clear, objective notes made in tutorials in which you explored matters that had a significant influence on some part of your research. Make sure that your tutor agrees with the substance of such notes.

Glossary

A glossary is a list, with explanations, of uncommon and 'technical' or subject specific terms that you have used in your report. Your topic is mainly either academic or professional in nature and so you will have used terms from the vocabulary particular to your subject. Some of your readers may not be sufficiently familiar with your subject to know some of the terms. If it is likely that this will be so, then you should include a glossary.

Index

It is rare for an undergraduate project to have an index but some university schools or departments may require the inclusion of one. An index is a pointer to the locations in the text of particular words and terms such as subject concept terms, methods, theories, and names. If you have to construct an index, be aware that some terms have more than one meaning. Therefore, when selecting entries for the index, make sure that you understand the meaning that each entry has at its location or locations in your report. It is this meaning that you should have in mind when making the entry. The entries in the index are usually arranged alphabetically. Before you begin to construct the index, examine the indexes in three or four textbooks. 'Chase' a few topics in these books to determine how the indexes 'work'. How are entries made for terms that appear in several locations in the book? How are unusual terms dealt with? Has the indexer given a brief explanatory note to clarify such terms for the reader? You do not have to index every term in the report. Ask yourself what your readers might want to find of a specific nature in the report. This will help you to choose index terms.

The readers' five questions – and where they are answered

You now have the basic structure that you are going to use for your report and are aware of what should be written in each section. Readers of the report will have certain expectations of it. What are these expectations and how can you anticipate them? Most of those who have an active, decision-making interest in your research will have five questions that they may address to your report. Some of the readers may have only one or two of these questions. A properly structured report will guide the readers to the sections containing the answers to these questions.

1. What is the problem, circumstance, or situation addressed?

Answered in: Title

Introduction – terms of reference

Summary   – if provided.

2. How was the matter studied?

        Answered in: Methodology section.

3. What information, data were obtained?

        Answered in: Results section, and Appendices if included.

4. What interpretations, comments, and evaluations are made?

        Answered in: Discussion section
                         Conclusions section.

5. What action is recommended?

        Answered in: Recommendations section.

The three writing stages

One simple and helpful writing strategy is based upon the view that writing a report is a three-stage process – pre-writing, writing and post-writing. With the help of your tutor, select two or three reports prepared by students in previous years of your course. They should be reports that achieved good grades. Read these and discuss them with your tutor so that you are able to identify the sort of features that justified the good grades.

Pre-writing

It is in this stage that you define the purpose of the report, clearly establishing what it is that you want to achieve in writing it. You will have in mind that you want to explain precisely what it is that you have researched, why and how you researched it, and what the outcomes were. You will want to ensure that everything is so clearly, logically and systematically presented that all readers will be informed as to exactly what you have done, no more and no less. You should then write down your findings, notes about the information that you have captured from the literature and of opinions formed in discussions with your tutor, and organise them systematically to reflect the way in which you wish to develop your argument.

An important aid to this is the project proposal that was approved by your tutors, in which you will have systematically presented the project scope, aims and objectives and the justification for doing the research. Thus, you will have an important reference or benchmark against which you will be able to write your report. If you have adhered to the terms of your proposal, then you will automatically have a very good set of guides for use in composing the individual sections of your report *(see Appendix 6 Relationship of the Project Proposal to the Project Report)*.

Box 10.4:   Copyright

You have a scholarly duty to acknowledge all sources from which you have taken ideas to help with your project. There is nothing wrong with using such ideas so that you can, for instance, justify a certain procedure or explain a certain phenomenon. Almost all research work today builds on the work of others by using, for example, known methods or results. Remember to pay the intellectual debt that you owe to your sources; pay by attribution. If you use photocopies, diagrams, tables, charts or similar which you have taken from other sources, you should get the permission of the publishers or copyright holders and should certainly acknowledge all sources appropriately.

Writing

At this stage, you will have information from the literature review, from the investigation and from your discussions with your tutor and so will be formulating your ideas for discussion of the results. You should now begin to feed all this information into the appropriate sections of the report. Do not try to draft the whole report at one sitting. Indeed, you will quickly realise that it is too soon to draw conclusions and formulate recommendations. These should be left until you are writing the final draft, though there is nothing wrong with making notes of some tentative conclusions, but do not mentally commit yourself to them.

You will now realise how useful a properly structured project proposal is when you begin writing, and will find it a great help to have your writing governed by the sectional nature of the report. Be absolutely clear in your mind that what you write as a first draft is not going to be the final report. In the normal course of events, you will have several attempts at writing the report; perhaps some sections will require more attempts than others. It is very likely that you will write several drafts of the discussion section before you are completely satisfied with it. Never be satisfied with the first attempt at any section, no matter how in tune you are with your research and with the arguments that you wish to deploy.

Thus, the writing of your report is a lengthy process and this is why you are recommended to begin the writing up as soon as possible and to leave yourself several weeks at the end of the project period to complete the drafting. For example, writing of the introduction, in which you will present the scope, aims, objectives and justification, can begin very soon after the project has been approved. Similarly, you can begin the writing of the literature review section once you have started to capture and analyse the available literature. This will necessarily require progressive updating during the project but the bulk of it will be completed before the final writing up period. The section devoted to methodology can also be started early in the project period since you cannot start your research until you have settled on the methods that you are going to use.

First draft

When you start thinking about the first draft, use the recommended report structure to prepare an outline. It is logical, systematic, organised and differentiating of the ideas that you now have to use in writing your report. Whether you use the recommended structure or some other that you have provisionally agreed with your tutor, start drafting immediately. This is sensible as, in settling on a structure, however provisional, you will have begun to decide what should be written in each section of your report. Thus, you will allocate content; in some cases no more than a few short indicative sentences, in others substantial paragraphs.

At this time, do not worry excessively about matters such as grammar, syntax, spelling or even order of ideas. You will deal with these in later drafts. It is the ideas that you need to record. Put the draft aside for two or three days, during which time your thoughts will settle and your reading and thinking about the topic will develop further. At the end of this time, edit the draft. Reconsider the content and the overall structure. It is unlikely that you will be satisfied with what you have written. Your thoughts may vary from contemplation of a complete rethink and starting again with a blank sheet of paper to barely tinkering with anything. Both these extremes are bad strategies. Yet neither is an unusual state of mind to be in at this stage and does not suggest that you are not suited to project work or that you cannot write a report. If you really are unable to move forward, consult with your tutor, who will almost certainly have faced many students in identical situations. You are doing the project to learn and the tutor is allocated to you to guide you in that learning.

Second and subsequent drafts

When you have edited the first draft, again leave it for a few days. In that time, you will have further developed your understanding about writing, analysed more data and information, adding to what you know and so will be able to prepare a second, revised and extended draft, possible adding more detail to some sections and introducing content to others. Leave this draft as you did the first draft. Repeat this revising and leaving process until you are satisfied that you have incorporated into your report all that you consider necessary to tell the complete story of your research and to fulfil course regulations. This may mean that you write several drafts, may be as many as seven or eight versions of some sections. This is normal and will usually result in you having increasing confidence in your writing.

Final draft

You have now written the final draft of your report. Subject only to the discovery of significant errors or omissions or the failure to meet stylistic or administrative requirements, you are almost ready to submit the report to your tutor. The key word here is *almost*. You have four important things still to do. First, you must check the draft against the project proposal to make sure that you have met the aims and objectives or have included explanations as to why you may not have met some of them. Second, you must check it against the requirements prescribed in the course regulations. The third and fourth things that you have to do are to edit the draft and to sub-edit the draft. These are two distinct processes so do them separately even though you may perceive a slight overlap between them, which is not a problem.

Editing is mainly directed at checking the content to ensure that it is of the right quality in academic and intellectual terms. This is the last opportunity to check the accuracy of facts and figures – text and graphics, and formulae, and logicality of arguments. Do not tinker but work through the report systematically and objectively. Sub-editing is concerned with the quality of administrative technicalities such as spelling, vocabulary, syntactical and grammatical errors, accuracy of referencing, and typing and layout errors.

The final draft is also the last opportunity for you to proof-read for plagiarism. Plagiarism is defined as representing any idea or work of another as your own knowingly or when you ought reasonably to have known, and has been discussed in Chapter 1. A precaution that you can take is to develop the practice of always documenting the source of every idea, even yourself as a source, at the time that you obtain or have that idea. Your university will have a code of practice in which the penalties for plagiarism are spelled out. They will be severe.

Post-writing

Now you can finally settle your mind and establish confidence in the work that you have done. Leave the final draft for a few days so that you can become somewhat distanced from it, at least in time. Then, as far as you possibly can, read it as if somebody else had written it. When you have read it, attack it. Examine the way in which you have written every element of the report. Challenge each element in turn from both the clarity of writing of it and from the validity of its content as you have presented it. Do you now accept your choice of topic and your definition of it? Does your justification of it stand close examination in the sense that your argument for it as a piece of worthwhile work stands up to challenge? Do the scope, aims and objectives successfully meet your challenge in the sense that you have so clearly and unequivocally met and explained them that they are completely acceptable and supported by the outcomes? Remember that, at this stage, you are concerned with how persuasive your writing of these elements is, in other words, how good the argument is that you present in your report equally as much as the quality of the academic content.

Some style features

During the making of your report, it is important that you pay close attention to your writing style. Why should you do so? Remember that the first contact that most readers of your report may have with you is your report. If your project is work-based, these readers may include senior management in your organisation, and possibly potential employers. Therefore, it is in your best interest to ensure that it is of a high quality. The quality will depend not only on the content or even the choice and use of the methods but also on the way that you present what you have done. Style is an important feature in achieving the necessary standard of presentation. Good style can add to the persuasiveness of your report. Some style elements are considered below.

Accuracy, brevity and clarity

These are the ABC of report writing and together with simplicity, are major contributors to gaining and holding the attention of readers. Therefore, avoid word redundancy, and sentence and paragraph complexity. Readers are busy people. To them, time is critical. Repetition in a report adds time and possible confusion in reading and will be a cause of loss of brevity and clarity and of the attention of your readers; avoid it.

When you begin to write your report, you should be full of ideas and will not want to forget them as the writing progresses. One result of this is that you will write in rather long and complex sentences, possibly using too many words to express many of your thoughts and opinions. When you return to what you have written, you will be faced with a morass of words. You have been wordy, somewhat unstructured and grammatically unsound and repetitive. Do not worry. This is quite common and is easily corrected. It was important that you got your ideas down on paper to avoid losing them.

Now you can begin to refine these ideas. Correct your grammar. Check the words that you have used to express certain ideas. Are they long and technical and could you replace at least some of them with shorter, more commonly used words? Have you created long and complex sentences that contain several clauses and that require much effort and time to work out precisely what they mean? Is there intricacy and complexity where simplicity and clarity would be much more valuable? One way to test this is to read your text aloud. Is it easy to read with ease and to create the necessary flow and emphases that should convey the sense of what is written?

An interesting way to check the readability of your report is to calculate the Fog Index. Take a sample of your work, count the number of words and sentences in it and work out the average length of a sentence. Now count the number of words longer than two syllables. Work out what percentage they are of the total number of words. Add together the average sentence length and the percentage figure of the longer words and multiply by 0.4 to obtain the Fog Index for the sample. The value of the Fog Index for this paragraph is 10.4. The ideal Fog Index is said to be 7 or 8 and any writing with a figure above 12 is considered to be a difficult read. The method of calculation seems odd and illogical yet it does provide a relatively crude guide to clarity.

Do not be persuaded that your report is too complex and difficult to understand if your Fog Index values are nearer to 12 for samples of your work. Most project topics are professional or academic in nature and such subjects have their own specialised vocabulary. Many professional and technical terms are multi-syllabic. Some parts of your report may require quite intense discussion that calls into play many specialised terms. This will result in some sentences and paragraphs being very rich in specialist vocabulary and occasionally quite long, leading to high Fog Index values.

Continuity, flow and uniformity

Do not borrow the words of others. It is usually easy for the reader to see the joins when a writer has imported parts of another author's document. Also, relying closely on words from the text of some of your documentary sources may open you to the accusation of plagiarism, even though it may be unintentional. Your readers will not know that it is unintentional.

Colloquialisms and clichés

Try to avoid using these. We use colloquialisms and clichés frequently in everyday conversations. We understand them and they often act as a condensed form of speech. There is no harm in this because our conversations are with people who are in direct contact with us and we can usually clarify any misunderstandings that may arise from their use. However, they are junk language and usually lacking in the precision needed in a report. Something that has begun to appear in GCSE schoolwork is the use of 'texting language' with its accompanying abbreviated spelling. Some students use this automatically. Do not use it. It is a form of colloquial language that has developed for economic reasons.

Impersonality and formality

Use a formal, impersonal style. A report is a formal document and, as such, should be free of the use of personal pronouns and of loose and informal expressions however acceptable they may be in conversation. The main focus of your report is its subject not its author. The only occasions on which the personal form is acceptable are when it occurs in a quotation that is being used, when specific instructions or directions given by people named in the report are reported verbatim, or where the focus of your research is or includes people as individuals.

Technical and complex terminology

The vocabulary of a specialist subject has been developed to enable those involved in the subject to express their ideas succinctly and clearly and so it is essential. However, it is possible to fall into a trap of your own making by using jargon for the sake of impressing. Exercise care in the choice of terminology, use a thesaurus and a dictionary to check terms, and use common sense. Use a subject specific thesaurus and dictionary to check terms when the topic of your research is relatively intense academically, professionally, technically or scientifically.

Grammar

Much written work is devalued, even debased, because of lack of attention to grammar and much student work is subjected to substantial criticism due to poor grammar. It has become apparent over the past 30 years or so, that many students lack detailed knowledge of English grammar. However, you should realise that there is a significant advantage to be gained from adhering to many of the rules of grammar. Good grammar and clarity of expression of ideas go hand in hand. It is not suggested here that you should use the rules of grammar with utmost rigidity. Slavish conformity could, itself, lead to loss of clarity. Good reference sources to use are *Fowler's Modern English Usage*, *The Oxford Guide to the English Language*, and *Brush Up Your Grammar*, by Michael Cullup (1999).

Over-qualifying

Beware the adjective and adverb rush. It is fairly common for students to qualify a particular noun with several adjectives or a particular verb with several adverbs. This can lead to difficulties for the reader since it may take several readings to grasp the point being made. For example, 'knowledge management is the most important, significant and critical process in preserving the market position, profitability and innovative capabilities of British companies in the rapidly developing and changing, increasingly competitive global market place' could be clarified by breaking it down into two or three sentences. The ideas in the following sentence could usefully be presented in two or three sentences, each of which should include explanations of the reasons why the behaviour was reprehensible: 'The researcher worker's behaviour was morally, ethically, socially, psychological and professionally reprehensible'.

Litotes

This is the expression of an affirmative by the negative of its contrary, for example, *not inconsiderable, not unindustrious.* Be sparing with these and, preferably, do not use them. They can be striking if used rarely but become affected and troublesome if used frequently. They have featured in students' reports, perhaps in attempts to 'tone down' criticism.

Blandness

Do not be bland, facile, evasive or non-committal. If you have something to report, report it objectively. Do not be afraid to be direct, to get to the point, to commit yourself on paper. If you have results that suggest something controversial, do not be afraid to report them. However, make sure that you check and recheck these results before reporting them. On the other hand, if there is nothing to report about an aspect of your investigation, then state this so that your reader is not left uncertain about what you may have discovered during your research.

Exaggeration

Do not exaggerate. Exaggeration devalues a report. Too frequent use of emphasis – such as superlatives and extreme forms of description – reduce the impact of what you wish to communicate. In everyday conversation, we often hear the words *brilliant, marvellous, outstanding* and *excellent* to describe circumstances, performances, events or occurrences that a generation ago would have been regarded as quite ordinary or even mundane. It is not unusual to find over-qualification and exaggeration together. The following was encountered in a student report: *It was a brilliant, excellent and quite outstanding piece of work.* This sort of excessive emphasis devalues the work being reported. If you emphasise everything that stands out, how can you make an impact on the reader?

Generalisation

Do not generalise from the particular without very good justification for doing so. Generalisations must have firm foundations in fact and you must be able to show how they are developed from data or information gathered in your research. Always make sure that you have sufficient evidence to support your generalisations. The arguments you use to justify them must be logical and systematic and will rely on that evidence.

Control opinions and influences

Do not state opinions as facts. Do not present assertions as facts. Just because you declare that something is so does not make it so, however strong your declaration. If you think that a statement you have made is an assertion, ask yourself the question: *What is the evidence for it?* Make sure that there is evidence and that it is strong enough to stand up to challenge.

Influence may become evident as bias. You may be biased because of the extent and depth to which you know your subject and your commitment to it. Influence may result from pressure exerted by people interested in your research. Time limitations imposed upon your work may unintentionally bias the results, for example, because reduced time for data collection means that your sample sizes may be too small for meaningful analysis. It may be that, to meet the time constraints, you have been 'carefully selective' of samples, choosing instances that are easily accessed, readily to hand or simple to process. Your objectivity must extend to control of your opinions and of the influences on your work and their potential effects. You may find this difficult in circumstances in which your tutor or workplace supervisor has a strong personality and has very determined views on the topic that you are investigating. This may result, for example, in unintentional bias creeping into your work because your analyses and interpretations of your results are 'force fed' by someone else. Remember that the project is yours and, no matter how strong the opinions of your tutor or supervisor, they can be wrong and are if they instruct rather than advise or guide. You have done the work, you are closer to it than they and you are entitled to present your opinion in your report, but you must be able to justify your position.

Some technicalities of report writing

You are responsible for the content of your report and for its preparation as an information vehicle. There are some points of an administrative significance that you must keep in mind when writing the report since they will contribute to the credibility and information value of the report. They will help to put a good finish to it.

Confidentiality

Make sure that information you intend to include in your report and that you have gathered within or without your organisation is not confidential and so you are prevented from using it. This applies to information that you generate in the project as well as to information that you may have extracted from internal documentation or received in conversation. If in doubt about any information or data, check with responsible people. You must clear all information with an authorised person before publishing it in your report. For example, if you have done a work-based project, the information and data that you generate or accumulate and reorganise in the project will normally be the intellectual property of your employing organisation and so it will be the right of that employer to determine the level of confidentiality attaching to that part of the content, and the use you may make of it in your report.

Checking

You must ensure that any facts such as quantities, figures, formulae, and the names of people, places, events, products, materials, or services that you have included are accurately and correctly presented. Always check and recheck; it may seem to be a chore but it is a very significant quality factor. You owe it to yourself and to all those who have been involved in your research in some way, to be precise and correct as far as is possible in what you report.

Editing

Edit every *sentence* and every *paragraph* to ensure that your meaning is clear; do not just read for overall sense. Check the flow of ideas from sentence to sentence and from paragraph to paragraph. Ensure that there is a logical development from one section of your report to the next. If you have word processed your report and have cut and pasted parts of the text to reshape one or more sections, you may have introduced some oddities of expression. Be sure to examine such parts of the text even more closely. Compare what you have written with what your stated intention was that you set out in the project proposal.

Proofing

Proof-reading is not easy but it is an essential process in your project work. It requires time and care. In the extreme, it may mean the difference between success and failure of your project. A good proof-reader will spot errors in layout, typography, page and section numbering and labelling, and word forms, poor relationships between diagrams and text, inconsistencies in diagram legends, and even errors of fact. Get someone else to proof-read the final draft with you. You may be too close to your report to spot obvious errors of fact, transcription, representation or spelling or even something as simple yet blatant as the repetition of common words – *'the'*, *'if'* and *'of'* often being doubled. Bearing in mind what can happen at this stage when making corrections and revisions, it is essential to leave good time for writing and editing the report. However, resist the temptation to tinker. It can be disastrous. It is sensible to rethink the golden phrases that you coined to express certain ideas, but beware of changing for the sake of changing.

Spelling

Use an English dictionary such as *The Shorter Oxford English Dictionary*. Use spell checkers carefully – some have North American spelling. If in doubt, always check and remember that dictionaries usually give more than one meaning to many words, so be sure that you examine all alternatives when checking. Remember that a spell check does not inform you whether a word that you have chosen is the correct one to use in a particular context.

Choice of word

Get your vocabulary correct. Using the wrong word in a particular context may result in a loss of accuracy, even offence. Consider the difference between the following:

> He was an inept choice for the job.
> He was an inapt choice for the job.

This is quite a simple example but the level of offence that the first observation offers to at least one person – the one who made the choice – is substantial. Another example of a word that is being used incorrectly more often now a days is *'less'*. Even some reporters for the BBC have been heard to refer to 'less people' in particular contexts, for example, 'less pupils are taking languages at A-level'. 'Less' is a 'mass' noun and is incorrect for the context. The correct word is 'fewer', which is a 'count' noun. A good English dictionary used in conjunction with a good English thesaurus will help you to avoid poor choice of words.

Structure

It is worth reiterating the importance of structure. Good, well-written, well-structured, well-presented reports will attract attention and will promote a good image of the writer. A well-structured report will lead your readers systematically through your investigation from inception to completion, answering any questions that they may have as they read. Conversely, badly structured, badly written reports will promote a bad image and will cause the reader to lose interest in the work.

Summary

Now that you have read this chapter, you will understand why you should prepare to write your report. Preparation is a key process; the better the preparation the better the report is likely to be. You will be able to plan your writing in detail, recognising the significance of the proper use of language and of structure in the making of your project report. Much is involved in writing your report and so the chapter begins with a definition of what a report is and its purposes are explained. In knowing your readers, you will be able to determine precisely what is necessary to answer the writer's and readers' questions and so choose a structure and develop content suitable to report your work. You now know how important and how easy it is to maintain quality control of your writing. Ensure that you have access to reference works such as an English dictionary, a general English language thesaurus, and an appropriate subject-specific dictionary and specialist thesaurus. Also, sensible use of books on style and quality of English will help to ensure that your grammar, writing style and vocabulary are of a reasonable standard. An authoritative guide to citing information sources should be kept readily to hand because information is available in so many different formats. Finally, you are the author and you are the editor and sub-editor of your report. These are responsible 'posts' and you must take them seriously. Editing and sub-editing are the last opportunities for you to ensure a good report.

Further Reading

Bowden, John (2004) *Writing a Report: How to Prepare, Write and Present Effective Reports* (7th edn). Oxford: How to Books.

Cullup, Michael (1999) *Brush Up Your Grammar*. Tadworth: Right Way.

The New Fowler's Modern English Usage (1998) (3rd edn). Oxford: Clarendon.

Oxford English: a Guide to the Language (1992) edited by Ian Deal. Oxford: Oxford University Press.

Appendices

Appendix 1:   Sample Project Record Forms

PROJECT TITLE:				
Activities list No.:				
Code	Description	Start date	Finish date	Progress report

PROJECT TITLE:				
Start date:				
Code	Key Activity	Duration	Dependencies	Done

PROJECT TITLE:			
Correspondence List No.:			
Item No.	Description	Date received	Date replied

Month	Sept	Oct	Nov	Dec	Jan	Feb	Mar	Apr	May	Jun	Jul	Aug
Administration	*	*	*	*	*	*	*	*	*	*	*	*
Tutorials	*		*		*			*			*	*
Establish aims, obj	*											
Literature search	Initial	Ongoing	*	*	*	*	*	*	*	*	*	
Identify methods	*											
Draft proposal	*											
Provisional plan	*											
Draft Introduction		*										
Gather data, etc.			*	*	*	*	*	*				
Draft discussion					*			*		*	*	*
Draft report									*	*	*	*

Appendix 2:   Sample work schedule, weekly breakdown

Week	Monday	Tuesday	Wednesday	Thursday	Friday
1	Tutorial; select topic	Start literature review	Discuss lit. rev. with tutor	Agree topic: define it	Identify aims, objectives
2	Tutorial on methods	Select possible methods	Draft proposal	Tutorial on proposal	Redraft proposal
3	Open project files	Design documentation	Design instruments	Test instruments	Tutorial on instruments
4	Plan project	Prepare work breakdown	Create time line	Tutorial on plan	Revise plan
5	Lit. rev. continues	Lit. rev. continues	Review aims, objectives	Review plan	Begin introduction
6	Review lit. search strategy	Lit. rev. continues	Redraft plan	Tutorial on plan	Review introduction
7	Lit. rev. continues	Lit. rev. continues	Review methods	Tutorial on literature	Lit. rev. continues
8	Select methods	Review instrument design	Select population for study	Select sampling method	Tutorial on sampling

Appendix 3:   Literature Item Review Record Form

Item No.:	Location of item:	Date reviewed:

PROJECT TITLE:

Full bibliographic citation:

Purpose of reading the item:

Brief notes from content of item:

Main points gained from item:

Opinion of content:

Contribution made to investigation (e.g. methods, theories, data/results):

Thoughts triggered as a result of reading the item:

Appendix 4: Literature Item Location Record Form

PROJECT TITLE:		
Literature items reviewed: List No.:		Start date:
Item No.	Description/Citation	Location

Appendix 5:   Steps to Making a Written Proposal

Preparing	Identify target readership – tutors, supervisors, and examiners.
	Define why the proposal is being made.
	Outline the topic of interest.
	Consult relevant documentation – the 'literature'.
	Define unusual terms.

Planning	Establish the sections needed.
	Put sections in order.
	Identify and list what goes into each section.
	Create timetable for work.

Drafting	Create working title – *acts as a focus*.
	Avoid interruptions to flow during first draft.
	Draft a section at a time – *initially*.

Editing	Review draft – *content*
	– presentation.
	Be ruthless – *seek economy, clarity, and accuracy*.
	Check facts, figures, names, etc.
	Check spelling, grammar, style, etc.

Producing	Beware last minute changes.
	Note that a proposal is a 'working document'.
	Take care.

Appendix 6: Relationship of the Project Proposal to the Project Report

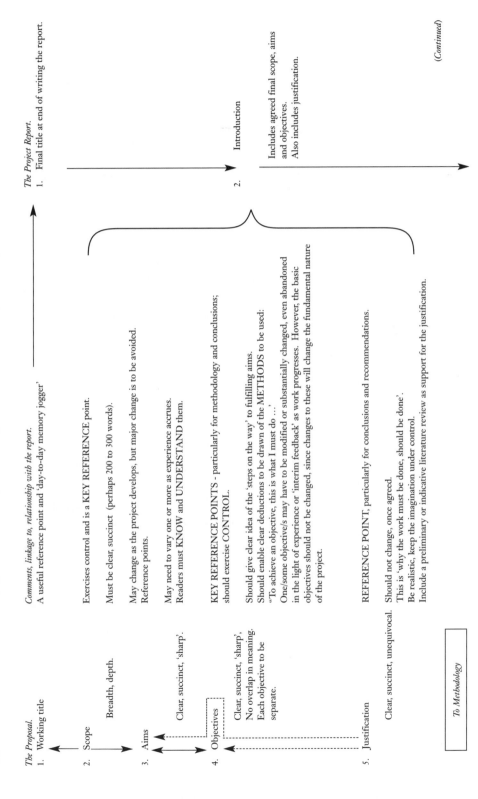

The Proposal.

1. Working title

2. Scope

   Breadth, depth.

3. Aims

   Clear, succinct, 'sharp'.

4. Objectives

   Clear, succinct, 'sharp',
   No overlap in meaning.
   Each objective to be
   separate.

5. Justification

   Clear, succinct, unequivocal.

Comments, linkage to, relationship with the report.
A useful reference point and 'day-to-day memory jogger'

Exercises control and is a KEY REFERENCE point.

Must be clear, succinct (perhaps 200 to 300 words).

May change as the project develops, but major change is to be avoided.
Reference points.

May need to vary one or more as experience accrues.
Readers must KNOW and UNDERSTAND them.

KEY REFERENCE POINTS - particularly for methodology and conclusions;
should exercise CONTROL.

Should give clear idea of the 'steps on the way' to fulfilling aims.
Should enable clear deductions to be drawn of the METHODS to be used:
"To achieve an objective, this is what I must do ..."
One/some objective/s may have to be modified or substantially changed, even abandoned
in the light of experience or 'interim feedback' as work progresses. However, the basic
objectives should not be changed, since changes to these will change the fundamental nature
of the project.

REFERENCE POINT, particularly for conclusions and recommendations.

Should not change, once agreed.
This is 'why the work must be done, should be done'.
Be realistic, keep the imagination under control.
Include a preliminary or indicative literature review as support for the justification.

The Project Report.

1. Final title at end of writing the report.

2. Introduction

   Includes agreed final scope, aims
   and objectives.
   Also includes justification.

(Continued)

To Methodology

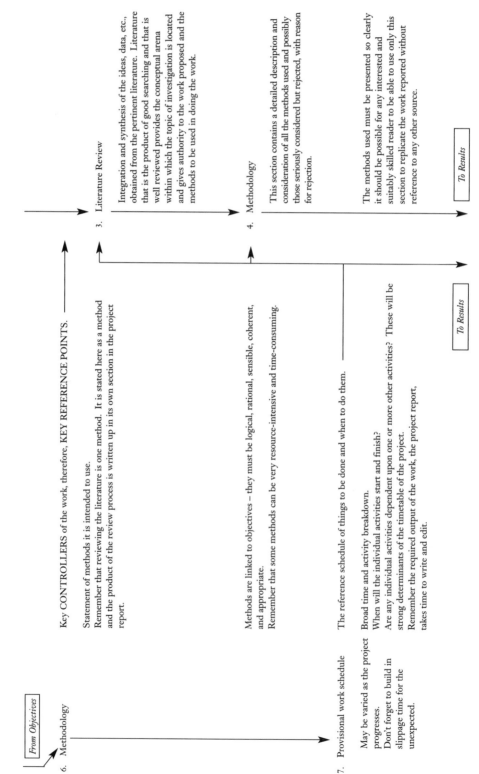

From Objectives

Key CONTROLLERS of the work, therefore, KEY REFERENCE POINTS.

3. Literature Review

Integration and synthesis of the ideas, data, etc., obtained from the pertinent literature. Literature that is the product of good searching and that is well reviewed provides the conceptual arena within which the topic of investigation is located and gives authority to the work proposed and the methods to be used in doing the work.

4. Methodology

This section contains a detailed description and consideration of all the methods used and possibly those seriously considered but rejected, with reason for rejection.

The methods used must be presented so clearly it should be possible for any interested and suitably skilled reader to be able to use only this section to replicate the work reported without reference to any other source.

To Results

6. Methodology

Statement of methods it is intended to use.
Remember that reviewing the literature is one method. It is stated here as a method and the product of the review process is written up in its own section in the project report.

Methods are linked to objectives – they must be logical, rational, sensible, coherent, and appropriate.
Remember that some methods can be very resource-intensive and time-consuming.

7. Provisional work schedule

May be varied as the project progresses.
Don't forget to build in slippage time for the unexpected.

The reference schedule of things to be done and when to do them.

Broad time and activity breakdown.
When will the individual activities start and finish?
Are any individual activities dependent upon one or more other activities? These will be strong determinants of the timetable of the project.
Remember the required output of the work, the project report, takes time to write and edit.

To Results

From Methodology

5. Results

Data and information gathered as a result of correct use of the selected methods are presented in this section without evaluation or critical comment. Significant amounts of data presented in tabular or graphical form are best put into appendices. Include summary presentations of such data in this section, as summary graphics and tables. Do not start discussion of results in this section.

6. Discussion

This section requires a major intellectual contribution from the researcher. It must contain a critical and analytical consideration of the results obtained in the research. It must also contain pertinent data and information gathered from the literature integrated into or synthesised with the results of the research undertaken. The results of research must be considered critically in relation to the expressed aims and objectives. There should also be a consideration of problems, resolved and unresolved, that were encountered during the life of the project.
The extent to which objectives were attained should be shown and there should be an explanation of non-attainment or partial attainment of any objectives.

Reflection on the project as a whole and an estimation of the practical worth and professional and academic value of the work will be important in highlighting the contribution to the subject and to professional practice.

7. Conclusions

Absolutely dependent upon the Discussion.
Are the aims and objectives realised?

8. Recommendations

Absolutely dependent upon the Conclusions.

Notes

1. The project proposal is a separate document from the project report.

2. The arrows indicate significant, even critical dependencies between sections, within the proposal and within the project report, and between the proposal and the report.

3. Before you make any changes to Scope, Aims, Objectives or Methodology, you are strongly advised to consult with your tutor and obtain agreement in detail on the specifics of any changes.

4. Content that may be confidential to any organisation or person connected with the research in any way must be cleared with that organisation or person before inclusion in the project report.

5. Information, data and any other content of the project report obtained from any published or unpublished source must be clearly and formally attributed to such a source.

6. Assistance, guidance or any form of input to the research provided by any person or organisation must be acknowledged.

7. Citations, references, footnotes, and entries in the bibliography must conform to an accepted academic standard.

8. You are advised to ensure that the format and layout of your project proposal and of your project report conform to the standards described in the project documentation issued to you by your tutor.

Appendix 7: Checklist for Determining Confidence in your Methodology

Questions to ask of your research design	Yes	No
Is your research question, your hypothesis, the problem you intend to investigate, or the focus of your research, clearly defined and described?		
Is your overall methodological approach sound and clearly explained?		
Have you justified your choice of methods, shown their validity, and clearly and specifically explained each?		
Have you the expertise to use the proposed methods, data and information analysis techniques, and essential equipment and software?		
Have you explained how you will manage your methods?		
Are the research focus, the aims, objectives, methods, and data and information analysis techniques logically related?		
Have you clearly and fully explained your data and information collection instruments?		
If your research includes a survey, have you ensured that your survey instruments will be pilot tested?		
Have you clearly and fully explained the data and information analysis procedures for each aim or for your research question?		
Have you briefly explored the advantages, limitations and potential problems of your proposed methods?		
Have you assessed the risks of methodological problems occurring?		
Have you described how you will manage these risks?		
Have you carefully considered all relevant ethical matters?		
Have you the skills necessary to interpret and present your results objectively, clearly and succinctly?		
Has your tutor approved your methodology?		

Appendix 8:   A Method of Working on the Literature Review

Explanation of the subject of the review

What do you want from the review?
  Subject context/understanding/personal briefing?
  Methods of working?
  Research instruments?
  Phenomena/data?
  Explanations/interpretations of phenomena/data?
  Theories, opinions, arguments?
  Some or all of these, and more?
  Names of people, organisations working in the subject area?

Definition of the subject of the review

Prepare initial concept map.
  Select significant terms.
  Note why they are significant.
Formulate initial search strategy.
  Note how and why this strategy has been formulated.

Determination of initial criteria for grouping notes from the literature

These can be based upon the answers to the initial question above.

Selection of appropriate searchable media/sources

Take advice from your Faculty librarian, or bibliographic specialists.
Note the media selected and why they were selected.

First search

Examine hits.
Read selection of hits – *make notes.*

Revise concept map?
Modify search strategy?

Second search

Examine hits.
Read the additional items – *make notes.*
Reflect on what you have learned so far.

Begin first draft of review

Sketch out a plan of the review.
Identify what needs to be included – *consult with tutor*.
Arrange notes from search hits on sketch.
Identify possible gaps in coverage of your topic.
Use identified gaps to revise search strategy again.
Begin writing; do not worry about style, etc. at this stage.

Search using revised strategy

Examine hits.
Read informed selection of hits – *make notes.*
Fill gaps in sketch.

Write draft

Leave to 'settle' for a few days.
Read draft critically.
Identify gaps in coverage – *there may still be some.*
Gather information to fill gaps.
Identify weaknesses in your 'argument'.
Review and rethink arguments.
Reflect on what you have learned so far.

Revise draft

Proof-read
Edit – attack the review, discuss with tutor.
Sub-edit.
Reflect on what you have learned so far.

Write final version

Proof-read.

Edit – do not be afraid to make changes but do not tinker.
   Take advice but be careful and wise about how you use it.

Sub-edit.
   Recheck headings, subheadings, and layout for consistency, accuracy.
   Recheck references for accuracy and consistency.
   Check grammar, syntax, style, spelling, and typographical errors.

Appendix 9:   Databases

The Internet provides information on virtually the whole of recorded human knowledge. Much of this is organised in databases dedicated to specific subjects, types of publications, or materials targeted at specified interest groups. These databases are compiled and maintained by specialists in the particular fields covered and access to them is controlled. Your university library will normally be able to provide you with access to a reasonable selection of them, depending upon the fees and conditions imposed by the operating body. Access to many databases is controlled by password and there are usage fees to be paid. Your university will subscribe to several and this will cover use by registered members of the university.

Databases that could be the source of useful information for your project are given below but this list is far from exhaustive. The details given here include the national coverage, the main language of the content, format of entries, types of publications covered, time period covered, and subject coverage. The library staff will be able to give you more detailed information on which databases are available and explain how to formulate effective searches. As many databases have their own search engines and search techniques, it is best to use your university library subject specialists for advice and guidance in their use. Therefore, the search engines and techniques for the databases listed here have not been included.

BATH INFORMATION AND DATA SERVICES (BIDS)
International; mainly English; bibliographic details from journals, abstracts; 1981 onwards; multi-disciplinary.

BRITISH EDUCATION INDEX (BEI)
UK; English; abstracts, journal literature from 1976, British theses from 1950; all aspects of education.

BRITISH HUMANITIES INDEX (BHI)
Mainly UK; English; 320+ journals and magazines, newspapers – UK and US; 1962 onwards; art, business, culture, literature, motion pictures, politics.

BUSINESS SOURCE PREMIER
International; English; abstracts, full text, images; 3,300 English language business journals; 1990 onwards; subject coverage includes accounting, business education, business law, economic development, management, marketing, public administration.

COMPASS – The British Museum (BM)
International; English; images and accompanying text of 5,000 objects in the BM collection; architecture, art, design, history.

CONTEMPORARY AUTHORS

International; English, French; indexes, full text; books, journals, medial adaptations; 1819–1994; 100,000 modern authors including novelists, poets, screenwriters, non-fiction writers, literature.

DATASTREAM

International; English; statistical, graphical; share price data on all UK quoted companies and some on companies in EU countries, USA, Canada, Australia, South Africa, and some Far Eastern countries.

DESIGN AND APPLIED ARTS INDEX (DAAI)

International; English; abstracts; over 500 design and craft journals; 1973 onwards; coverage includes architecture, art, design, fashion, graphic design, interior design, jewellery, packaging, textile fabrics, typography, and vehicle design and construction.

ECONOMIC AND SOCIAL DATA SERVICE (ESDS) International

International; English; statistical data; major international statistical datasets from IMF, OECD, UN, World Bank; 1960 onwards; statistical data.

EDUCATIONAL RESEARCH ABSTRACTS (ERA)

International; English; abstracts; selects abstracts from seven major abstracting journals that cover over 500 journals; 1995 onwards; coverage includes educational systems, and school management and organisation.

EDUCATION RESOURCES INFORMATION CENTER (ERIC)

USA; English; abstracts; over 100,000 full text non-journal documents issued between 1993 and 2004, and more than 1,000,000 citations; 1966 onwards; coverage includes adult education, education research, educational psychology, teaching.

EMERALD Fulltext

MCB Press journals; English; abstracts, full text; 130 academic and professional journals; 1989 onwards; 130 titles; coverage includes economics, engineering, hospitality, library science, personnel management, training.

EMERALD Reviews

International; English; abstracts; more than 150 leading management journals from around the world; 1988 onwards; all aspects of management including marketing, human resource, hospitality and tourism, information management.

EUROPE IN THE ROUND

54 European countries; English; current; full text, statistical and graphical material, images; statistics, maps, photographs; audio materials, text; coverage includes business, economics, econometrics, statistics, leisure and tourism.

FAME

UK and Ireland; English; full text, statistical and graphical material; data on 1.3 million UK and Irish companies; 1994 onwards; coverage includes business enterprises, corporation reports, finance, marketing.

FILM INDEX INTERNATIONAL

English-speaking countries; English; indexes, statistical material; over 100,000 films indexed, biographical information on 40,000 personalities; 1930 onwards; actors, directors, motion pictures, theatrical producers and directors. Regarded as the definitive online resource on entertainment films and personalities.

GLOBAL MARKET INFORMATION DATABASE (GMID).

International; English; full text, statistics; market analysis reports, consumer lifestyle reports; 1977 onwards; includes general economic and demographic statistics for over 200 countries, market data for consumer products, economic and market forecasts.

GROVE ART ONLINE

International; English; indexes, images; articles, biographies, country surveys, links to images from galleries and museums worldwide; architecture, art, artists, photography.

HOSPITALITY AND TOURISM INDEX

North American and International; English; abstracts; journal articles, books, case studies, conference proceedings; 1965 onwards; hospitality and tourism.

IMAGES OF ENGLAND

UK; English; images, text; to cover 370,000 images of listed buildings; architecture.

INDEX TO THESES

UK and Ireland; English; abstracts, index; higher degree theses accepted by universities in UK and Ireland; 1716 onwards; 479,162 theses.

INTERNATIONAL BIBLIOGRAPHY OF THE SOCIAL SCIENCES (IBSS)

International; 70% in English; abstracts, indexes; journals, books; 1951 onwards; economic development.

INTERNATIONAL FILM ARCHIVE (FIAF)

International; English; abstracts, indexes; 300 journals; 1972 onwards; motion pictures, television.

MOVING IMAGE GATEWAY
International; English; moving images, images; collects websites that relate to moving and audio images; multi-disciplinary.

NATIONAL STATISTICS ONLINE
UK; English; full text, statistical; UK official statistics including press releases, time series data and National Statistics publications; UK statistics.

OXFORD DICTIONARY OF NATIONAL BIOGRAPHY
UK; English; full text, images; up to 2001 – includes only dead individuals from or connected with the British Isles; over 50,000 biographies.

SCRAN
International; English; images; 325,000 images, video clips and audio files from 250 international collections in museums, galleries, archives and the media; architecture, art and design, social studies, tourism.

SOCIAL SCIENCES CITATION INDEX (SSCI)
International; English; abstracts, indexes; 1,700 social sciences journal, plus relevant articles from 3,300 other journals; 1981 onwards; coverage includes anthropology, criminology, information science, marketing, planning, women's studies.

SOCIAL SCIENCE INFORMATION GATEWAY (SOSIG)
Internet-based service of selected information; an online database of thousands of proven quality Internet resources each selected by a librarian or academic.

SPORT AND LEISURE INDEX
International; English; abstracts, indexes; journals and magazines; 1986 onwards; biomechanics, leisure, sport.

SPORT DISCUS
International; English, French; abstracts; journals; 1974 onwards; dance, physiology, recreation, sports sciences.

STUDIES ON WOMEN AND GENDER ABSTRACTS ONLINE
International; English; abstracts; journals, books; 1995 onwards; coverage includes education, employment, history, social policy, sociology.

TATE ONLINE
UK; English; full text, images; digitised images of contemporary and British art; art.

UK DATA ARCHIVE

UK; English; statistical material; holds the largest collection of digital data in the social sciences in the UK, houses a major collection of computerised historical material; social sciences, statistical data.

UNITED KINGDOM OFFICIAL PUBLICATIONS (UKOP)

UK; English; indexes, full text; publications of Parliament, government departments, government-funded bodies and public corporations; 1980 onwards; legislation, political science, politics.

WEB OF KNOWLEDGE (WoK)

International; English; abstracts, citations; journals, reports, conference proceedings, books; 1981 for SCI, SSCI and AHCI, 1990 for ISTP; multi-disciplinary. Provides access to Science Citation Index, Social Sciences Citation Index, Arts and Humanities Citation Index, and Index to Scientific and Technical Proceedings.

WORLD ADVERTISING RESEARCH CENTER (WARC)

International; English; abstracts; full text, statistics; journals, conferences papers, case studies, abstracts from other publications; coverage includes business news, consumer research, demography, econometrics, market research.

ZETOC

International; English; indexes; 20,000 journals and 16,000 conference proceedings are scanned annually; 1993 onwards; research. The database includes 15 million article and conference records.

Bibliography

Allan, Barbara (2004) *Project Management: Tools and Techniques for Today's ILS Professional*. London: Facet.

Anderson, Valerie (2004) *Research Methods in Human Resource Management*. London: Chartered Institute of Personnel and Development.

Bell, Judith (2005) *Doing Your Research Project*. (4th edn) Buckingham: Open University Press.

Blaxter, Loraine, Hughes, Christina and Tight, Malcolm (2001) *How to Research*. (2nd edn) Buckingham: Open University Press.

Boje, David M. (2001) *Narrative Methods for Organizational and Communications Research*. London: Sage Publications. (Sage Management Research series.)

Bowden, John (2004) *Writing a Report: How to Prepare, Write and Present Effective Reports*. (7th edn) Oxford: How To Books.

Brewerton, Paul (2001) *Organisational Research Methods: A Guide to Students and Researchers*. London: Sage Publications.

British Standards Institute (2000) *Project Management: Part 3: Guide to the Management of Business Related Risk*. London: BSI.

Brown, Mark (2002) *Project Management: In a Week*. (3rd edn) London: Hodder & Stoughton. (From the In a Week series.)

Bryman, A. (2004) *Social Research Methods*. (2nd edn) Oxford: Oxford University Press.

Burns, Robert B. (2000) *Introduction to Research Methods*. (4th edn) London: Sage Publications.

Buzan, Tony (2003) *Use Your Head*. London: BBC Books. (See particularly *Mind maps*, pp. 80–139.)

Chapman, C.B. and Ward, S. (2003) *Project Risk Management: Processes, Techniques and Insights*. (2nd edn) Chichester: Wiley.

Cresswell, John W. (2003) *Research Design: Qualitative, Quantitative, and Mixed Methods Approaches*. (2nd edn) London: Sage Publications.

Cullup, Michael (1999) *Brush Up Your Grammar*. Tadworth: Right Way.

Dayman, Christine and Holloway, Immy (2002) *Qualitative Research Methods in Public Relations and Marketing Communications*. London: Routledge.

Fielding, Nigel (ed.) (2003) *Interviewing*. London: Sage Publications. (Sage Benchmarks in Social Research Methods series.)

Fink, Arlene (2003a) *The Survey Handbook*. (2nd edn) London and Thousand Oaks, CA: Sage Publications. (The survey kit 2; 1.)

Fink, Arlene (2003b) *How to Manage, Analyze, and Interpret Survey Data*. (2nd edn) London and Thousand Oaks, CA: Sage Publications. (The survey kit 2; 9.)

Gilham, Bill (2000) *Case Study Research Methods*. London: Continuum. (Real World research.)

Graziano, Anthony M. (2004) *Research Methods: A Process of Inquiry*. (5th edn) London: Pearson.

Gregory, Ian (2003) *Ethics in Research*. London: Continuum. (Continuum Research Methods series.)

Gunter, Barrie (2000) *Media Research Methods: Measuring Audiences, Reactions and Impact.* London: Sage Publications.

Halding, Luke (2005), History of Modern Man Unravels as German Scholar is Exposed as Fraud. *The Guardian*, 19 February.

Hart, Chris (1998) *Doing a Literature Review: Releasing the Social Science Research Imagination.* London: Sage Publications.

Heerkens, Gary R. (2002) *Project Management.* New York, NY: McGraw-Hill. (The *Briefcase Book* series.) (See particularly Chapters 3, 4, 6, 7 and 8.)

Kaplan, Elaine (2001) The International Emergence of Legal Protections for Whistleblowers. *The Journal of Public Inquiry*, Fall/Winter, pp. 37–42.

Lashley, Conrad and Best, Warwick (2003) *12 Steps to Success.* London: Continuum.

Martin, Paula K. (2001) *Getting Started in Project Management.* Chichester; New York, NY: Wiley. (The Getting Started In series.)

McQueen, Ronald A. and Knussen, Christina (2002) *Research Methods for Social Science: A Practical Introduction.* Harlow: Prentice Hall.

Metcalfe, J. E. and Astle, C. (1995) *Correct English.* Tadworth, Surrey: Clarion.

Moore, Nick (1999) *How to Do Research.* (3rd edn) London: Library Association Publishing.

The New Fowler's Modern English Usage. (1998) (3rd edn by R.W. Burchfield) Oxford: Clarendon.

Orna, Elizabeth with Stevens, Graham (1995) *Managing Information for Research.* Buckingham: Open University Press. (See particularly Chapter 4, pp. 59–73.)

Oxford English: A Guide to the Language. (1992) edited by Ian Deal, Oxford: Oxford University Press.

Powell, Ronald R. and Silipigni Connaway, Lynn (2004) *Basic Research Methods for Librarians.* (4th edn) Westport, Conn.: Greenwood.

Project Management Institute (2004) *A Guide to the Project Management Body of Knowledge: PMBOK Guide.* (3rd edn) Pennsylvania: Project Management Institute.

Project Risk Analysis and Management Guide. (2004) (2nd edn) High Wycombe: APM Publishing.

Quantitative Methods. (2000) (3rd edn) London: BPP Publishing. (Business basics series.)

Rudd, Shirley (1989) *Time Manage Your Reading.* Aldershot, Hampshire: Gower.

Saunders, Mark N. K., Lewis, Philip and Thornhill, Adrian (2003) *Research Methods for Business Students.* (3rd edn) Harlow; New York: Prentice Hall.

Swinscow, T.D.U. (2002) *Statistics at Square One.* (9th edn) edited by Michael J. Campbell. London: BMJ Books.

Thomas, R. Murray (2003) *Blending Qualitative and Quantitative Research Methods in Theses and Dissertations.* Thousand Oaks, CA: Corwin Press.

Travers, Max (2001) *Qualitative Research through Case Studies.* London: Sage Publications. (Introducing qualitative methods series.)

Wengraf, Tom (2001) *Qualitative Research Interviewing: Biographic Narrative and Semi-Structured Methods.* London: Sage Publications.

Wilkinson, David and Birmingham, Peter (2003) *Using Research Instruments: A Guide for Students.* London: RoutledgeFalmer.

Yin, Robert K. (2003) *Applications of Case Study Research.* (2nd edn) London: Sage Publications. (Applied Social Research Methods series.)

Young, Trevor L. (2003) *The Handbook of Project Management: A Practical Guide to Effective Policies and Procedures.* (2nd edn) London: Kogan Page.

Index